What people are sa~~ying about~~

99 Reasons to Forgive

Geoff Thompson encourages us all to become brave hearts on our life journey and to look within for the courage and wisdom we urgently need not just to forgive others but most important of all to forgive ourselves. An empowering and truly liberating read from a remarkable and resilient thought leader and spiritual pioneer that I can't recommend highly enough.
Theresa Cheung, *Sunday Times* bestselling dreams and mystical author

What Geoff Thompson brings to this book is so much more than his wisdom – which is broad and far reaching – he also brings himself. In bringing himself he gives the reader his hard-won compassion towards the human condition; our inner condition. Where we have been wronged and are the victim of injustice Geoff speaks to the self within, beyond our ego and offers his knowledge of how we can set ourselves free. His personal knowledge of unconditional love is the authority with which he speaks, and his voice of love reaches deep into the darkest recesses of our psyche and whispers, "First you must love yourself." This is the place where forgiveness begins, and this book will set you free to forgive yourself and break the cycle of revenge towards others that holds you in its grip.
Colm Holland, author of *The Secret of the Alchemist*

A deep and insightful guide to forgiving and finding freedom.
Etan Ilfeld

99 Reasons to Forgive provides us with the guidance and support to embrace the healing power of letting go.
Geoff's writing beautifully carries essence and compassion

alongside a truth and wisdom that can only come from having truly lived and embodied his message.

In a society so often obsessed with achievement and ascension Geoff provides an invitation to descend, going down into our wounds where we can find the magic of forgiveness and love.

This book will nourish something deep within its readers and provide hope in times of suffering.

I am always grateful for Geoff's work which inspires me to live with more compassion, truth and love.

Pat Divilly, *Pat Divilly Podcast* and #1 bestselling author

99 Reasons to Forgive

And Revenge Ain't One

99 Reasons to Forgive

And Revenge Ain't One

Geoff Thompson

BOOKS

Winchester, UK
Washington, USA

JOHN HUNT PUBLISHING

First published by O-Books, 2023
O-Books is an imprint of John Hunt Publishing Ltd., 3 East St., Alresford,
Hampshire SO24 9EE, UK
office@jhpbooks.com
www.johnhuntpublishing.com
www.o-books.com

For distributor details and how to order please visit the 'Ordering' section on our website.

ISBN: 978 1 80341 134 7
978 1 80341 135 4 (ebook)
Library of Congress Control Number: 2022935926

A CIP catalogue record for this book is available from the British Library.

Design: Stuart Davies

UK: Printed and bound by CPI Group (UK) Ltd, Croydon, CR0 4YY
Printed in North America by CPI GPS partners

We operate a distinctive and ethical publishing philosophy in
all areas of our business, from our global network of authors to
production and worldwide distribution.

Contents

To the Ein Sof: this work belongs to you
To Sharon the best part of my every day
To Mark, for showing me God in stillness

Thank you to:
Marina Cantacuzino for her constant support and
wonderful introduction to this book
Jo Lal for an inspired first-draft note
Everyone at John Hunt, for their belief and kindness
Gabriela for graciously creating and managing my Instagram
page
@ geoff_thompson_official

About the Author

Geoff Thompson is a BAFTA winning screenwriter.

Author of close to fifty books, he has appeared on the *Sunday Times* Bestseller List several times.

(Extracts from) his first book, *Watch My Back*, have been adapted into a stage play, a BAFTA nominated short film, and a BIFA nominated feature film.

His first stage play, *Doorman*, won him an invite into the Royal Court Young Writers Group in London.

Geoff has penned multi-award winning films for luminaries such as Ray Winstone, Paddy Considine, Orlando Bloom, Maxine Peake, Anne Reid, Alison Steadman and James Cosmo.

Geoff's musical for theatre, *We'll Live and Die in These Towns*, was staged at the Belgrade Theatre Coventry in 2018 to great acclaim.

He is also one of the world's highest ranking (8th dan) martial artists.

Black Belt Magazine USA named him: "the most influential martial artist in the world since Bruce Lee."

But I say that even as the holy and the righteous cannot rise
beyond the highest which is in each one of you,
So the wicked and the weak cannot fall lower than the lowest
which is in you also,
And a single leaf turns not yellow but with the silent
knowledge of the whole tree,
So the wrong-doer cannot do wrong without the hidden will of
you all.

Kahlil Gibran
The Prophet

Introduction

I have spent a career trying to unlock the mysteries of forgiveness, attempting to excavate and unpick how people make peace with their demons and find compassion for those who have hurt them. In 2004, by creating a platform for personal storytelling, I set out to establish a space where anyone could explore this most contentious and contested of topics. I have also been at great pains not to present forgiveness as an imperative and I have stressed the greyness of this most oblique of subjects. Within the nuance, the complexity and uncertainty I have hoped that people might find some clarity.

In many ways therefore Geoff Thompson and myself could not be more different in terms of our approach to promoting forgiveness. Geoff, who has had the profound experience of forgiving a great harm, imbues forgiveness with the transformative force of medicine. He has had to encounter the darkest of places in order to reach for the light; and by going deep into his own psyche to explore spirituality he's been able to explain to the rest of us the enormous value and power of forgiving. He is convinced that only forgiveness can enable us to escape "the prison of an abusive entanglement."

I, on the other hand, do not come to this subject as someone who has experienced an intolerable harm; I have had nothing major in my life to forgive, although of course like everyone else I've had plenty of grudges and grievances to navigate and contend with. I am a journalist, an investigator, a storyteller, and I prefer to position myself somewhere in the middle, weighing up a balanced approach to the limits and possibilities of forgiveness. I have resisted any imperatives around the need to forgive, and have often spoken about the dark side of forgiveness: how if you make it a duty it can easily become an oppression.

I don't think Geoff would disagree with me on this last point even though he is someone who absolutely knows the strength of forgiveness and is certain of its efficacy. And the strange thing is that even though I'm not in favour of persuading people to forgive, *99 Reasons to Forgive* is probably the most persuasive document I have ever read in terms of presenting forgiveness as a remedy, as a panacea for all ills that can cure pain and unlock misery. If you are stuck and weighed down by intrusive negative thoughts, or if you are locked into the story of an injustice, then *99 Reasons to Forgive* may very well provide you with the answer of how to become liberated from the trap of resentment or self-blame. The clear and unequivocal message here is that it is precisely in the wound that the gift lies. And the gift of forgiveness is vital because in the words of Desmond Tutu it can draw out the "sting in the memory that threatens to poison our entire existence."

It was several years ago that I first got to hear about how Geoff had forgiven his abuser and so I invited him to come along and share his story in a male prison as part of The Forgiveness Project's offender programme. As Geoff spoke, I watched the men lean forward, listening deeply; I saw how they dropped their defenses and then confided in him about their own vulnerability and brokenness. They seemed to understand for the first time how forgiving themselves and others could help them take back control of their lives. Geoff's message about forgiveness makes sense to people because this is not about reconciling with someone else, but about reconciling with ourselves. His forgiveness comes white-hot from the whetstone and is necessary to sever the ties. Reconciliation in this sense means making peace with a painful event and allows people therefore to find resolution and move on.

Since that prison event, I've heard Geoff tell his story to a range of diverse audiences. Every single time he leaves them in little doubt that forgiveness isn't some soft option that might let others off the hook, but rather an energetic life force which can change personal paradigms. *99 Reasons to Forgive* feels like a book written from the summit of the author's life, one that has emerged after years of studying the esoteric and the metaphysical. By distilling his many discoveries and experiences into this extraordinary publication, he reveals the very essence of what it means to forgive and in so doing a kind of alchemy takes place, allowing all those who go on this journey with him the chance to finally utilize the potency of forgiveness.

Marina Cantacuzino
Founder, The Forgiveness Project
https://www.theforgivenessproject.com/

Author's Foreword

You are suffering.

I understand.

That's probably why you picked this book up, why you paid out good money to own these bound pages, why you have invested your time and no little courage to have this tome in your possession – *you are suffering*.

I understand you and I understand your hurt.

You are in pain, and I am going to suggest in these pages that forgiveness might be the remedy to your ills. I will propose that forgiveness is a panacea, not only for the problem that currently entangles you, but it may also be the key to unlock many more of your pressing miseries.

My suggestion might immediately offend you; it may bring you to anger, or rage. Perhaps you will feel like throwing this book into the nearest fire and burning it cover-and-page because you are so affronted by even the suggestion that what happened to you is in any way forgivable: "You don't know what he/she/they did to me."

I don't know what was done to you, that's very true, but I don't need to know.

It may be vital for you to tell your story, maybe you will need – like me – to tell it a hundred times on a thousand different occasions in order to let go of the pain as part of your healing, but what was done to you, why it was done, where and how it was done are not important in the process of forgiveness: it gets in the way when you allow the gravity of your abuse to qualify the level of grip you use to hold onto it.

I don't need to know what happened to you.

I do, however, care about your situation. I care about you and I care about your suffering... I care enough to sit here, in no small amount of personal discomfort (I have put this writing off for months), and fill these pages with words of truth, when my lazy, lower, click-bait self is compelling me towards a myriad different distractions, a thousand fun things are calling me, and none of them involve telling my story *again*, talking about forgiveness *again*, bringing out my dead again, taking the sharp pin of deep-enquiry into the crab-shell of my heavily fortified mind again and again, to pick out the last juicy remnants of my pain.

Why should you listen to me?

Because I suffer and because I care enough to bleed my suffering into this ink.

Like everyone who has been privileged to live on this spinning planet, I have had my moments, my days, my weeks, and months, *sometimes years* of insufferable, lonely, lonely, torment.

I know what it is to suffer.

If you have ever woke at four in the morning, day in day out for months on end, damp and cold with sweat, the demon of depression squatting heavy in your chest, wondering if you can crawl through another *long day*, doubting that you even want to, you know what suffering is.

To have lived as a human in this sheath of skin is to suffer.

Welcome to planet earth.

Why should you listen to me?

I care so much that I ache.

I am urgently compelled to sacrifice the body and blood of my learning to this book.

This is food and drink for the hungry and the thirsty.

I am a man that has escaped the burning building of abuse and depression. Not easily, I have to say, and not quickly or cleanly either. But escape I did. Before I found the exit-door marked forgiveness, I took many wrong turns. I tried a door called revenge: I became an elite martial artist and nightclub bouncer, and I used my killing tools to bludgeon my way out.

It did not work. I tried the door called blame: but when I flirted with blame, the blame was never ending, and the number of people who became blame-worthy multiplied exponentially until I hated nearly everyone. I tried the door called self-pity, I spent many desolate years marinating in my own sorrow, using misery as a poor excuse to give up on life and feed on the sympathy of others. But my pity-party attracted a house guest called depression, and that bastard bled me until I was pale and impotent and useless. I spied a door called medication too and snatched at the handle in the hope of a healing balm, but a smog of misery came down over me with the first prescription and I was cast into my own private episode of *The Walking Dead*: I threw the tablets in a river before the chemical cosh completely lobotomized me. I followed the sirens of iniquity too and self-prescribed for a long time – violence, sexual pornography, alcohol: the usual suspects – they promised me salvation but delivered only damnation: these vices-with-voices led me so far astray I worried at times that I might never find my way home.

I did eventually work my way out, and, after a period of profound relief, I suddenly realized that there were family and friends and associates and perfect strangers still trapped in the burning-building, loved ones who did not know how to escape.

I have reentered the inferno (to continue the metaphor), not to compel you to follow me, or ask you to believe me, or purchase a course from me, or profess me a living guru, rather I return, and I return and again I return to advise you that there is definite route out, I am certain because I have found it, and I can share my learning if you have the ears to listen.

I was needlessly tortured, just like you.

I have escaped the suffering.

That's why you should at least hear me out.

Preface

Forgiveness is a volatile subject.

Of course.

We know this much already.

It would seem that the general masses are not too keen or not yet ready to forgive their (elected) enemy, and so remain suspended in an uninformed state of perpetual angst, exhausting unfathomable amounts of seminal energy, which could be better utilized in pursuit of creative generation or regeneration, rather than in the destructive pursuit of witnessed revenge.

How much more could the individual, the community, the city, the country, *the world* achieve if the greater majority of its creative juices – its attention – were not stolen by the hidden enemy of ignorance?

I confess that I write this book as an idealist.

But I am not one to preach theory from the pulpit of unseasoned theology or theoretical academe. Of the two methods of learning, I have found that discovered knowledge is far weightier than book learning. I am an empiricist. Mine is a tested and proved study. As far as practical forgiveness is concerned, my savvy was birthed in the theatre of war; I have been, and I continue to be in the field of play.

My words carry with them the historicity of personal research, both as an ardent and dogmatic grudge-bearer, and later as a man of peace and redemption.

I have held grudges and been incarnated into an emotional inferno because of my error (the flames of my anger always burned me before they ever reached my enemy).

I have forgiven and been soothed in the cool waters of grace.

I have also *been* forgiven and felt the savage scold of burning coals heaped upon my head by the bestower.

My intention with this book is to find the rub of truth (as far as forgiveness is concerned) and stay in that freeing discomfort for the duration of the writing. Hopefully, if I can achieve my aim, this will be beneficial to you the reader (hello there!) and it will be instructional for me the scribe: I am still very much working on this stuff myself.

I will be writing this book and offering advice and direction from my standing as a seasoned and senior martial artist teacher (I hold the rank of Hachidan: 8th dan black belt), and very much from the budo[1] perspective of my art. As practiced players in the deadly game of combatives, we perceive problems as a sign of life. We view any kind of opposition – violent or otherwise – as a ready form of (internal) resistance training, the catalyst to forced and accelerated growth. We develop our game, and we advance our character and perfect our technique by welcoming (sometimes even seeking out) and overcoming these problems. Just by framing difficulty in all its forms as an opportunity to grow, we dismantle much of its machinery.

At the end of each chapter, I will offer a Budo Practice to help enhance your strategy, and throughout the book proper I will garnish the teachings with as many true examples of budo efficacy from my own life as my editor will allow.

Before beginning the study proper, I'd like to clarify exactly what forgiveness is – the "giving over" of sin, "forgiving it from our minds" – and what forgiveness definitely is not: it never was, it never is, and it never will be "letting them off with it."

This is the greatest stumbling block in any discussion regarding forgiveness: nailing down an exact definition.

Nearly everyone I speak to about forgiveness, almost without exception, assumes that if we forgive someone, we are automatically freeing them from responsibility, they are no longer culpable for their crime, we are offering them pardon, a get-out-of-jail-free card, which means they are (in common parlance) "getting away with it."

We are assured in the Buddhist canon that it is not the

abuse of others that keeps us locked to the wheel of misery and sadness, it is our own ignorance.

One thing I have learned and one thing I know is this: no one gets away with anything. Not ever. Even a basic enquiry into the great earth and its laws will confirm that this is a reciprocal universe, and the law of compensation reigns.

The Oxford English Dictionary informs us that forgiveness means to "stop feeling angry with someone who has done something to harm, annoy or upset you; to stop feeling angry with yourself."

Notice that the denotation mentions nothing about letting someone off with a crime, pardoning bad behavior, or standing as judge and jury over the perpetrator of an abuse. In fact, it says nothing about the offender at all, the definition is entirely dedicated to us, *the offended party*; it is about us freeing ourselves from anger, annoyance and upset, it has nothing to do with anyone else.

There has been so much written over the years about forgiveness, about whether we should forgive, what it means to forgive, who benefits from forgiveness when it is bestowed and what the limitations on forgiveness might be. I wonder sometimes if the most important truth about forgiveness has been lost in the emotional deluge that rushes in every time anyone mentions it as a viable problem-solving tool.

Perhaps if I can furnish you with the essentials of my own learning it may offer a clearer view of the freedom we all long for.[2] Or perhaps my words might offer a little balm to get you through another *long day* if you are currently suffering.

I am often advised (or warned) not to mention God or religion whenever I approach the subject of forgiveness, certainly when talking to the masses. People will switch off, I am assured, people will be offended, affronted, they might even attack you.

I will not be heeding this advice, as well meaning as it might be.

There is nothing I will not employ in my quest to drive home my point.

If the word God offends you, I am already your teacher.

I have opened a learning portal for you, an avenue of enquiry, the gateway to future healing.

If religion is an offence to you, why is it an offence to you?

What is your "house ghost" trying to hide?

What is it distracting you from?

And why are you taking heed of an angry inner voice, a weak sub-vocalization, a false personality that can be so easily baited by ink on a page?

What I will do, if you are still there (are you still with me?), is qualify any mention I might make of the divine. My intention with this book is not just to shed a little light on the subject of forgiveness, it is also to offer avenues of further enquiry, paths you might follow after you have placed this book down. There are great teachers out there and many of the best are waiting for you in the esoteric books of aligned philosophy.

It would be a shame to miss these giants of learning for want of a little enquiry.

You won't get through your current crisis without some form of invisible support, of that I am certain.

It doesn't really matter what you call this lofty assistant, what *is* important is that you learn to access it with genuine, courageous, open-minded curiosity. If a voice jumps into your consciousness and insists that *any* door to learning need remain shut, you should question that voice and demand qualification.

The help is everywhere if you open your heart.

The help will be eternally illusive if you come to this subject with prejudice already loaded into the game console.

My Story

I'd like to start the book proper by briefly telling you my story.

The lessons I aim to present in this book demand qualification. The worst thing you can do is take travel advice from someone who has never left home.

I was groomed and sexually assaulted at the age of eleven years.

Let's start with that shall we.

I was abused by a trusted and beloved teacher.

I was so disturbed and frightened and confused and derailed by this assault that my life was never the same again after that fateful night, back in 1972. I went to bed as an eleven-year-old boy, when I woke up the next day, I was a hundred years old.

I have written much about this incident. It has found form in articles, books, a multi-award-winning short film (*Romans 12:20*), a controversial stage play (*Fragile*), a TED Talk and more recently a critically acclaimed feature film (*Retaliation*) starring Orlando Bloom and Anne Reid.

I would recommend that you refer to these writings if you want a more comprehensive understanding of the incident itself. Enough to say that (specifically) the grooming and the subsequent assault devastated me as a boy, emotionally crippled me as a youth and greatly impaired me as an adult.

If the initial harm had been captured and arrested immediately after it had happened, much of the damage that unfolded over the next thirty years could have been prevented, of that I am sure. What had been installed as parasitical malware in the mind of this sensitive, vulnerable boy could have been quickly detected and keenly removed, perpetrator brought to justice and the wheel-locked boy emancipated before any further damage could be done.

This did not happen.

I had been quietly conditioned all my life, you might say I was "gaslighted" or groomed by the mores of my culture and the precepts of my class never to challenge middle-class authority figures. I was a meek, under-educated boy from a jittery working-class world where we were warned never to bring shame to the door. Shame was the enemy of my generation; we were more afraid of public humiliation than we were of an assassin's bullet.

Conditioned shame kept me from sharing my experience with anyone for a long time.

I was also groomed by my abuser.

Post-abuse I did not think, "Why has this happened to me?" I thought (and this was how I'd been positioned to think), "This is my fault. I did something wrong, I brought this on myself, I deserved it."

By the time I did find the courage to share it with loved ones (two years later) I was met with a polar reception: cold hard fear: cognitive dissonance: ignorance.

I needed a hug.

I needed to be held.

I craved reassurance.

I desperately wanted to be protected.

Instead, I felt questioned and doubted by loved ones who were as dissonant and afraid as I was: why hadn't I mentioned the attack sooner? Why had I taken so long to tell them? The questions may have been innocent enough, but for a young boy already disturbed and imbalanced by interference, the enquires seemed implicit with doubt, intended or not, and I immediately felt as though I should never have shared my secret.

I am sure this is not how it felt to them.

I am pretty certain that they were worried sick when I told them and that the subsequent schema of worry never truly left them... but it was how it felt to me.

Assurance was not forthcoming because (I can see in retrospect) my family were frozen by shock and by fear: they were confused. Their reception was not a lack of love or empathy, they could not have loved me more, it was simply a lack of understanding. I'd dropped a truth-bomb in their

Sunday morning kitchen, and they were so busy trying to fire-fight and gather the broken fragments of their homeostasis, that they would not have had the wherewithal to stop in the middle of this emotional tumult and console me.

My family did not know how to deal with this situation.

They are beautiful and dedicated and protective, they loved me very much. They wanted to confront the situation, they wanted to call my abuser out, get the police involved but I begged them, I cried and begged them not to do this, I couldn't cope with that kind of attention.

I was too afraid.

The thought of anyone else knowing, the very idea of a fuss being made, of the police getting involved, of my friends at school knowing frightened me more than the abuse itself.

I felt dirty.

I felt vile.

I felt absolutely unlovable.

I asked them not to take it any further.

They did not take it any further.

My self-disgust felt like ten-thousand inhabiting creatures crawling under my skin, all at the same time.

By this time, the parasite of abuse had already burrowed deep, it had set up home in my young psyche, it had commandeered much of my autonomy (it stole my free will), certainly it had invaded my thinking, and controlled much of my volition: I could no longer even trust my own mind, let alone my own hands.

(My juvenile misreading of) the familial reception I received on confessing the abuse only confirmed (to me) what this parasitical inner voice had already suggested – I was a piece of shit: this was all my fault: I must have led him on in some way: I should never have told anyone... I should never, never, never have told anyone.

Number one rule of any parasite, the demon of scripture:

keep your abuse secret, tell no one.

But what we bury becomes disease: we are as sick as our secrets.

I kept it secret from then on and over the next thirty years I paid for it with crippled self-esteem, psychotic jealousy, bouts of debilitating depression *so many depressions*, self-harm, sexual self-harm and later, when I built a tank-like carapace around my wounded child, violence, a battalion of violence, I used physical force as a means of protecting my sensitive underbelly *and it worked*.

For a while it worked.

Anyone that got too close got knocked out. End of story.

I became good at violence.

It was what I did.

In a well-reasoned but ultimately misdirected attempt to overcome my inner fear, the existential self-disgust, I became a highly potent, highly graded martial arts guru and a nightclub bouncer; I bashed the heads and broke the ribs and snapped the teeth of hundreds of displaced enemies in a decade long rush of blood-red vengeance.

It was only after nearly killing a man in a car park match-fight that I turned to a higher guide and ended my covenant with the martial way.

This experience led me towards writing which became my mode of enquiry, my path to repentance and redemption and ultimately, the exorcism of a devil that had been implanted in me as an eleven-year-old boy.

My pen became a resurrection stone.

My healing proper began one Sunday morning when I was having breakfast in a local café. It was early. The place was empty. I *thought* it was empty. I looked across the room, and there, sitting at the table opposite me was a frighteningly familiar face.

I was in my late thirties at this point. I weighed in at an

impressive sixteen stones. I was a lump (as they say around these parts). I was a veteran bouncer with hundreds of fights under my belt, never losing, not once. I was qualified in more martial arts disciplines than you could shake a stick at. (At that time) I was 5th Dan, master grade in the hard art of Japanese Shotokan. I could maim and kill in thirty different languages but... when I caught a glance of this man sat opposite me in a Coventry café all my physical prowess fell away like shed skin. I was eleven years old again. I was impotent *again*. I felt the weight of his menace from across the room. It completely overpowered me. I trembled with fear. I'd vowed if I ever saw this man again, I'd kill him dead, just as I had already murdered him a thousand times, in moments of wild, and unedited reverie. I'd trained for it, this had been my raison d'être, it is what got me to the gym three times a day, *every day* for thirty years. All my preparation, all my training in the art of the kill, my plethora of impressive fighting techniques from every exotic martial art failed me when I saw this man again.

I wanted to run away.

Not because I felt my art would *literally* fail me in a physical affray. No. Not that. I had a history of making violence work against men steeped in brutality. I did not doubt the efficacy of my art; what I doubted was the potency of my intent.

I was already spilling into the budo by this time, the esoteric end of martial arts, where the *lesser war*, the exoteric battleground, was a mere candle flame when measured against the inferno of the *greater war* on the enemy within.

I was a senior level martial artist, so budo was already calling me and of course I'd stumbled over and flirted with the metaphysical and the power-potential of forgiveness. I'd even taught the theory to my own students but here, now, on the cold-hard floor of reality, with my nemesis only feet away, I knew, I absolutely, categorically knew that I was being summoned, I was being recruited into the higher echelons and the payment for entrance was right before me.

I knew that if I could forgive this man, if I could stand before him knowing that *physically* I was capable of stopping his breath, but chose instead to show mercy, my initiation into the hidden arts would be guaranteed. But – and this is the reason why the shake and the tremble and the doubt had reached the edges of all of my limbs – I was terrified of entering this encounter without the protection of my massive and impressive physical arsenal. I feared I'd be a powerless boy again under the maul of a beast, that I would be devoured without my martial skills.

I knew innately (I don't know how, probably a subtle communication from my soul) that I had to lay down my arms and enter this affray with only one weapon. In esoteric warfare this is always the weapon of choice... Truth.

I had the truth.

There is a beautiful verse in the Kabbalah that says, "If you would forgive someone, first injure them." On the surface this appears to be oxymoronic, a kindness juxtaposed by a violence. In exegesis, however, the meaning is explained: parasites by their very nature will not give up their living host without a fight. Why would they, the human being is a literal bank-raid, he is a walking, talking easy-access, bait-clicking foodbank. When we "forgive them from our minds," we are in effect exorcizing the demons from their squat in us, which means that their source of sustenance (us) has been removed, and they will perish. So, in order to make their removal easier we must first diminish their strength by injuring them.

How do we injure them?

We mortally wound them with honesty and truth.

Let me explain: People who exploit others often do so in blatant ignorance, they employ lies, half-lies, rhetoric and weak rationalization to justify their actions, hide from their sin and deny their abuse. When we proffer them truth – in other words when we destroy their rationalization and denial with cold hard facts – we weaken their stronghold, and removal by forgiveness becomes that much easier.

The man who sexually abused me lived his whole adult life in shameless ignorance to his crimes, rationalizing his abuse of children by convincing himself that he was doing no harm and that the children he groomed were somehow complicit; in his sickness he believed he was developing a loving, nurturing, natural relationship with the boys he gaslighted. I killed this dark lie in one fell swoop, when I confronted him in a Coventry café and "injured" him with the light of undeniable, incontrovertible truth:

This man was an abomination, he was a walking lie.

I had the cutting sword of light.

This man was a shadow, a shade.

I had knowing.

This man was wall-to-wall ignorance.

I had the truth.

I can't tell you how scared I was, how much I wanted to walk away, to run away, how tempted I was to pretend I hadn't seen him, pretend I hadn't heard the call of spirit, pretend, pretend, pretend I didn't know that violence does not solve violence, that hate does not heal hate, that fear does not erase fear.

The gap between me and this man was probably only a few feet, but it felt like a million miles, and I very nearly listened to the eleven-year-old boy who spoke in my ear and pleaded with me to look away, to walk away, to run away like my very life depended on it.

I could have walked away, no one would have known.

Only… I would have known.

I would have known, and I could not live with that.

I stood up. I climbed out of the dugout of my café chair. I walked across the no-man's-land of McDonald's café in Walsgrave, Coventry and I stood before the man who abused me as a boy.

He looked at me, his face a knot of confusion underscored by a nervous smile.

"You don't remember me," I said, emotion trembling through my vocals, ready to erupt into a chaos of weeping or a riot of war, I did not know which.

"You don't remember me but when I was a boy you sexually abused me."

His face twisted, first towards denial, then in the direction of confusion. Lastly, I saw fear alight on his brow.

He made to stand up.

"Sit down!"

It was a command; it was not a request.

He did not resist me.

He sat.

His gaze found the table, then the floor; he looked anywhere he could to avoid my eyes which were set and firm like black marbles staring out of a bronze statue: they were beacons of certainty.

"You abused me when I was a boy: you *fucked* my life…"

His mouth opened in defense, in defiance, more denial that died before it could even reach his tongue.

"But you need to know…" I continued, "that I forgive you. I forgive you."

The second *forgiveness* was for me and not for him.

I needed to reiterate my words with the double-tap of certitude.

I forgave him.

I did not let him off.

That was not what happened here.

Pardon was not my intention.

My intention proper was to recover from this man something he'd stolen from me some three decades before: a light, an innocence, my will, a part of my soul.

He had it in his keeping. I wanted it back.

I also wanted to return what was his, and I only understood this properly many years later after much contemplation, after much heartache and inner search, after a higher communion with the frequency of love.

When I was eleven, he stole my goodness, *my kingdom* and he replaced it with his evil, his ignorance, a schema of lies and fear, and this was my opportunity to give it back.

This vampire had left a bleed in me thirty years before and he had been feeding from it remotely, even in the absence of being and across time and space, and now I was returning it to him.

If this all sounds a little esoteric it's because it is.

But that does not mean it lacks potency, quite the opposite.

The esoteric is only esoteric until it becomes known.

It always sounds whimsical until you witness for yourself its boundless power.

Prior to this day, I had tried physical revenge many times and many times it had failed me. The men I fought and defeated, my "victories" outside nightclubs and bars, in road-rage incidents and on the streets of my home city, did not sate me or ease me or remove my fear.

Like the hydra of myth, every time I took a head, a new one grew in its place.

As fast as I could decapitate one, it was replaced by another.

It took me a decade of blood on the pavement before I could see this.

The violence I inflicted on others only fed the violence resident in me.

It fed my insecurity *fat* until I was almost lost to a dark covenant, with base brutality and evil.

I had tried the legal route too, just for your information: I was spat out by the judiciary after one interview with a clumsy, ill-prepared copper who seemed more interested in whether or not I enjoyed the abuse than he did in capturing a known pedophile. The crime was historical (he told me). The incident was unwitnessed (he reminded me). My word against his, I was assured. I also suspected the policeman felt the abuse was not serious enough. My body was invaded but I was not raped, only my young mind was savaged, and that does not show up on evidential photographs, it does not read "serious" to a jury uneducated in the psychology of sexual abuse. There is no way they could truly understand unless they'd experienced it themselves, how the young plastic brain is twisted and distorted by interference. They could not know how it leaves a victim in a perpetual state of fearful anticipation for the rest of their lives unless they are able, somehow, somewhere to arrest it and clean it out. And the longer it is left of course, the more difficult this becomes. The roots of abuse tangle themselves around the organs and the psyche of a victim like bindweed. Not even the practiced scalpel of a skilled surgeon would be able to cut-out this root without also killing the invaded synapses and organs.

Only love has the power to remove abuse once and for all, and love of course is injected intravenously when we employ the weapon of forgiveness.

I had tried the physical, I had tried it to death and nearly ended myself in its pursuit. I had followed the judicial route only be told (to quote), "We can't do anything with these pedophiles unless we pretty much catch them in the act."

All I was left with was the metaphysical and I just needed to be brave enough, smart enough, controlled enough to give it a try.

I told him I forgave him twice.

As I walked away, job done, the beginning of my healing, he stood up from his chair, he looked at me, and he put his hand out nervously.

His fingers were trembling.

He wanted to shake my hand.

I knew what he was asking.

I knew.

Are you forgiving me or are you *forgiving* me?

I shook his hand.

My forgiveness was complete.

My soul was retrieved.

I gave him back his darkness, the hot coals, the parasite of his abuse.

This, this, this was only the very beginning of my healing.

Listen, I was nearly forty years old at the time, the crime was committed against me some three decades before. His parasite, *this* parasite, had been living in me for a long time. It had acted in me, it had acted as me and through me for many years. Which means I had accumulated a lot of negative karma when I acted inappropriately, when I was unwise or unkind, when I was outrageous and violent. I acted in these ways unconsciously and at the command of a damaged psyche and as a form of displacement, but nevertheless I did act, and I did do a lot of bad things and the consequence of my actions *the history* was stuck in the plumbing.

Thirty years of unconscious living was not going to disappear overnight just because I'd forgiven my abuser. Even though *I was not myself* when I did all those terrible things, they were still done on my watch and so it was my job to clean up the mess. Like Odysseus returning home from the Trojan wars, only to find his palace at Ithaca overrun by evil, I had to win back my kingdom, and pay back my debts.

This would take another twenty years of hallowing, of purging and cleansing.

This is a story in and of itself. It is not one that fits comfortably into the narrow confines of this book. For those looking to hear more about my regeneration into a sane human being, may I refer you to my memoir *Notes From a Factory Floor*.

Suffice to say that forgiveness removed the original cause, and I was now left with the job of cleansing the effects of that cause and the effects of the effects.

Every effect becomes the cause to the next effect ad infinitum unless the moving object of karma meets with an obstacle or a greater force.

When we forgive someone, they should be very afraid. It means we have given them over to the law of reciprocity. It means we have let them go.

My abuser had his own karma to meet.

He could no longer sustain himself on my energy.

I had severed the link of hate and fear when I forgave him.

Some years later I heard the news that this man had killed himself in a hotel room in London. An angry mob of historical crimes had finally caught up with him and, before his victims could see their day in court, he ended his life at the end of a short rope.

Someone asked me on hearing the news, "What do you feel?"

I said, "I feel compassion."

That was the moment I knew I was completely free.

Compassion is a non-local power: it always dissolves evil.

I would later use this reference point, this certainty to dissolve other grudges when life presented me with pain and abuse and betrayal, and I needed a sound strategy to redress the balance.

I have earned certainty with forgiveness, the result of my own personal experimentum crucis, the conclusive proof that the hypothesis of forgiveness works in the real world against real-world problems.

Whilst I don't expect you to believe me, whilst I implore you not to believe me, I hope to inspire you enough with this small treatise on forgiveness to go out and be your own proof.

If my proof of efficacy acts merely as a creative spark that you might develop into the flame of bona-fide certainty, my job will have been done well enough.

In the title of this book, I promised you **99 reasons to forgive,** and I aim to start with **freedom**.

You are never free while you are bound to another by the glue of resentment.

Freedom is the first reason to forgive.

Reason One: Freedom

Most of us think we are free.

We believe we are free human beings.

I used to think I was a free man.

I wandered my small patch of planet earth for many years announcing my freedom and revelling in the emancipated life I lived *but it was a lie.*

I knew it was a lie.

Everyone else knew that *their* freedom was a lie too, even though none of us dared voice it, even though not one of us was brave enough to *admit* our prison with its invisible bars and amorphous doors and covert guards and high, high walls.

This was certainly true for all those in my world, growing up in industrial, working-class Coventry.

Fear stood wall-and-sentry around the orbit of our tiny realities. The bars were our false beliefs, the circumference of our cells marked the level of our enquiry: small. The heavy steel doors were built from our many unchallenged cognitions. Our burly guards were the conceptions and unquestioned precepts of our education. The family, the friends, the environment with its ancient laws and its dogmatic mores made sure that we did not challenge these perceptions. We were so busy trying to make the rent and feed the kids and keep up with the current needs and wants that few of us found time to challenge our existence or even find thinking-time to meditate on the fact that change might be needed or even possible. And for those of us who did venture to the periphery of our set limitations, it felt as though we would have to take on the whole universe if we were to break through the meteor belt of conditioning.

These prisons had no independent selfhood: they were not real.

They were mere conceptualizations with the forms and

aspects that constructed a living prison, with the façade of a free world.

They were made this way to prevent the inmates from ever knowing that they were incarcerated.

How can you escape when you are not even aware that you are imprisoned?

The devil, as they say, was never so happy when he convinced people that he did not exist.

There are many things that imprison us, conceptions all, and this in itself is a line of enquiry that I would encourage everyone to explore.

The Buddha tells us that all suffering finds its route in ignorance.

When we don't know the rules, we can't play the game.

That's one thing I am sure of: *this is a game.*

It is a game that must be played but can't be won.

It is a game of souls, and the stakes are high.

Death is lurking around every corner; evil is crouched outside every open door. And there is only one guarantee; you will be challenged the moment you wake from the sleep of ignorance and stake your claim to genuine autonomy.

Thomas Aquinas defines freedom as the result of consistently using free will to make choices that accord with wisdom and love. When we lose our ability to do this, because our autonomy has been impaired or stolen, and we make bad choices, we become imprisoned in and determined by the subsequent reality that these actions create.

The first glimpse of freedom occurs when we awaken from the conceptual dream and recognize that money, wealth, privilege, accumulation, accolades, the respect of our fellow man etc. – *they do not lead us to emancipation.* Quite the opposite. Craving for and needing anything always, inevitably, leads to suffering. I read a very apt postcard once, it said, "I am free… between concepts."

Awakening usually occurs when we suffer a crisis or experience a mind-expanding spiritual epiphany. We think we are free but as little as a negative Twitter post or an unkind review or a curt e-mail or a bad-news-phone call can climb inside us, trigger our feral body chemistry, and steal our vital attention like a thief in the night; it can spiral us into a day, a week, a year, a whole lifetime of anxiety. Or we are courted and distracted and derailed by the same energies, wearing a different disguise: flattery, faux kindness, favor, peer-review, or the fluttering-skirt of sexual arousal.

We will not be free until we become impervious to the rush of all these passions.

We are not free, not necessarily because we lose control of our sovereignty at the first sign of physical or psychological arousal; rather we lose our sovereignty because we never had sovereignty in the first place. We have no center, so our body chemistry, the *adrenal-army* and the foot-soldiers of anxiety and fear are dumped inside us like a cluster-bomb.

We are controlled by our body chemistry.

Until we find a center and bring the endocrine system to book this will always be the case.

We are scattered because we do not know, or have not yet identified our true I, the eternal part of us that is invisible and indivisible; the permanent, stable, unchanging self that is unmoved by *the ten thousand things* of the world.

This is a whole area of investigation of course and not within the context of this book which is specifically about the benefits of forgiveness. If I can refer you to my tome, *The Divine CEO*, you will find a more comprehensive guide to finding the self and winning personal autonomy.

Freedom, or the quest for it, is worth every one of your hours and your very last penny in its pursuit. And if freedom, from sadness, from suffering, from the residual ache of historical abuse is your goal, there is no better place to start the search than by looking at the things that currently stand between you and your liberation.

I can remember some years ago when I carried a grudge towards a close friend who had betrayed me in the most indefensible manner. I told myself that I had forgiven this man because, as an aspirant of all things spiritual, I felt as though I *had* to say that. In truth, every time I heard his name, even in casual conversation, my hackles would rise, and my adrenalin would drip-drip and internal dialogue would spiral into projections of anger and betrayal and revenge.

I convinced myself that I had forgiven him, but my body signals told a different story.

I spoke to my Intuition in a meditation.

I made an enquiry.

I said, "What is it with this man? Why is he still stirring up these emotions in me? I've forgiven him, job done, move on, next lesson please."

(After He'd stopped laughing) my Intuition spoke to me, "You haven't forgiven him."

"I haven't? How do you know I haven't?"

"Because he still affects you, he still controls you."

"Controls me?! I don't think so."

My Intuition reminded me of the facts: "You overhear his name, you see his face, you hear his voice, and he climbs inside you, he hijacks your body chemistry, he steals a day, he pilfers a week, or a month: he rapes your attention. He controls you."

Silence.

Good point.

"How will I know when I've forgiven him?"

"You will know you have forgiven him when his name, his voice, his face triggers nothing but compassion."

"Compassion! But..."

"He's still controlling you. He is riding your senses like a stallion."

More silence.

This was true.

It was true. It was uncomfortable to hear, and it was unacceptable.

My Intuition spoke to me again, "Any grudge you hold, even for one man, is an obstacle between you and your freedom."

I would never be free while I nursed resentment for anyone because it meant that anyone (even if he were a *no one*) still controlled my body chemistry.

That meant he controlled my free will, he controlled my attention-energy; literally.

And, as I mentioned earlier, freedom is what results when we consistently use free will to make choices that accord with wisdom and love.

He controlled my mood (mood is radically altered by adrenalin), he controlled my actions (we often lose control and make the wrong choices when under the cosh of fear), he controlled my health (adrenalin closes down immune function, leaving us open to disease). My potential to work was inhibited: how many man-hours are lost each year to stress? He even affected and hijacked my personality because anything that controls your senses invades your mind and works your personality like a marionette.

When I realized that I was controlled by the object of my resentment, that my life had been commandeered and that it was a clear and pernicious barrier to my potential to fully flourish as a human being I ended my grudge towards this man immediately. I also realized (more on this and other health aspects in a later chapter) that the object of my arousal was feeding off my essential energies. When we harbor hate or anger or fear for anyone, our *strong emotion* forms a link or a bond between us and them, an ethereal intravenous drip that allows them to vampire our essential energies from distance and at will.

By finding forgiveness for this man, compassion, by enlightening my ignorance, I was able to sever that feed and break free.

To get through this earthly sojourn, soul intact, fully realized, I need all the energy I can get.

It is essential then that I prune all subsidiary roots, that I contain my vital sap, so that (to paraphrase Blake) it can rise powerfully in one direction and not be pilfered by blood-sucking parasitical grudges.

The false ego feeds off drama.

It feeds off pain and conflict.

It holds onto grudges like a gannet.

It is delicious to hold grudges because something inside us, our own negative inclination, or the adverse forces, loves to feed off pain.

The mystic Eckhart Tolle calls these subpersonalities **pain-bodies**.

He assures us that pain-bodies feed off other pain-bodies.

Pain-bodies feed off any kind of drama and there is no bigger drama than a betrayal or an abuse or a personal affront.

The parasite of grudge feeds off pain.

If it feeds off pain, this means that it is not you, it is not your true self, it is not your unique identity.

How do I know?

Because the authentic self feeds only from love and love is veiled by resentment like the sun is covered by a rain cloud.

If the acrimonious-personality feeds off pain and you can establish and qualify that *this is not you*, this is not your best game, then it is logical to conclude that you are not free and you are not free because you are not you, even if it feels like you are. And it does feel like you, of course; one of the deceits of the pain-body is to subtly take over your personality by enticing you with tasty, salty, dirty emotional bait.

Once you engage it, it becomes *you*.

For the entire duration of your engagement, *it* thinks it's you and (more worrying) you think it's you.

It is not you.

Anything that marinates in drama and feeds off pain and delights in fantasies of vengeance and rationalizes bloody revenge is not by any stretch of the imagination you: not the real you. Once you can categorically establish that it is not you, that it has stolen your identity, your autonomy, your body, your life, you can set about eschewing it, denying it, learning its tricks, exposing its traps, interrupting its strategies, and starving it out – *it is not you!*

There are whole books on how to do this; *The Power of Now* by Eckhart Tolle being the most accessible.

It is a study and a discipline to do battle with these semi-autonomous thought-forms, but in succinct vernacular it is simply a matter of starving them out by refusing to emotionally engage them. They are fed and watered, they are sustained and strengthened by our emotional engagement, by our identification with them.

When we engage shadows, they thrive.

When we deny shadows, they atrophy, they die, they fall away.

Emotional engagement of negativity in any form (anger, rage, jealousy, revenge, self-pity, depression, sadness, greed, envy etc.) is an asinine and conceited indulgence in the hook-and-bait that dangles before our attention. The great mystic Richard Rose reminds us that, "We take the bait at our peril, we take the bait at high cost; our own freedom."

You are not free while you hold a resentment: that is fact, and it is reason number one why you should take a torch to your rancor and put it to the fire.

The principal reason why we hold onto acrimony in our life – and I know many people who have spent their entire lives locked in its prison – is ignorance.

If you study the Buddhist liturgy or the Judaic exegesis or delve into Christian mysticism or mine the rich vaults of Islam or Sikhism or the Holy Vedas, if you study these historical works and reduce their teaching to the one word that explains our current suffering on the great earth, that word would be **ignorance**.

Generally, and specifically people are ignorant of themselves, they are ignorant of their biology and their psychology, and they have no great understanding of their metaphysical origins, or the effect their own actions have on the reciprocal world around them. Most people still live in ignorance of basic universal laws, the purpose of these laws and their own individual responsibilities within them. Even a brief scan of the daily tabloids and the evening news bulletins with their reports on the *bad news* around the world *("if it bleeds, it leads")* is enough to immediately tell you two things: 1) the world at present feeds mostly off negative energy, and 2) many of the people in power are as blind to universal law as everyone else.

Many of the people we follow *our elders, and our leaders* are blind, they don't know where they are going, and even though we can clearly see that dishonesty and deceit and denial is rife in the halls of power (they don't even bother to deny it anymore) we still pretend we haven't seen it and we continue support their tenure with our tick in a ballot box.

This may sound like a sweeping statement, and I implore you not to take my word for it. You must look for yourself. You must find proof for yourself. If a leader (or anyone else) is dishonest, if he lies or omits truths, if he deceives in his public office or her private life (in essence, they are not different), if he cheats, if she slanders (even subtly), they do so because they are ignorant of the law. If they knew the law, if they truly knew and understood it, they would never tell another lie, they would never knowingly deceive again.

Position and power and privilege are no assurance of

knowledge; they guarantee only one thing: that the people on public platforms have understood enough about society to turn its engine.

In other words, they know how to operate in the explicate world, but have yet to fathom that there is a higher law in play, in the implicate order. Wrongs that might be escaped in the lower realms are always picked up by the higher law.

Science tells us that there is an explicate law, and there is an implicate law, an inner and an outer reality. Things may seem as though they go unnoticed, and unpunished in the explicate order, but they are seen in the implicate order, they are meticulously recorded in an amorphous ledger, brought to balance at the appropriate time and always in equal measure.

This ignorance of law is responsible for the small wars you have in the microcosm of your own mind every day; it is also responsible for the big wars we see in the world at large. So, it is no good blindly following what others are telling you, you have to learn it for yourself.

When you are able to shed light on ignorance you have opened the door towards free will and freedom.

Seek first the Kingdom of God.

You have probably read or heard a million times biblical phrases like "seek first the kingdom of heaven," "enter the land (of Milk and Honey)," "enter the promised land," etc.

The root word for land is "will."

When we are directed to "seek first the kingdom" we are being encouraged to "seek first the will... then all good things will come unto you." The will (referred to in esoterica as "the body of conscious will" or "the causal body" or "the bliss body") is personal autonomy. When we have control over our own will, we have "entered the kingdom," "the land of milk and honey," the will is "the promised land" because it offers us direct access to "all good things." It is also called the causal body because it is the part of us that wills or creates causation in the world, and causes are the building blocks of this manifest world. Once we have won back the will/personal autonomy (or, won back our kingdom), we can use that will to connect to the Tao (the way) and we can willingly engage with and utilize the natural forces of the great earth: we can become one with them, we can make choices that accord with wisdom and love, and that will lead to a sustainable freedom. In other words, we find the rhythm and vibration of our own will and we connect it to the rhythm and vibration of the universe, so that we become one with its immense powers.

People want to change the world, but they have not even developed a strong enough will to change their own waist measurement, they have not used their will to change their eating habits, they do not have enough power of will to stop themselves from gossiping about their friends outside Costa on a Friday afternoon. How strong is your will if you can't use it to control one of the smallest muscles in the body: the tongue? It is easy to kid ourselves that we have control of will, because we have met with some success in the world, but until we can use our will to live consciously and make wise choices every day, to be self-aware, to self-observe and be virtuous we cannot lay claim to the kingdom.

Winning back the will (which leads to freedom) is our first and foremost job.

Without it there can be no advance. As the soul awakens in the body (the birth of consciousness) it is going to need an iron will in order to follow out the commands of destiny.

This chapter is insisting that freedom is the first and prime reason why you should forgive. It is worth everything, all the discomfort and work, to win your free will and claim your personal freedom.

In Arabic the word for forgiveness is Musa'ma'ha; the same word can also mean "free."

To forgive someone from your mind then, is to become free from them.

Before we can forgive, we first have to spread some light on what forgiveness actually is, and perhaps more specifically, what it is not.

As I said earlier, forgiveness does not mean we are letting people off with the crimes they may have committed against us or against society.

We don't even have the power to forgive (in that sense), pardon is not a human imperative, it is a divine attribute.

We do not have the power to forgive others.

We do not even have the power to forgive ourselves.

We do, however, have the power to give our complaint over to a Power that does.

One of the myriad names for this Power is Reciprocity, the law of compensation.

This is the subject of the next chapter and the second reason why we should forgive.

Budo Practice

In the many stations of martial arts training, our ultimate goal is personal emancipation, freedom from the parasites of fear and conditioning. Like a tiny acorn lying on a forest floor, our desire is to reach our full Oak-like potential. This can only be achieved if all impediments to growth are first identified, and then systematically removed.

The **Oak-stem borer** – a tree parasite – is only 5mm in size, and yet this tiny creature can devour an entire Oak: first it attacks in the small branches at the top of the tree or on small side twigs. Then, hungry for seedlings, the oak-stem borer larvae will tunnel in the twigs and then down into the main trunk to the root collar. One small parasite can quickly become a legion, in the tree, and in us if we do not arrest their relentless assault.

I have to say that the majority of martial artists do not achieve their final goal of emancipation; they unfortunately get lost along the way and never reach this lofty place, but for those that do, the rewards are boundless.

In this practical addition to chapter one I would like to encourage you, the reader, to make an honest, unedited, and relentless inventory of all the feelings and emotions, the resentments and grudges that currently stand between you and your freedom from fear. You may not think so, but these untreated emotions are parasites that will at the very least stifle your full growth, and at worse bore in and feed off your root-collar energy until you are little more than a walking husk.

Write them down.

Even if (at the moment) you feel they are legitimate grudges, put them on the page anyway, look at them, and see them for what they really are. Whether you justify them or not, you cannot escape the fact that they bleed your resources, and more often than not, postpone your life. I nursed many "legitimate" angers about being abused as a boy, some that I dared not voice for many years, for fear of offending my mum, or my dad, or God. It was only after I wrote a fearless stage play (called *Fragile*) that the parasites of blame and anger and dissonance presented themselves (on page and on stage) in their full regalia. An interesting thing happened when I put my rage to the page: a wise inner voice looked at my presentation and asked me to qualify each of the many blames. Was the abuse really my mum's fault, because she let me stay overnight at the Boy's Club where I was abused? Was it my really my dad's fault? My father had visited the martial arts school and the teacher, and he had spoken to him prior the assault, just to make sure that he was safe, to assure that I would not be harmed in his care. My dad came to the school, straight from the pub and I allowed a negative inner voice to convince me that he was staggering drunk (he was not), that he was pissed, and that he wouldn't have been able to identify a pedophile if one fell out of the sky and hit him on the head. As much as I adored my dad, the parasite of blame had bored into my consciousness, and I found myself secretly hating his very bones. It was his fault, I told myself. And then there was God, even He came in for a vile, unqualified rage: "Where the fuck was you?" I found myself asking.

Writing that play freed me.

The list of endless blames, the unqualified angers and the debilitating confusions and the fathom-deep rage that I removed from my mind and placed into ink, washed clean the doors of my perception and I was able to see for the first time that what happened to me was sad, it was unacceptable, and it was damaging but there was no one person to blame: even the teacher that abused me was a victim in his own way, of darker forces, of a sick and deranged mind, of a childhood that too would have been littered with damage. All I felt after writing down my dramatic itinerary, and bringing it into the light of day, was unadulterated, undiluted, unconditional love. Man, I have never felt so much love, for my mum, for my dad, for God *and yes*, even for the man who groomed and abused me. Love. Compassion: that's how I was finally able to exorcize him... but more on that in a later chapter.

Once the obstructions have been listed and named, once you have brought them to light, they will lose much of their sting. They feed in darkness these parasites, and they thrive on not being seen.

Once you have written down every resentment and anger (fill your boots: the more detail you are able to bring to the page, the better the process will be; split every log, lift every stone), you can set to work on removing their obscuration through a process of individuation.

The bad news is that your free will is always compromised by your karma, the drama you are determined to act out today was written to the page by the causes of all your yesterdays. You have no choice but to follow the direction of the dramatist. But there is some good news: karma can be changed because you *are* the dramatist. Even if you did not directly write the historical abuses with your own pen, you are the person that gets to choose how you react to that consequential narrative: perhaps I can't change what happened to me yesterday, but I can definitely choose how I respond to it today. Once we understand that the lines we write in the present moment determine the acts and scenes of our future reality, we can begin to clean and edit the old script with our positive choices, and write a shiny-new story with our current actions.

If I buy a house, only to find on my first day that the plumbing is backed up and blocked, I can either sit around complaining, trying to figure out which of the previous tenants was to blame, and if they are going to be punished for their negligence, or I can roll my sleeves up and get to work clearing the shit from the pipes. I know one thing, they are not going to clean themselves, and marinating in my own anger and self-pity, is not going to get my toilets flushing again anytime soon.

Individuation might sound complicated, but in reality, it is simply an exercise in observance: you allow the feelings and thoughts and confusions (blocked in your plumbing) to rise in your mind (just as they usually do), and then watch, observe them, witness them but without identification, without emotional engagement.[3] It might be difficult at first, but it will get easier with practice. Imagine that your wild and volatile emotions are like the throwing wind and thrashing rain of a hurricane, and you are sat in the very quiet center of it all, in the eye of the storm, looking out.

If fear rises, watch it rise, follow its course, feel its keen sting, acknowledge the feeling of wanting to react, either by lashing out, or by retreating to your safe place, and remind yourself that without your identification, it cannot persist for long: employ *choiceless awareness*, just be the witness, patiently watch. Dare yourself to observe until the feelings eventually withdraw. They will withdraw. They have no power, they have no reality without your permission: you are a god over these feelings and thoughts and emotions, and if you command it, they no longer exist. All the time you are acting as the passive observer, remind yourself again and again why you are refusing to engage with the negatives: they are parasites; if you engage them, you engorge them. If you don't engage them, they will withdraw.

I have three key words I use when the passions rush my mind door, and the feelings and emotions whisper doom and depression in my ear: **practice, practice, practice**. The second I become aware of an imminent assault, I say to myself (aloud or sub-vocally), "Time to practice." The word *practice* acts as a Pavlovian action trigger; the moment I say it to myself, and believe it, my state tips from helpless ignorance to conscious, courageous curiosity. An interesting thing happens when you start to use your shadows as target practice; as curiosity and enquiry are engaged, fear and dread are disengaged. It is as though the pain-body instantly notes your change of state, realizes that you are no long easy meat (quite the opposite, the hunted has become the hunter) and either diminish their assault, or retreat completely. There is a powerful verse in *The Tibetan Book of the Dead* that I love; it suggests that when monsters rise in your mind to claim you, all you have to remember is that they are monsters of your own creation. When you consciously and deliberately make this distinction, **recognition and liberation are instantaneous.** I would strongly suggest that emotional crisis is not just a good time to be curious and practice, it is the only time: Generals do not prove their battle strategies in the dry safety of a warm classroom, they make their gains and earn their stars in the blood-red theatre of war.

When you are prepared to sit in the initial discomfort of a passion-assault and absorb 99% of its wild bluster, what will be left after the storm has passed will be a rainbow of new consciousness, the shimmering diamond hidden in the rogue winds of adversity. If you do nothing more than sit in the discomfort and watch and wait until the weather has passed, this gift will be presented to you by the enemy turned emissary. The courage and the wisdom developed by the process of choiceless awareness, develops the internal musculature needed to handle the rush of new knowledge that the god of ill winds blows in.

I will return to this technique again throughout the book.

Reason Two: Reciprocity – The Law

In Buddhism there is a great emphasis placed upon understanding Dharma or law. Failure to understand law is ignorance, ignorance leads to craving and grasping or clinging, which is the root cause of all suffering.

When we carry resentment and feel damaged or maligned or disrespected or hurt by the attitudes and actions of others, we suffer. When we wish to remove this suffering, it causes craving or grasping; craving relief or remedy, grasping for change or ease. This grasping becomes the cause of still more suffering and the perpetual wheel of discomfort, sometimes outright pain, continues.

The main reason many of us suffer is because we want to see justice, we need to witness sentence being dealt to our persecutor, and if this doesn't happen, for whatever reason, we suffer even more.

This is the first level of ignorance: it is where many people remain stuck.

It often interrupts, postpones, cripples, or even ends people's lives.

Science assures us that man, as a whole, is made up of many component parts. Each part is essential, and each part is connected to every other.

If we carry an unhealed wound from a past relationship, the resentment does not remain isolated, it permeates every aspect of our lives, just like a single component (a frayed bolt or a broken cable) on a huge airliner can compromise, even bring down the whole plane.

Trillions of cells in the human organism can be damaged and destroyed, by one faulty perception that has been allowed to bloat: we do not have to look too hard or too far to find proof of this in our history books.

I once worked with a young woman whose whole life had been destroyed, leaving her with debilitating depression and other connected mental health problems, and all because her first husband was abusive and she felt *she believed* he was never rightly punished for his crime, by society, by the judicial system or by God. When I tentatively suggested that she could free herself from the tyranny of depression by forgiving her former spouse, she turned on me in bristling anger and confusion and said, "You have no idea what he did to me."

When she calmed down, I said gently, "It doesn't matter what he did to you. What matters is, he is still doing it, even in his absence, and he will continue to hurt you whilst you hold onto the grievance." I added, "You can free yourself from the suffering by forgiving him from your mind, by letting him go."

She would not even contemplate this as an avenue of possibility (or even enquiry), she was too bitterly obsessed with how her life was over and he was off "swanning it" with a new partner and a new child and a new life.

Life (she assured me) was not fair.

She assumed that he'd completely escaped the consequences of his actions.

She clung to her depression like a life-raft, her wound became a drowning identity.

She violently kicked to the curb any notion of a cure which did not include her ex being publicly shamed, and severely punished. She craved relief and cried for balm whilst all the time immersing her engagement and identification in the very perceptions that were causing her suffering.

I met another fascinating man, Chris Lubbe, former friend, and bodyguard to South African president Nelson Mandela. Chris had spent time in prison on Robben Island with Mandela and in our brief, serendipitous meeting he told me many stories of demonic torture and divine miracles in that forsaken place. One of the most revealing stories was from their post-prison years when Mandela, newly elected president of the troubled country, was putting together a multiracial bodyguard detail. He told me how Mandela insisted that he (Chris) and the other black BGs work side-by-side with their white counterparts. Chris was perturbed to say the least. He was being asked to work cheek-by-jowl with his former enemy, men who had beaten and tortured him in the apartheid era. Chris felt it was an *ask* too far but Mandela insisted that the healing of the country had to start from the top down, with the healing of its leaders. How can you ask the country to replace bombs and guns and conflict with peace and love and understanding if the leaders themselves could not achieve it, if the so-called hierarchy could not lead by example?

The white bodyguards viewed the black bodyguards as terrorists, people who tried to bring the country down and bomb its police.

The black bodyguards viewed their white counterparts as racist oppressors, murderers, and torturers.

Through a slow and painful process of *truth and reconciliation*, these men and women sat around the table, aired their angst, and worked through their own prejudices and ignorance. Eventually they were able to find enough reconciliation to work together in the vanguard that was to start the whole country on the long and slow path towards freedom.

Mandela understood law.

He understood that everyone had their part to play in this unfolding drama of South African politics, and there would be no resolution without honest discussion. He knew too that hate and anger would not solve the problems that they now faced.

Both sides had tried the warring route, and both sides had failed.

The anger fed the anger, the hate fed the hate, and even when it was well intended, the violence always rebounded on itself. It was time for a new energy, and that energy (as Mandela himself said) was love.

It was the suffering in SA that had awakened love, and now it was moving through the troubled country like ink through water, with one man – Mandela – at the helm. In his memoir, *Long Walk to Freedom*, Nelson Mandela reveals candidly how his thirty years in prison had shown him this truth. He said that, as he drove out the prison gates on his last day of imprisonment, his first day of freedom, he realized he had a choice to make: let go of the hatred, his sense of righteous injustice, or be plagued and controlled and consumed by it forever. He knew that if he did not let go of anger and leave it at the gates of the prison, he would never be free from it.

He made the choice.

He let the anger go.

Although I am sure he must have had many testing moments where his famous temper threatened to erupt in moments of high pressure, he never again let anger rule him.

Mandela also understood his own personal role within that law: to lead by way of example.

As president of South Africa, he began working the law to the good, with the men and women closest to him.

The healing of SA is, of course, an ongoing process, but it has begun, and I feel sure that, in time, the country will finds its peace.

My friend, depressed over the abusive treatment of her ex, did not believe in the law, she would not contemplate the law or even listen to rational explanations and stories about the obvious power of law.

She did not believe me when I told her that her healing lay in understanding, and not in revenge and anger.

Chris Lubbe and his comrades took Mandela's word; they trusted him and were enabled and freed by what they learned through a very painful, but ultimately healing process.

So far, my friend has still not recovered from her mental

health problems, but that does not mean she is forever lost. In the future her return, her health will always only be a single decision away.

I am aware that I have mentioned *law* several times already without really qualifying or quantifying it.

So, what is this law and why is it important?

The law I am speaking of is the law of compensation, or the law of proportionate returns, often called Karma in the East, better known in the scientific West as cause and effect, or reciprocity, or *the principle of causation*. This is known in science as Newton's third law: for every action there is an equal and opposite reaction.

This is the law and understating it is imperative.

We can't even begin to find freedom or peace if we don't have a profound understanding of causation. If we don't understand or believe that our actions, *everyone's actions*, have consequences, if we believe for even a second that some people escape the effects of their actions, then we will always be taking one step forwards and two steps back. We will forever be at the mercy of our own ignorance, planting nightshade in the soil of our lives and wondering in dismay why it did not sprout into an apple tree. We will be relentlessly in retrograde because we have not yet understood the basic law of the universe in which we live.

If we don't understand causation, how it works, why it works, when it works and its absolute nature, we will always be experiencing negative effects in our lives, and in our universe, and then wondering *what the hell just happened*. Or we may be subject to a positive consequence, but not fully understanding how we did it, how it worked, and why it occurred: this means we will be unable to consciously repeat and replicate our success in further encounters with the world.

One of the reasons we are able to deny causation is because of time; more often than not, there is a time lag, a distance or gap between the initiating cause and its inevitable effect, so it is easy to assume that a particular cause was effect free, or that a crime was left unpunished, or a good deed went without appropriate reward. Often (also) someone may commit a crime against a person or against society and escape judicial law (the explicate order), and people say, "See! I told you. It doesn't work. He committed a crime, and he escaped the law. Where is the justice?"

This usually happens because people are generally unaware of the implicate order, they do not believe in karma, so they deny universal reciprocity. They mistake judicial law for universal law, and because the perpetrator escapes his day in a public courtroom, they think he escaped the consequence of his actions.

He did not, he has not, and he could not.

Universal law is meticulous. It is a self-levelling force that repairs and repays every right and every wrong in its own time, at its own pace and in its very own individual way **without our need to witness it**. Causation does not even limit itself to a single incarnation; debts and credits left unpaid at the end of one life-span roll over to the next generation and the next generation ad infinitum until eventually the books are balanced and all debts are paid.

Our internal debts and profits are left as an inheritance for our offspring (what we do, and who we are in society will affect our children and our family), we leave them the cellular inheritance, often called *the genetic curse* (if the debt is negative) or *the genetic gift* (if it is the positive).

I spoke with a young man once who was perturbed at the very idea that his wrongs might somehow, somewhere affect his daughter to the negative. He didn't think this was fair and rebuffed any suggestion that it might be true. His opinion was strong, but it made no difference to the law, his angry denial did not affect the ebb and flow of causation. The law is not altered by opinion, any more than the force of electricity would be affected by your assessment of it; you either understand it and respect it and use it to the good, or you get fried, it is that simple, *and* it is not personal.

Even a cursory investigation would reveal the truth of this reality.

Everything we do affects our offspring, of course it does, the effects of our actions on our children is astonishingly real. And, as I said to the young guy, if you don't want your negative living to affect your *innocent* child, there is an easy solution: don't live negatively. Use your free will to make wiser, kinder, more loving choices, and make your child's inheritance a good one, a positive, affirmative treasure.

I believe people know *at some level* that their actions have consequences but prefer to remain in denial and postpone (repayment of) their debt to some date in the future.

A couple of years ago we screened a feature film (*Retaliation* – starring Orlando Bloom and Anne Reid) at the Edinburgh International Film Festival. It is a powerful movie based on a particularly troubling aspect of my life; its message is about the metaphysical power of forgiveness. The film (spoiler alert!) culminates with an abusive priest burning himself to death in a field after he is confronted (and forgiven) by one of his victims. Unable to deal with the "coals of fire heaped upon his head," the priest takes his own life. Unbeknown to the priest, his young niece wanders into the park and witnesses the burning. Although the child does not immediately understand what she is seeing or the fact that it is her beloved uncle who is on fire, the message was clear: the consequences of our actions do not end at the point of our death. The law of causation does not stop, rewind and start again from the beginning. This game of souls is real, and the effects of our living are stored in the console so that we are forced to start again from the point where we left off.

If I score low grades in high school, I will carry those marks forward with me into college or university; my start-point at university, will be my end point at high school. Similarly, the debts and loans I incur, on entering university, are carried over and paid back in the years proceeding my matriculation into the workplace. This is not Monopoly (the board game) we are talking about here; we can't accrue massive debt today and then start again fresh with a clean slate tomorrow, without first making recompense.

Now there are many reasons why you might expect someone to be offended by this muscular film; violence, violent language, self-harm, and visceral sexual self-harm to name but a few.

Do you know what offended people the most?

The scene at the end where the child witnesses the fire.

The financer of the film had asked us to remove the scene.

He found it deeply offensive but – when we asked him why – he could not qualify his complaint. The film distributors also called for it to be removed; again, without articulating what the offence was. We eventually managed to save the scene (and in saving the scene we saved the film). At a post-screening Q&A session one particular film reviewer was incensed by the scene and asked me to explain why I wrote it. I told her simply that our intention was to portray reciprocity in as clear a manner as possible. We (as film makers) wanted to show that the abusive priest may have killed himself, but his debt still remained, it had to be picked up, carried forward and paid for by his family.

I told her this, but I figured she already knew, because she complained, nearly crying, "Why would you do that to us?"

What she was really asking was, *Why would "I" do that to her?* Why would I feel the need to remind her of this uncomfortable law?

I didn't do anything to this lovely lady.

All I did was write a film and tell the truth. And I made sure that the integrity of the film and the truth were protected.

No matter how unpalatable it was, my job (and the directors' and actors' job) was to ensure that the truth was not diluted or removed by frightened financers and windy sales agents and film reviewers living in denial.

She asked the wrong question.

The right question would have been, "Why would I do that to myself? Why would I do that to my children, to my family, to my tribe, why would I do that to my world?"

She knew the law.

Of course, otherwise why the great offence, why the cryptic and emotional question? She understood causation, but she did not want to understand it, she would rather forget she knew, and she was offended that I *as the writer* might remind her with a short scene in a small, micro-budget, independent British film.

At some level we all know but acknowledging our knowing can be painful. It reminds us that we use our free will to make life choices that will bring suffering to ourselves, to our kith and kin, to the world at large and yet we still do it. We still choose our pleasure, knowing that it will be a torture to those we love and that is hard to live with.

Denial is less painful in the short term.

In the long term it is disastrous because debt is accumulative, it is compound, and over space and time the interest only grows.

Our present actions affect our future freedom.

Our present actions affect our children's future freedom.

You are unlikely to fully understand the law from this one small book.

At best it will act as an intercessor, timely information that interrupts your denial and inspires (or scares) you onto the right path.

If you already understand causation, this book will be a validation, it will underline, *perhaps crystallize* your own knowing.

I hope at least that it awakens your conscience or provokes

your interest or tickles your curiosity enough to excite further investigation. Being as blunt and as succinct as I can, I am making a strong statement that **no one escapes the consequence of their actions**, not the rich, not the privileged, not even royalty.

This realm has rules, it has laws: no one escapes them.

If you haven't seen this for yourself, it is not because it's untrue, it is because you haven't looked hard enough yet, you have not been brave enough to do the rigor.

Access to this truth is equitably available to everyone. It offers emancipation to those who search out and learn its ways, it delivers great profit to those who heed its rule.

What qualifies me to make a statement like this?

Because I've lived it, in extremes.

I was in denial for many years about law.

I caused great harm, to myself and to others, with my clumsy living and my ignorant denial. If I am going to write a book worthy of your attention, I feel duty-bound to either tell the truth or put down the quill and take a job on the shop-floor again, where I swept floors and swapped porn in the factory canteen, and pathetically complained that this world was "not fair to people like us."

When I say *no one escapes the law*, of course that includes you.

For me, I am already certain of the law and equally certain of the part I am called to play in it (more on this presently). I have, as the Irish are apt to say, *been around a few corners*. I have hurt people, I have damaged people I love, family, friends, wives and lovers; I have hurt my own children with my selfish life choices and my ugly actions. I have damaged them with my ignorance, and I have seen the scars and the insecurities and the suffering it has heaped upon them as they grew into adults. Although they love my very bones and would take a bat to anyone who uttered a bad word about their dad, I know (and they know) that I have been responsible for much of the suffering they have experienced as adults. Whilst I do all I can now as a conscious being to redress my many wrongs, I cannot in all conscience deny that I see the consequence of my actions every day in the faces of all my adult children.

I am a seer.

It is painful, being able to see.

It is painful to see clearly where your actions have had their effects on the world and its people.

It is also a tremendous gift to be a seer.

It is a grace to see clearly and without doubt how potent your actions are, how certain their effects will be and equally how you can change the course of your life for the better by choosing kinder, more responsible, loving actions in the present moment.

It also gives you an understanding and a genuine compassion for those who do not yet understand the law and who therefore cannot ride the wave of reciprocity by marrying their actions with its awesome power.

I have studied the law to a profound degree by living and by observing the consequences of my own living.

In my lifelong, in-depth study of this law, I have split every log, I have lifted every stone.

My findings are the painful treasure of a sixty-year excavation.

I am left in no doubt of the compensation that awaits all actions and all beings of action in this correlative territory we call home.

My certainty leaves me in awe of its power and in wonder at my potential as a vehicle for this preternatural force. How much good can I do in the world, how much joy and profit and healing and instruction and direction, how much guidance can I offer to my fellow beings now that I have understood and am learning to master this law.

The gist of this chapter lest I lose my way is this: forgiveness is not within our remit, it is not a human power, it is a universal attribute.

You can abandon your belief that you have to enact vengeance, or seek revenge, or witness justice; all you have to do is let go of the anger and fear, let go of the dissonance, shed your rage like an old coat and give the debt over to the force that "levels the hills and fills the valleys."

That's what forgiveness means: **give it over.**

It is not your job to forgive.

It is not your dharma.

You can't forgive anyone, but you can give it over to a power that can.

You can pray for others if prayer is within your vernacular of living or feel pity for them if it is not. The remedy of compassion is there too, for anyone that seeks it, and if there is one thing I am certain of it is this: compassion is a non-local power that melts bitterness like butter on a griddled sweetcorn.

It is popular these days to say things like, "Before you can forgive others, you first have to forgive yourself." Or, "Forgiving yourself is much harder than forgiving others."

We say this as though it is fact, and in stating it (or reading it or hearing it) over and again it eventually becomes the go-to maxim, our pseudo truth, even though it is a full-fat lie.

While we still believe the lie, we are not going to look for the truth.

A friend of mine complained once that he was being savagely attacked by critics, even though (he insisted), "I have done nothing wrong." In truth, everyone knew that he had done a lot of unkind things to others in the past, but he seemed unable (or unwilling) to admit it. I said to my wife, "Why do you think he won't look for the truth?" She said, "Because he believes he already has the truth."

We don't look for solutions if we don't think we have a problem.

We can't forgive others.

We cannot forgive ourselves.

With *their* debt, all we can do is give it over to the Great Bailiff.

With our own errors, we are gifted with the power of repentance.

We cannot forgive ourselves, but we can stand before our error, accept full responsibility for it, and allow the law to determine the nature and the measure of our penalty.

I must stipulate here that, though you may seek one, and though you may find one a comfort in times of moral suffering, you do not need a priest or a rabbi or any other mediator between you and God. It can help to talk with someone ordained, a person of faith that you trust to hear your confession, without judgment, certainly it can help to bring about the conversion of sin when we speak our guilt out loud (the word "conversation" comes from the root word *conversatio* meaning to convert). Our public confession can injure and greatly weaken the sin that lives in us as a blackmailing parasite, and for this reason alone, voicing our wrongs to any objective, non-judgmental ear, ordained or otherwise, can be a good thing, but, ultimately you are the prime mediator between your sin and the forgiveness of that sin by a conscious, self-levelling but ultimately loving Law.

Neither can a minister guarantee you forgiveness, even the Pope himself cannot settle your account if your public confession is incongruent with your private devices.

If you are truly repentant, however, if your conscience aches with the deep suffering and weeping regret of your mortal or venial errors, no other mediator is necessary. But your own mediator "conscience" is in itself a non-local power, it is a divine gift that cannot be bought or sold, bartered for or earned, no public donation or private pledge can beget this Grace: all we can do is prepare the ground, by suffering our sin, surrendering ourselves to penitence, and praying for mercy.

Once you understand law, once you know the universal way, you stop chasing witnessed revenge and you start courting personal repentance.

This is where I found myself all those years ago in that Coventry café, facing down my nemesis and offering him something I could not really deliver: pardon.

I have the ability to let go of my enemy and give him over to law, but I don't have the ability to pardon him; that job falls to a greater power than I.

After I shook the hand of my abuser, I felt proud of myself. I had forgiven a man who had done me a great disservice. But as I walked away, and in the coming months and years I realized *I understood* that my gesture, as well meaning and courageous as it may have seemed, was a quiet conceit. By evicting his fat parasite from my being, my awareness expanded into the vacated space, and I was able to see what my ignorance had been hiding from me all along.

It became clear to me that I was the one that needed forgiving.

I'd been so busy looking at what this man had done to me (and looking for revenge), that I had completely blocked out what I had done to others. I had hurt many people in my busy helter-skelter of a life and only ignorance had protected me from its glare. I was not just busy railing against him, I was also double-busy calling out the corrupt politicians and the greedy bankers and the violent fundamentalists in society. In the middle of this projected shit-storm of judgment, I'd failed to recognize the obvious: that I harbored a corrupt politician in me: I was my own personal greedy banker selfishly looking at what life could offer *me*. And the violent fundamentalist was so close to the surface that he was threatening to pierce my skin and act out at any moment.

The despots that I so despised in the world were in me.

Only my amateurish projection had hidden them.

I had a lot of work to do and none of it involved trying to bring the unjust to rights; all of it involved bringing myself to book.

We fall foul of the law because we *choose* to not understand the law.

We choose to not understand the law because to understand reciprocity in the general is to understand it in the particular. To see the truth in the macrocosm of the universe out there is to see the truth in the microcosm in here. We do not want to remove our indignation, *our resentments* because to do so would reveal much: that it is not within our power to forgive, that the law we live under is absolute, it favors none: that we are evading our own sins by hiding them under the shadow of others'. We also realize innately that the work we need to do on ourselves – personal repentance – is very real, it is urgent, it can only be achieved whilst we occupy a physical body, and we have no clear idea how long we have left to use this fleshy-spaceship. Whether we will leave this coil in fifty years' time or be snatched from the corner of our kitchen this very afternoon, no one knows.

Time then is of the utmost importance.

We must live like this is our final hour and immediately (if not sooner) get to work on ourselves. It is very freeing when we are able to let go of the judgment of the world (not our job) and get on with our own repentance. We recognize the folly of trying to fix the problems of the movie from the level of the cinema screen and instead get to work on the projector, the film, and the focus of the lens etc.

It is all our fault.

Once we grasp the basic tenet of causation and understand the nature of the connected universe (everything affects everything) we see that a cause *here* creates an effect *there*, not just in your own private world but everywhere in the universe at large ("many a little makes a mickle"). If you drop a pebble *anywhere* in the water, the ripples are felt *everywhere* in the pond. With our actions (no matter how small) we contribute to everything that occurs everywhere and at all times.

We are personally responsible for everything that happens in the world, good, bad, or indifferent.

We feel disparate and disconnected from (and innocent of) crimes and atrocities that happen in someone else's country, in someone else's city, in someone else's back yard; but when you understand cause and effect, you recognize that everything we do affects everything in the world, sometimes in a very individual, personal way, and sometimes in a collective manner. All of our actions collect in the universal body, together with the compound interest accumulated by delayed redress and unpaid debt and, over time and space, they rebalance themselves like a ledger sheet in a large conglomerate. Like the intricately connected human biology, the world-body feels the joy and suffers the pain of every part. If I stub my toe on a sharp edge, the ripples of pain will be felt in every one of my trillions of cells from the soles of my feet right up to the crown of my head. Equally, the joy of witnessing an act of love through the pupil of my eye will fill my whole being with the same effulgence.

Karma is like a huge fatberg that forms in our drains and blocks our systems, *we all contribute to it.*

It is built up of a plethora of disparate, foreign objects, flushed down the toilet or thrown down the drains by millions of people; they are discarded and then forgotten about.

Years, sometimes decades, *even generations* later, the underground city-plumbing blocks and bursts, and everyone is affected.

Few would consider that they were to blame for the blockage.

The single condom, the pan of cooking-oil, the baby-nappy, or *the odd wet-wipe* or sanitary towel – thrown down the toilet in a moment of thoughtlessness, long ago and long forgotten, would (surely) not have caused the explosion of detritus ten miles, twenty miles, a hundred miles from their home.

If you are part of the problem, you are all of the problem.

If you contribute to any part of the blockage, you are automatically and equally responsible for all of the blockage.

Cause and effect works on the same principle.

Because we do not commit large scale crimes, the kind that gets us noticed by the constabulary or makes the daily news, we think we are innocent, law-abiding citizens, but the small acts of unkindness we participate in every day eventually add up to a fatberg of big effects that will eventually have their say in parts of the world and on people of the world that we think are nothing to do with us.

If everyone dumped a granule of salt in the fresh water supply every day, it would not be long before the water coming out of our taps became undrinkable. And when this finally occurred, we would likely say to ourselves: "Not my fault. I only put a granule a day in the water, what difference would a granule of salt make?"

My friend violently resists the idea of karma, of causation; he angrily denies any kind of rational law that allows innocent children "to be raped and killed" (his exact words) in war-torn countries. And yet he will happily lap up sexual pornography from the World Wide Web, where the pleasure-masks of the performers are wafer-thin and the demonic torture and systemized depravation of somebody's son, somebody's daughter, is bursting through the screen for anyone with eyes to see and ears to hear. When we view the porn, we actively and willingly contribute to the abuse and the rape. When we indulge in any of the pornographies (food, sex, violence, gossip) we are playing our part (and taking our pleasure) in all the pornographies that occur under God's blue sky.

Every single stone thrown into the water causes a ripple.

By the time the accumulative waves build into a violent riptide at the furthest corners of the pond, it is impossible to identify which individual pebble initiated the wave, or indeed which caused the most damage. It is the collective power of all the pebbles and all the ripples that cause devastation in a place that might seem completely disparate and unlinked to the initiating cause.

The wave phenomena can work for the good or for the bad.

If my actions are creative, if they come from love, I can play my part in untold healings and inspirations all around the globe. Lord Krishna is offered a small handful of rice from one of his devoted followers. The man is poor and embarrassed by his paltry offering, but the Godhead assures him, because he offers it from a place of love, as little as a handful of rice is enough to feed the Lord and the whole of his universe. When we recognize that we have an effect on everything, it inspires us to affect everything in the best possible way. When we understand that "everything" includes our wife, our son, our sister, our father, of course we are even more encouraged to make kindness our gold standard.

If I feed the roots, I feed the whole tree.

If I put poison into the well, the whole village will become sick.

I felt revulsion, a jolt of denial when I first realized that the whole of reality is relying on me to stop contributing to the vice of the world with the poison of my righteous anger, my rationalized judgment, and my ignorant prejudice.

My friend rails at the torture of innocents while he necks a prime rib and dips his chips into the pooling-blood of an "innocent" animal, slaughtered somewhere far from public view: throat slashed, veins bled, decapitated, hung upside down on meat hooks, hacked into joints with a very sharp knife, called something more palatable than its true name, and then cooked as a feast on a Sunday barbecue for family and friends. We call the pig bacon or sausage or ham, we call the cow steak, or sirloin, and we call the majestic Deer venison. We name our meat, so it sounds like it is something that didn't have a face, something that didn't have a heartbeat or a blood flow or a mother and father or indeed a soul with its own journey to undertake.

If a bird lands in a tree (to paraphrase da Vinci) the whole world changes.

Everything affects everything.

Animals are not excluded from the karma-equation just because we have dispirited and disinherited and renamed their species, so that we can consume them without too much guilt.

If it sounds as though I am on a radical campaign against meat eaters, I am not. I am writing what I have learned so that I can relay to you the reader and reiterate the truth to myself.

Everything we do in this world comes at a cost, to you, to me and to everyone else. And that cost *will* be met by us all, if not sooner, definitely later.

The innocent gossip we partake in (it is not called *character assassination* for nothing) is not quite as innocent as it seems.

It is not an action without consequence.

Whilst this might seem like small-change in a corrupt world, it becomes (like all causes) part of a larger conglomerate when it joins together with all the other *inconsequential* actions and builds into a monster that clogs the plumbing of a street, a city, a country, even a world. We rationalize our actions as "hardly worth mentioning" but if we follow Kant's categorical imperative (**if everyone did what they rationalize as harmless, all at the same time, would it still be OK?**) we would be less likely to see our anomalies as pedantic nothings and start recognizing their accumulative threat.

Miniscule germs of negativity become world destroying diseases if they are left unchecked.

When we inject our karmic poisons into the veins and arteries of the world every organ is affected.

Another reason why we so easily and so quickly dismiss causation as a working law is because, although the universe is absolute, a unified body, most people do not see it, rather they view it only in its reductionist state: a collection of disparate parts, unconnected, neither affecting the other.

Cause always has an equal and opposite effect, whether we witness it personally or not. It will be "equal and opposite," there will be a proportionate compensation for every action, but it may not necessarily return in kind, or in a direct, linear manner, and it may not (it often does not) always return immediately or in an immediately recognizable form. The aligned charity you offer today, your £1, your £10, your million dollar gift, might not return to you directly from the source of your giving or in the money-method of your donation; it may return in good health, a fruitful relationship, or as an opportunity that appears completely disconnected from your initial offering. Equally, the bad seed you sowed (you know, the one you thought that no one saw, that was forgotten about, that you'd gotten away with) might return in a completely foreign manner. It may be separated from the cause by time and space, it might be referred or truncated; it may look so different from the seed you planted, that you (are able to) convince yourself that the crisis that lands on your doorstep today is random, unexpected, undeserved, and unkind.

If you understand causation, you stop railing against the gods when difficulty visits. You immediately recognize that a boomerang you sent out into the world all that time ago has returned to the hand that threw it.

When someone ran into my parked car (I was in the house) and wrecked the whole back end of my posh Jag, my first thoughts were not *Why has this happened to me? I've done nothing wrong*; my immediate response was, *I must be out of alignment.* My second thought was in a similar vein: *This is the effect of something (or some things) that I did in the past, even if I don't immediately recognize what I did or when I did it.*

Everything has a cause, and if an effect finds its way to us, we have to either assume that the effect is ours (displaced, truncated or direct), or flail around in denial and self-pity, gnash our teeth and moan and complain about the random uncertainty of a savage universe. This (the latter) is not intelligent; better to spend your time investigating the nature of law, and gaining a little knowing, some certainty about the realm we call home, so you can be less reactive and more proactive as you travel through your current incarnation on this spinning planet.

Ultimately, all effects, local and remote, personal, and impersonal have a shared but ultimately unknown genesis. Everything that ever happened in the history of the world affects everything that ever happens and ever will happen. Unless we are omniscient, unless we are able to know every action by every creature that ever walked the earth, we will never be able to find the exact, original cause of the myriad, often confusing, seemingly random and senseless phenomena that we witness in our lives, on our TV screens and in the newspapers we read every day.

Whilst we cannot know the exact and unique cause of anything in the particular, we can know the cause of everything in general.

This knowing (that our actions will add to the effects of all other actions) inspires us to employ due diligence in the world, and act only in a way that is kind and beneficial to everyone. This might sound confusing, but you can simplify it greatly by vowing to only use your free will to act in a way that accords with wisdom and love, and only make offerings in the world that come from a place of righteousness.

Be kind.

What constitutes righteousness and love?

Well, that's the purpose of this world, to work hard at understanding the general law, to garner and grow a body of wisdom, and then discern what is right and wrong *for us* within it.

We can only do this when we know ourselves.

When we know who we are, we can consciously place our beliefs under the scrutiny of law. It will show us soon enough what is aligned and what is of a lesser good. When we hit the right path, and take our instruction directly from wisdom or Intuition, and work with the gold standard of love, we will be able to see the benefits of our work in the consequence of our actions.

The Judiciary

None of this, as true and as right as it is, means in any way, shape, or form that universal law negates the need for judicial law (only that it supersedes it).

After all, the seventh Noahide Law is "the obligation to establish courts of justice."

We need courts of justice.

Judicial law can be, and often is a legitimate arm of reciprocity.

Unlike divine retribution, societal law is made and maintained and enforced by man. Man, by his very nature, is a corrupted being, and so his laws or certainly the enforcing of his laws are prone to lapses in judgment, misjudgment, wrong judgment and often no judgment at all. Whilst we may look to it and lean on it and trust it to a degree, judicial law does not have the final say when it comes to the rights and wrongs of judgment.

Neither does the assurance of a divine and absolute law excuse us from the responsibility of being good citizens. If we are witness to wrongdoing, it still falls on us to point it out, to call it out, and to insist that the error be policed so that victims of abuse may have their day in court. Neither does it deny us our right to follow all avenues of compensation, so that we too might see social justice and bring our persecutors before a judge and twelve good men.

It is not a case of one or the other.

Sometimes judicial law and karmic law are good bedfellows,

and the higher assists the lower in bringing crimes to redress. But the judiciary cannot be relied upon as the final arbiter of justice. As far as the universe (and the law of compensation) is concerned, our wrongs *will* be righted but retribution may not come in the way we hope for or indeed expect; it could be redressed in any number of a billion different ways, many of which may occur outside a court of law and far away from the eyes of man. *Just deserts* might be served seconds after an abuse, in which case you are able to witness instant karma. It may be years, or decades before you get to see justice served. It could arrive at a different time and place, on a disparate continent and from a seemingly unconnected source; you may not be around to see justice at all, certainly not with your own eyes, but it will happen.

This delay between cause and effect, between action and consequence might seem *to the human sensibilities* an infuriating and senseless rule but, speaking personally, I have been grateful for it in my own life. I have been very appreciative of the karma-gap when it came to the many crimes of the personality Geoff Thompson. This time-delay has been kind to me, it has given me the golden opportunity to see the error of my ways and repent willingly before repentance became an urgent and enforced matter. Better to pay your own debts by confessing and repenting than to wait for the fates to spring the bill of "consequence" upon you when you least expect it. It is much more potent to willingly repent. Waiting to be dragged kicking and screaming and in denial into the higher or lower courts of law (by a force that has been patient with you for long enough) is a disempowering and painful experience.

Repentance

When I use the word *repentance*, I am aware of its biblical connotations, the hard and dogmatic language of a jealous god.

This is not how I intend it to sound.

The word repentance sounds severe, and I know it gets a bad rep because it is so often personalized, associated as it is with the punishment and revenge of a humorless and unseen deity. To me, repentance means "return," return to the still center, return to good, return to alignment, return to the authentic self, return to homeostasis (our natural balance), a return to kindness, the return to God.

This is the one command of the Christian God, it is the panacea of the Buddha, it is the essential instruction that Lord Krishna offers to the prince of the world, Arjuna Pandava, when he falls into fear on the battlefield. In Judaic liturgy, we are assured that we do not have to "go to heaven or cross seas to know this command, it is already in our hearts, on our tongues." The cardinal precept of the Old Testament – all the other commandments being human refractions and imaginings – is "return to me."

"Return to me" is the whole of the Torah, and the path of return is in you.

To repent also means *repair*, it means *refuge*. To repent is to make a personal inventory, but not of the wrongs that others have done to you: I am talking about the wrongs that you have done to others.

Make a list of your wrongs.

Offer apologies where you can, make amends if they are called for, accept due punishment if that is what your crimes demand: and do it all willingly, with no complaint.

When I repent (and I have had much to repair) I am just grateful for the opportunity to lift the burden from my conscience.

It is a massive relief to unburden yourself.

It is a true gift that we all have the opportunity to return to peace.

My advice to all those brave enough to take this opportunity is this: accept responsibility for your wrongs, accept the consequence, the punishment, the suffering inflicted on you by your own conscience; even more importantly, whatever it is you have been doing wrong, stop doing it right now, today, immediately: don't increase your debt by continuing your crime.

Stop doing the wrong thing.

Break your covenant with evil (the subtle or the substantial).

When we return to religion – religion in the true sense of the word: "realign to good" – when we stop flirting with darkness and engaging with unkind ways, we are repenting.

When we replace our dark habits with good deeds, we are repenting.

When we stop making negative judgments of others and start making positive adjustments to ourselves, we are repenting.

This is what the Christian Eucharist teaches us: when we sacrifice our body and blood in the loving, willing service of others, our own sins will be wiped clean in the process.

When we study scripture and talk from love and act with grace: when we refrain from greedy ambition and eschew selfishness and embrace a selfless way, we are repenting.

When our teacher (the soul) talks of love and his teaching speaks of love and the community we keep is wall-to-wall love, we are really repenting.

Burnt Offerings

Just in case there is a danger that either you or I lose the thread of this chapter, let me throw out a quick reminder of why we find our self on this page and on this particular aspect of forgiveness: forgiving others is not our job. Forgiving ourselves is not our job.

Pardon is not a human power; it is a divine attribute.

To forgive is not to let someone off; vengeance belongs to the law, and it will repay.

Revenge (or reciprocity) belongs to the law; it does not belong to us any more than the force of a hurricane or the geography of its wrath or the path of its destruction belongs to a feather that happens to have floated in its way.

We have the power to "give over" our complaint to the force of reciprocity.

We have the power to recognize and understand this law and willingly put the body and blood of our sin – the allegorical meaning of *burnt offerings* – into the fire of this force, remove our sin, and return to our original nature.

That is what this chapter is about.

This is the law, and it will not disappoint.

Repentance is called "burnt offerings" or "the animal sacrifice" because the sin is literally incinerated, and the vapor consumed into the fire of grace. The animal soul – known in psychology as the false ego – is sacrificed, leaving room for consciousness to be revealed.

I have just published a book (2021), a memoir called *Notes From a Factory Floor*. It is 320 pages of confession of repentance, and of admittance. It was the most painful, willing body-and-blood sacrifice of my animal soul that I have ever made. It was my burnt offering, recorded in ink and crucified on the broken hill of public opinion, and divine judgment. The day I finished the first draft of *Notes* I received a literal download of divine manna: 20-chapter headings for a second tome of revelation called *The Divine CEO*. I was out walking when a ka-ching of chapters fell into my mind like a silver dollar jackpot from a Las Vegas slot machine. They fell so quickly that I had to record them in my phone and send them to myself as e-mails lest I forgot them before I returned home. The book took me eight weeks to transcribe to the page (it would have been quicker if I'd had the stamina). I wrote 150,000 words, mostly arcana that I was not previously aware of before.

Notes was my burnt offering; *CEO* was the reward.

Notes was my repentance; *CEO* was the *knowing* it revealed.

Notes was the sacrifice of my animal soul on the holy pyre of self-honesty.

CEO was the eye of the soul, opened as a consequence.

Notes was the death of the old me.

CEO was the anointment of my soul.

I mentioned briefly that the dharma or the law has two distinct parts: the general and the specific. The law in general is all about understanding and employing the force of reciprocity. In the specific it is about discovering our unique, individual purpose within it, our personal job in the great work or the divine plan.

The specific will not be revealed until we first find certainty with the general.

Once we understand law, once we believe and trust that it is real, we reveal who we are – the true Self. Once we know who we are, what we are here to do, the part we are called to play in the world, our purpose for being is revealed.

If you think of yourself as an organization, purpose is the holistic property within it that attracts corporation. Corporation doesn't exist without purpose; it could be defined (to paraphrase my friend, the author Sky Nelson-Isaacs) as "a group of people coming together with a specific and agreed purpose."

This is what happens metaphysically when you find your true purpose, a corporation is attracted to you like metal filings to a magnet; in fact (from my experience) once you have found the *why*, the whole universe conspires to help you in your quest.

If you want to be a vessel for real power, find your true purpose, and power will be an immediate adjunct.

There is nothing as potent as a righteous purpose.

The quickest way to find the Self, and thus reveal purpose is to first remove all the things that you categorically know are not you.

Make a list (check it twice) of all the mistakes you have made, that you are making, and those that you may continue to make tomorrow, if your habit is not arrested. One by one, strike them off until you are stripped back to the base-metal of your true identify. The hallmark of your purpose is blueprinted there, but you will not be able to read it clearly until the last layer of dirt and grime, the residue of wrong living, has been removed.

Once you find your own unique code, you will have a new covenant; you'll be connected to a divine sat nav that will direct all your future actions, street by street, road by road, city by city and eventually, world by world.

I could not have found this refuge, this return, had I not first understood the law.

It would have been impossible had I not willingly paid my debts to the bailiffs of reciprocity. Had I not taken time out to do the rigor and clear my own personal obscurations I would never have seen or understood divine law. I had to resign my pseudo reign as the arbitrator of law before I was gifted the true crown of personal sovereignty.

Step one was to understand the wisdom of the law until I reached the place of certainty.

Step two was to actively work with the law, dealing with the things that were mine to deal with (my own debts), giving over those that belonged to the law (other people's debts) and learning to know the difference between the two.

This – the action – is known in alchemy as **the red phase** of turning lead into gold. It is when we take our learning out into the world and use it for the good of others and for the good of ourselves.

Repentance is work; be in no doubt, it is arduous labor, it is not for the faint of heart or the weak of will. As Dante reminds us in his Cantos on the Inferno: "Your fame is waiting, but you will not find it from a cushion or from your bed."

Reciprocity is not only a good reason to forgive (or *give it over*), it is also a gift.

It is a non-local power, a divine attribute, one of the many boons we receive when we understand law. How wonderful that we have been given such a powerful asset.

A hidden secret has been revealed to us: that the universe is not arbitrary, or random, or unkind; it is a knowing and knowable force with laws that are very profitable to those of us who understand its ways and utilize its potency for the greater good.

We can also (of course) use our earned certainty to avoid the unnecessary tortures that come as a result of ignorance and misuse of this law.

Repentance is the greatest of gifts because it allows us all a second and a third and a fourth chance (ad infinitum) to get it right, to reassess our lives, to return to the source of our nature, and realign to our ground of being. How amazing that even the very worst of us have been afforded the opportunity to climb off the merry-go-round of greed and pain and suffering and start all over again from the beginning.

Understanding the law of compensation, and our ability to repent has a significant by-product and this is the third reason why you should forgive... it is incredibly good for your health.

Budo Practice

I was in a newsagent in Euston Station London, buying a magazine to read on my train journey home. I noticed that the man behind the counter looked subdued, perhaps depressed: I could hear sadness in the dull timbre of his voice. "How are you today?" I asked, sensing that a positive engagement might offer him a little balm. He looked up at me, surprised that I (or anyone) had taken the time to notice that he was out of sorts, let alone enquire as to his state of play.

"Problems!" he said, as though he had too many to mention, and they were too complex to be articulated, let alone solved.

"Problems are a sign of life," I said.

His face lifted up curiously.

"What?"

"Problem are a sign of life," I repeated.

He was alive. The only people without problems, are buried in oak and silk under six feet of muddy soil, marked by a marble headstone.

I was informing him, in as few words as possible (the circumstance did not allow for a lengthy discourse) that he was still breathing, and his problems were a sure sign of that.

His face broke into a broad smile, and he nodded his thanks: I made my way to the train.

It is easy in the rush and tumble of our day, in the helter-skelter of human living to fall into the trap of thinking that problems are impediments, that they are a hinderance to our day, our week, our year or our life. By simply changing perspective and looking at things from a different angle, from an anabolic perspective, the mundane can immediately become the magical, the workaday humdrum can become a masterclass in life.

My daughter Jennie has just completed her master's degree in Psychology. It really stretched her both physically and mentally. At one point she rang me up crying: "I don't understand any of this," she complained, referring to her latest assignment, and hinting that she might have made the wrong decision when she enrolled in the course, six months earlier. She was unhappy.

"If you understood it," I reminded her, "the course would be a waste of your time, and the accreditation at the end of the course would not be worth the paper it is written on. You have taken on this course precisely because you don't understand, and you want to."

I reminded her that she was not there to be happy, she was there to learn.

I also encouraged her to talk to her teachers and keep talking to her teachers (that's what they are there for) until she did understand.

She was doing a master's degree specifically to improve her

mind-body. The process of expanding our conscious awareness is, of course, uncomfortable. As the Greek author Aeschylus reminds us, "He who learns must suffer." This is the first law of Zeus: "No wisdom without pain."

But through this expansion, life automatically offers us a greater array of opportunities.

Martial arts students came to my class – and some of them travelled from across the planet to be there – precisely because there were things that they did not understand, and they wanted to learn by placing themselves in front of a teacher that did.

One of the students complained that he was not enjoying the course, "Where's the fun?" he asked.

If he was looking for fun, he was in the wrong class.

This training was not about fun, I had no interest in fun, I was not there to pander to his whims, or wipe his arse, or entertain him; I was there to facilitate his growth, and there is no growth in comfort.

We are all blessed to be in a body, we are highly privileged to be sojourning on this living, spinning classroom, heavy as it is with restrictions; our great earth is so infamous in the universe that even the great Buddhas incarnate here, just to perfect the way.

Perspective is everything: "Two men look through prison bars," Carnegie instructs us, "one sees mud the other stars."

In my own martial arts class, we created an artificial environment with limitations in the form of rules, and regulations. These restrictions were deliberately drawn and strictly observed in order to draw out, expose and correct a student's weakness and also to highlight and accentuate their strengths. We called this method of budo practice "restriction training": we developed our technique through the strategy of deliberate restriction.

I view the law of reciprocity in the great matrix of life as a macrocosm of my martial arts class, the Great Earth is the ultimate restriction training.

I would like to encourage you, the reader, to alter your whole perception of reality, and view it as a living classroom, a learning environment extraordinaire. Rather than falling into the same old self-pitying perspective as the masses, who view life as a meaningless torture chamber punctuated by an excruciating death, we can instead see every difficulty as a problem to be solved, every ailment as an ill in search of a cure, every ignorance, just one more class, one more paper, one more semester towards enlightenment. This makes life exciting; it gives it meaning and purpose. When you start seeing your current problems as latent potentials, you will (like me, like my better students) turn your whole life into a bespoke, advanced university course.

When I was depressed, depression became my study. Rather than take the quick fix solution that my doctor offered me in a brown glass bottle, I made my whole life a personal study into depression. I overcame this illness because I stopped waiting for someone else to take away my pain with a prescription, and I became an expert on the subject.

When I was assailed by fears, I wrote them all down on a piece of paper and confronted them one by one until I overcame them.

When I recognized that problems were a sign of life, and that it was through solving problems that I was able to learn and grow, I stopped running away from them, I stopped complaining about them, and I became Guinea Pig A in my own life: I leaned into the sharp edges, and I used my myriad problems as whetstones, to sharpen my intellect.

The budo practice in this chapter is just about a change of perspective. I would also encourage you to locate (what the mystic Gurdjieff called) your "chief feature" (more on this in a later chapter); this would be the one thing in your life that seems to dominate everything else.

As a younger man my chief feature was fear.

Once I overcame fear, all of my other problems fell into alignment and were quickly routed.

When you strike the shepherd, the sheep will scatter.

What is your chief feature?

Write it down. Look at it on the page. Be very curious about it. Watch how it weakens just by the power of being exposed to the page. Make a vow to overcome it. Make a plan to defeat it. Make a statement of intent that – come hell or high water – you are going to master your chief feature.

The brain has a curious quirk, it cannot process fear and curiosity at the same time. When we become curious about our fears instead of running away from them, the fears greatly lessen.

Reason Three: Health

You might not immediately associate ill health with bitterness and resentment, or good health with forgiveness, but the two are intrinsically and intimately and most definitely linked. Hopefully, the first two reasons may have already hinted at why forgiveness leads to good health. The moment we find certainty regarding the law of causation – and this in itself is a process that cannot be hurried – we lighten the load physically, physiologically, emotionally, psychologically, sociologically, and metaphysically.

Physically and physiologically, we stop infusing our human biology with dangerous stress hormones (more on this imminently) that poison the smooth internal muscles. We are always under the cosh of stress and anxiety when we carry a resentment or nurture a wound or house a fear or entertain anger or submit to dissonance.

When we are able to ditch our burden, emotionally we stop experiencing the drip, drip of existential angst, the anxiety of waiting for justice, the fear of the next e-mail or phone call or Twitter post, that become to the *worried waiting* the harbingers of doom. We stop hiding under the smother or our small, safe lives because we have become afraid of the world, afraid of those populating the world, afraid of the threat around every next corner, or the devil at every open doorway.

Sociologically we expand too, and to the extent that we shed our unqualified fears. We, by our very nature, are social creatures, and a large part of our essential human needs come directly from our interactions with other beings. To be apart from them because we fear our fellow hosts on planet earth is, by definition, a mental illness.

To live in fear is illness.

To live in ignorance is illness.

To take a lie and craft it into a "truth" is the very definition of disease.

Our whole body is ill at ease when we live in fear.

Fear is a virus: truth is the vaccine.

We live in fear because we lack knowing.

Ignorance – as I said in the last chapter – is to not understand law.

Ignorance of causation is like being placed in a wild jungle without knowing the dangers and its laws; you will probably be gobbled up by a hungry creature, higher up the food chain, on day one.

When we understand the rules, we can become king of the jungle; we can be promoted to the top of the established hierarchy.

We will always be ill whilst we remain ignorant.

Knowledge, *revealed knowing*, allows our world to expand, not just beyond our current locale, but beyond our present reality.

Metaphysically, we start to see that the sun and the moon and the stars are within us, literally, they are part of us, and we begin to experience the world as a malleable and collaborative and accommodating host. The universe itself will conspire to help us reach our potential when we understand the language of the world.

But that is all to come...

What I want to convince you of in this chapter is the benefits to your health (literal benefits) when you let go of your enemy, forgive her from your mind, leave him to his own destiny and start working on your own freedom from the tyranny of ignorance.

To understand the health benefits of forgiveness we have to first understand the dangers of the endocrine system, specifically adrenalin, and particularly a small, discreet hormone called cortisol, which is released during moments of stress to manage blood pressure.

I hope we all have a basic understanding already of the dangers of stress: high blood pressure, coronary disease, increased threat of stroke and heart attack, bowel disorders, urinary problems, low blood pressure, and impotence etc.

Actually, it would be easier to list the problems that are not a result of overactive adrenals.

The stress response, especially when it becomes habitual, affects everything in the human biology, and not in a good way. We hear all the time that stress is not good for us, but few people understand exactly why this is so. I did a master's degree with the Society of Martial Arts through Salford University, England, about the stress response. My thesis was later published as a book called *Stress Buster: How to stop stress from killing you.* More importantly I have had a lifetime of suffering with stress, post-traumatic stress and all the anxiety and fear you might associate with working for a decade as a nightclub bouncer. So, what I write here is gold, it is my master work, fired in the furnace of hard experience.

Stress is bad for us on several levels, and be in no doubt, if you are angry, afraid, nervous, anxious, jealous, envious, judgmental, dissonant: you become a stress-making factory, pumping unnecessary chemicals *every day* into a body that was not designed to cope with them, long term.

The stress response is meant to be an infrequent phenomenon, a last resort fail-safe, a supernova of adrenal-fuel, fired into the bloodstream to help us survive a life or death struggle with a wild beast that has caught our scent and desires our meat.

Studies have shown that when we have occasional spikes of adrenalin it can actually aid immunity, because the body releases lymphocytes (a type of white blood cell in the vertebrate immune system, including natural killer cells, T cells and B cells) that actively boost immunity and attack and remove any invading viruses. Things like cold showers and confronting fears (picking up a spider, doing a bungee jump etc.) have been proven to help boost immunity, for this very reason. But when fight-or-flight is not occasional and becomes the constant backdrop of our lives, the stress response that usually acts as our personal bodyguard, turns, and becomes our perpetual tormentor.

The stress response is supposed to be occasional and not habitual, because our energy is finite. The extra turbo boost of fuel called on in times of physical arousal is drawn from our own bodily reserves, and they are limited. During fight-or-flight, the boost of extra blood (spiked with adrenalin) needed for our rush to survive is drawn from all the areas of the body that are seen as subsidiary to our immediate needs and pumped to the areas of the body that are seen as vital in a life and death struggle.

The non-vital areas where the blood is drawn from are the immune system, the brain, and many other organs. It is transferred to the major muscles needed during fight-or-flight, like the legs, the arms, the back, the chest, and the lungs.

Our physical body literally trembles under the surge of increased blood flow.

This is fine, it could even be lifesaving if you need to run a hundred yards to escape a chasing predator. It is not so good if you have to go to work, hold a meeting, deliver a speech or simply get the kids ready for school and operate healthily in the everyday world.

This is the first and major threat to our health: the immune system all but closes down during periods of anxiety. This is not such a big issue if the stress response lasts its allotted span of thirty seconds to a minute and occurs infrequently. It is disastrous, however, if we lose control of our adrenals and they are triggering all day, every day. Not only are we left depleted of vital energy, we are also left without any defense against the virus, the cancer, and all the other parasitical marauders that are looking for a free meal and a place to call home.

The greater majority of serious illnesses today find their root, not in stress, but in the effects of stress, i.e., no immune function.

Holding on to the suffering of historical abuse can leave us in an acute state of anxiety, living in a vulnerable and defenseless body. We cannot defend our boundaries because the stressed biology has (unconsciously) drawn blood away from immune function and pumped it to body-parts that are in a constant state of high alert to a physical threat that might never occur.

We are, in common parlance, fighting on too many fronts, most of which are illusory, created only by an overactive mind.

In short, our adrenals are stuck in a perpetual state of anticipation.

The second major health threat to the over-stressed body is cortisol.

As I mentioned earlier, cortisol is an important hormone, it is very necessary if we find ourselves facing a genuine, physical threat, but it is very damaging in cases where cortisol has been released into the bloodstream but not behaviorally used.

In other words, the oversensitive brain senses a threat that isn't really there and releases hormones that are never really needed or used.

There is no saber-toothed tiger.

There is no hungry bear.

So where does all the extra fuel go?

If it does not find a behavioral release (fight-or-flight), cortisol (what I call the "rogue" hormone) turns in on us and acts as a caustic: it attacks our smooth internal muscles like the heart, the lungs, the bladder, the intestines, and the bowel. It travels through the bloodstream and up to the brain where it attacks and kills neurons. Due to its corrosive nature, cortisol has been heavily associated with Alzheimer's disease and dementia. On its lap of the bloodstream, it also scratches the inside of the arteries, and the fatty acids released in fight-or-flight get caught up in the damaged channels; this causes the furring and blocking we associate with angina and heart disease.

There is also the clear and present danger of displacement when we are perpetually stressed. If we release adrenalin that is not behaviorally utilized, the build of adrenalin in the bloodstream can be and frequently is displaced onto others, usually those closest to us. In psychology this is known by the acronym GAS (the General Adaption Syndrome). When we are stressed but find no behavioral release for the triggered hormones, the body eventually reverts back from the sympathetic response (fight-or-flight) to the parasympathetic nervous system, which is our normal physiological balance (known in psychology as homeostasis). So, we go from normal, to full-on adrenal alert then back to normal again.

But what happens to all the extra fuel, released but not used?

What happens to all those stress hormones?

What happens to the killer cortisol?

They stay in the body, that's what happens to them.

They stay trapped in the body, and they attack the internal smooth muscles leaving us with ulcers and furred arteries and all sorts of other horrible diseases. And, because the stress is not released, it can build up in the body like a pressure cooker, and we become (what is known as) *sympathetic sensitive.*

This means that we become oversensitive to any and every stressor.

Eventually, as little as the ping of an e-mail or the ring of a telephone can send us into a frenzy of adrenal release.

In this state, the compound buildup of adrenalin can make us react outrageously and inappropriately and disproportionately to the smallest stressors. People kill in road-rage attacks because a minor event in the car has triggered a major incident in the body.

This is all disastrous for our health.

It is also accumulative because the disproportionate anger we displace on our wife, our husband, the neighbor, a workmate, the cat or a complete stranger in the street is a cause with its own effects. If our behavior hurts the ones we love (or anyone for that matter), we start to corrode our social network, which becomes yet another stressor, and that is very unhealthy indeed.

Letting go of the hate, the anger, the resentment, the dissonance of old wounds greatly diminishes our chances of becoming unhealthily stressed; it increases our immunity (if we release the stressor, there can be no stress), it decreases our chances of becoming sick and, over time, it offers us back the most important thing that was lost in the fire; our freedom.

Health is the fourth reason we should let go of old resentments, give them over to a greater power than us, and take back our personal autonomy.

We can never be free while someone else has more control over our adrenals than we do.

So, the fourth reason to forgive is just that: personal autonomy.

Budo Practice

A common by-product of abuse is dissonance; we feel confused by what has happened to us, and it disables and dismantles our purpose for living, and this leaves us floating through the ocean of life with neither steer nor rudder. In the budo of this chapter I would like to ask you, the reader, to accept (temporarily at least) the fact that sometimes we cannot immediately escape our suffering, and often, the very act of trying to makes it worse. Once we acknowledge what we definitely can't do, we are then able to start looking at what we certainly can do. Perhaps I don't have the power to immediately remove the stressful feelings that are coursing through my body, but I absolutely do have the ability to do other things: I can eat healthy, I can go to the gym, I can fill my mind with positive and educational reading, I can go to church, I can help a neighbor, I can write a journal, I can cut the grass or call my mum.

As well as distracting you from what you can't do, all these feel-good occupations build your confidence, strengthen your will and help you to behaviorally release any trapped stress in your body that is looking for a healthy outlet: action gives hormones a surrogate release from the body, it offers them a legitimate and definite direction for the unreleased energy.

When we let go of what we can't change, and work instead on what we can change, often what we can't change changes all by itself. Make a list if you will.

You don't need to write down what you can't immediately change, you know what that is already. Instead write down what you can change, and immediately get to it. At first, it might feel uncomfortable to undertake these "necessary and possible" tasks when you are feeling so awful and stressed, but I would contend that your worse time is the perfect time to exercise your will. Anyone can get out of bed for a 4am meditation practice when their life is going well and they are inspired, but who can make the same commitment when everything inside them is insisting that they do the opposite. The more resistance there is to your task, the more powerful you'll build your will when you make yourself do it. In esoteric practice the will is seen as the working arm of the soul, that deep, sensitive part of us we call authentic. The will is also known as the "causal body," it is the penultimate sloka or sheath before the soul proper. It is often referred to as "the body of conscious will," or "the bliss body," because this is where we generate causes in the world. When we are abused, the body of conscious will is penetrated and a parasite left in situ. This leech, over time, takes over the conscious will, either partially or wholly and it acts in us, and as us and through us in the world, and its actions are not good, they are always perverted and often destructive. In other words, we lose our free will to the bloodsucker of abuse. Without control of the will, the soul cannot exercise its full grace in the world.

When we override this resistance by consciously engaging the will, when we act positively in the world, we begin the process of evicting this trickster, and win back our autonomy; we literally take back our body of conscious will.

You might see little purpose in doing the mundane when you are in pain, please let this budo practice be a reminder of your purpose: we are doing these jobs because it is our way of winning back the stolen will.

When St. Francis walked to Rome with his followers, to garner approval from Pope Innocent III to officially preach the gospel in Assisi, the Pope allowed Francis' tonsure with a caveat that he expected the barefoot monk to do "only the possible... but all of it."

(Francis was later quoted as saying: "Start by doing what's necessary; then do what's possible; and suddenly you are doing the impossible.")

This is the instruction I offer myself, in my own practice, and that I proffer to you now:

Do only the possible but do all of it.

When you do all of the possible, the impossible will look after itself.

That, my lovely friends, it worth getting out of bed for in the morning.

What can you do today, right now, to start the process?

Remember, these things are compound by nature; the more you consistently practice, practice, practice, the more inner power you will develop. And there is a bonus: the parasite that tempts you to inactivity, that tells you the world is a shit-storm, that there is no point in anything, that puts a hundred different obstacles in your way, gets burned up in the process of positive action, it literally becomes the fuel for your activity. In making yourself "do the necessary, then the possible," in forcing yourself to say what needs to be said and go where needs to be gone, you vaporize and convert the parasite, like wax melted and drawn through the wick of a candle to feed the flame: the devil that this morning was your nemesis, this afternoon becomes the fire that lights your path. The reason there is so much resistance to you exercising your will, the reason there is so much opposition to your action, and so many obstacles in your way, is precisely because this semi-autonomous thought-form knows this, and so will do everything in its power to block your progress: you end its reality when you begin your takeover. In this way the parasite can be a good thing, it is a reservoir of raw fuel if you have the will and the courage to act.

This book is a perfect example of the process in action. I am writing here a document on forgiveness, about winning back our will, and in the process, I am exposing the existence of the pain-bodies (and their modus operandi) that we all harbor. This process has created tremendous resistance in me, which makes it very difficult to sit down and put these words to the page. In making myself do the very thing I feel compelled to abandon, I turn the engine of my conscious will and these same forces are sucked in by the centripetal force of my action, and employed as a reluctant workforce, a raw energy source – they are literally converted from darkness into a light.

Even just reading about this process will empower you.

There is a light in these words (for all the reasons stated above), that will allow you to see what before was hidden. Now you see it, you can begin to act on it, and with the most powerful purpose of all: to win back your soul.

What can you consciously do right now to begin this process?

What job have you been putting off.

Who can you think of that might need your help?

Where can you go, what can you action?

Begin it now – the necessary, the possible, eventually the impossible – prove for yourself the efficacy of this budo.

Reason Four: Personal Autonomy

Everybody craves freedom, personal autonomy, the ability, and the God given right to choose their own path through life and make their own decisions.

But personal sovereignty needs to be properly understood before it can be rightly claimed.

Do we have free will or has it been commandeered by conditioning, by a subjective education, by dogmatic religious values, or immovable social mores, the rules of our culture, the expectations of our class, our own karma, and even the movements of the planets?[4]

Do we actually have free will?

Is free will possible in a universe so full of unknown rules and unseen powers?

Many people claim to have free will but confound their own belief in the way they live. Who can claim to have free will and yet still smoke cigarettes or take drugs or drink excessive amounts of alcohol or eat themselves into obesity and ill health or chase the siren of accumulation, even though it is clear to anyone with eyes to see that these addictions are both poisonous and imprisoning?

You might argue that each individual has the right to make such choices, even if they know the very choices they make will eventually kill them. But I have to ask myself: would anyone who was truly informed ever deliberately write their own epitaph with the evils that they inflict on themselves, on their children, on their friends, their family, and on their fellow man?

If they had true knowledge, would they really choose to harm their own offspring, with the decisions they take?

Even the small decisions that are not in alignment with kindness add to the overall karmic bill, a tab that has to be met at some point by the whole of mankind. Would anyone sane, would anyone intelligent or rational knowingly make bad decisions that – directly or indirectly – they and their loved ones will have to pay for?

I spoke with a friend who had embarked on an extramarital affair. He asked me for a little advice, and I offered him the sobering truth as I knew it, as a man who'd had affairs in the past, as a man with a history of hurting others and who had suffered as a consequence. I told him that the affair would damage his health, the health of his mistress, the health and well-being of his wife, and the husband of his girlfriend; their children and his children would all suffer at some point because of the affair. On top of that his moral and ethical shortcomings would gravely damage his own integrity. Our ability to trust and be trusted, in business and in life, is heavily compromised when we lose virtue. Who is ever going to really trust you in the world, when you betray your wife, your husband, your child, the people you love most?

You certainly lose faith in yourself, I know that much, and it is an immeasurable loss when we can no longer trust our own hands, when we lose connection with our highest values.

If you still choose illicit pleasure when you know that it is going to be at the cost of your child's health and happiness and welfare, that your pleasure will result in their pain, you know you are lost.

This is the advice I offered him.

He decided to continue the affair, anyway.

He took his pleasure knowing that it would result in the pain and suffering of his own child.

He did not do this because he was callous or cruel or deliberately unkind, he chose this path because 1) he was lost in the heady addiction, *the pleasure* of the affair and did not want to let it go, and 2) deep down he did not believe (or chose to deny) the law of compensation; he felt that he could have the affair, and keep it secret from his loved ones, and no one would be hurt.

He even managed to convince himself that the affair was OK, that his wife "didn't really understand him," that she didn't look after him, that he needed to feel loved etc. "We are just having a bit of fun," he told me. "It's not hurting anyone."

I did and said the same things many years ago because I too was ignorant.

My kids suffered because of my selfishness, my ex-wife was traumatized by my actions, and (as I said earlier) my damaged kids carried their mental scars into adulthood. I have to see my children every week, knowing the harm I did to them because I was such a selfish fool. I was lost in the seduction of an illicit affair, and I too felt I could trick karma, and work my way around an uncompromising law, and (as they say) have my cake and eat it.

I did not have – you might say that I had not yet earned – true *knowledge*.

When I say "knowledge" I am talking of course about the knowledge of law. This is a profound certainty concerning causation, an exacting law that ensures we all face the consequence of our own actions. With our ignorance (and all its foot-soldiers) we construct the walls and doors around our own prison and then we call it paradise.

If we have not yet transcended our conditioning, if we have yet to clear our karmic debt, we cannot yet say that we are exercising free will or experiencing autonomy. Conditioning, by its very nature, *conditions* us to turn left, to turn right, to go ahead, to fall back, and to push or yield with the decisions we make in our normal every day. Karma by its very law determines that we live today under the cosh and consequence of yesterday's actions.

In many ways conditioning and karma are the two arms of the same body: our conditioned beliefs heavily encourage or compel (often, violently force) us to act according to societal or cultural precepts or mores; this habitus literally constructs the reality we live in, it is the brick-and-mortar of our current paradigm. Our free will, and subsequently our autonomy is stolen by the consequence of our very own *unconscious* actions. We regain our free will, and activate personal autonomy, when we break these bad habits, and start to act in a manner conducive to the (consequential) life we would like to live.

We live and work within the confines of our own personal intelligence.

While we are conditioned, our karma will be repetitively set, so there can be no true autonomy.

Conditioning of course is subtle and, like the devil of lore, it works best when we don't know it exists. It is happiest and most effective when we don't believe it is there. When we awaken from the sleep of conditioning, when we identify that – like Moses on Mount Sinai – we are held in slavery by the Pharaoh of egotism, we too can demand that he "let my people go" and fight to win back our autonomy. Then we can say that we are awake, that we have seen through the illusion of freedom, noted our imprisonment-by-stealth, and start on the path towards emancipation.

Conditioning has to be broken before we can make any claim to freedom.

To be free we first have to ask ourselves a question: *Who is it that wants to be free?* There is a presumption that there is only one identity within us, but of course, we are all quietly schizophrenic, we all have many disparate voices in our head that we wrongly assume to be different aspects of the same personality.

Finding the true I, the authentic Self is the first step towards autonomy.

A friend of mine booked onto a weekend NLP training course held by two of the leading practitioners in the world. This system, they were told in the sales blurb, is *or can be* alchemical, it can give you the power over yourself and subsequently the power over others: to heal them if your purpose is altruistic or to manipulate them and snaffle their money if you are able to rationalize your stealing.

The two teachers in question were obese.

This is not a judgment; it is an objective observation.

During a break in the day, one of the teachers was talking to his students whilst chain-smoking cigarettes. Noticing the look of confusion on the faces of his acolytes, he said (regarding his smoking) *Wouldn't you love to be just like me, able to take it or leave it?*

Everyone in that room will have seen (and probably quickly denied) the truth: neither of their erstwhile teachers had free will or personal autonomy, despite their claims to the contrary, but none of them wanted to see it.

To admit their teachers' denial would be to reveal the denial in their own lives.

We can't help people to change their world when we still can't even wipe our own arse.

A student on one of my training courses told me how excited he was about human potential, our connection to *everything*, the power of metaphysics and our ability to use the mind to literally control and transform matter. All of which is true.

"When I tell my wife about it," he complained, "she just scoffs, she doesn't believe a word of it."

Of course she scoffs. Her husband is six stone (84 pounds) overweight and has an addiction to cigarettes and alcohol. She scoffs because he is not showing her the proof of his belief in the basic formation of his own body.

The magic has to start with us.

The magic has to be performed on ourselves.

This body and mind are the alchemy-lab and their transformation is "the great work," of course it is.

If he'd said to his wife, *I do have addiction problems and I am in the process of proving these methods on my own body and in my own life,* he may have found a sympathetic ear. But instead, he told her, and me, that his smoking and drinking were under control, and that he chose to be obese (he actually said *I choose to be "big"*) because "the extra timber" helped him deal with difficult customers in the pub he ran.

It is not our addiction that kills us, that leaves us slavish under its maul; it is our denial of our addiction that has us jumping from grave to grave.

We prove the magic on ourselves by killing the pseudo-masters and winning back the autonomy of our body, thus taking control of our own life.

We will, of course, always have to work around the law, causation will always place a caveat on our complete and absolute autonomy.

In a realm with any laws, we can never be completely free.

In Christian theology this is called "freedom under authority."

We are free, but under the authority of a greater force.

But the more self-control we are able to demonstrate, the more we expand in consciousness, the less laws we will be subject to.

When I was eighteen years old, poorly educated, ignorant of my own potential, oblivious to universal forces, my life was a shit-storm of laws: I was hemmed into a small existence, by the bars and walls of my own ignorance. As I expanded my awareness – through works, through study, through experience in extremes – I was able to lift myself to a density with very few laws.

What is available for one, is available for all.

Once we recognize that the force (God/Tao) favors those who surrender to it, we can connect to the universal-mother ship, and this authority will supply us with every bounty. Like a surfer catching the big wave, we will be able to harness the awe of nature to power our cause.

But what has this got to do with forgiveness? I hear you cry.

When we carry resentment, when we choose to stay in the pain of abuse, when dissonance, anger, hurt or sorrow binds us to even one person, we cannot claim to have full autonomy in our lives. When we are abused, when a crime is committed against us or against someone we love and we do not process the experience and forgive it from our minds we automatically become slaves to the orchestrator of our abuse, even in their absence, even if they are in prison, even when they are dead.

When we are abused, our assailants take something from us, a light, an innocence, our causal will, a part of our soul. In its place they leave something of their own; a darkness, an ignorance, a parasitical insect that feeds from us and off us over time and space. Because it is an active agent within us, it is also the cause of karma in our lives, and – as I mentioned before – karma (an action with a consequence) greatly impedes our free will and autonomy, because – like the Egyptian Pharaoh of lore, holding the Israelites in abject slavery – karma is a creditor and we its debtors: we have to slave until all of our dues are paid.

This is why in Kabbalah, the Rabbis encourage us to run after our enemy if we see him in the street and do charities for him because he may have something of ours, and we need it back. We will not reclaim it with anger and hate because anger and hate feed it. It resonates at the same frequency, so your suffering will grow muscular and strong on your hate.

The only way to win back our light is by accessing a higher frequency than resentment, which is compassion. Compassion is easier to find when you recognize that your enemy too, no matter how abhorrent, is captured, he too is a slave. The negative energy has possessed him to the point that it has become him, and he will suffer painfully as a consequence.

(In the field of quantum mechanics, this would be called "entanglement." We become so entangled with our abuser that "we cannot be described independently of the state of the other," even when "we are separated by a large distance.")[5]

Our basic human nature is goodness.

Anyone that falls outside of this exacting parameter is lost to their true self, and in need of our compassion.

This negative energy (I'll talk about this in greater detail in a later chapter) has been called many names in mythological and biblical tomes: evil, the devil, Satan, the Wetiko, Beelzebub, darkness, the beast, the shadow, shades, pain-bodies etc. There is not a single culture that does not recognize this energy-form in its mythology. And the deeper you delve into the esoteric (what is known as the "hidden works") the more prevalent its mention. If he (your abuser) is living in a state of depravity, it is because he too is a slave, a marionette to this greater force, and for that reason alone, he deserves our compassion.

The main reason I call for compassion is because it is *the* antidote to evil.

Compassion-energy supersedes the lower energy of abuse: it dissolves it.

Love, joy, charity, compassion, truth; they remove evil like a corrosive.

I mentioned somewhere else about "heaping hot coals" on the head of the enemy. When we call on compassion for our abusers, we recover our stolen light, and we return to them the "hot coals" of abuse that they implanted in us.

If you harbor hate, anger, dissonance, you set up home for evil.

Not just because it is a catalyst for the release of corrosive chemistry into your body and not only because it invades and snatches your peace of mind; rather it is deadly because these base emotions are an anti-virtue and they completely disconnect us from our source, from our sanity, and from our potential to fully unfold as living beings. Hate breaks the alignment to our true nature and with it our entire purpose in this life. Righteous

Religion – alignment to love – connects us to the authentic self, the authentic self is connected to the divine sat nav, our map, our unique charter, the street-by-street, road-by-road route through this holy incarnation.

While we are not aligned to purpose, we are fodder for every passing energy form, we have no protection (our alignment to kindness *our charity* is our protection), we cannot connect to and be nourished through or directed by our source if we are disconnected by resentment. Our potential is suspended until we stop feeding the parasite inside us and kill it with kindness.

People are often mortally offended when they are advised to "love your enemies, bless them that curse you, do good to them that hate you, and pray for them that despitefully use you, and persecute you." (Matthew 5:44-45)

They think that love is a soft solution to a hard problem.

Perhaps if I change the language a little it might help.

If you think of hate as a deadly virus and love and compassion as its antigen, perhaps it might be more palatable.

If hate is the virus, then love is the disinfectant "that kills 99% of all known germs."

I was abused at the age of eleven.

I told you this much.

I didn't see this man again for twenty years, not once, but he had left a germ in me, he left a parasite, and this stole a part of my soul. I was possessed by fear and dissonance. This fear had its own voice and it said to me, "What if this happens again?" The dissonance too spoke to me, and it asked, "Why did this happen, who let it happen, who is to blame – there must be *someone* to blame?"

I didn't know it at the time, but these two emotions were the main food source for the germ left in me by this man. The fear and dissonance led to anger, rage and depression. These "dramas" also fed the parasite until I felt like I was more parasite than I was human. When I later acted out and projected my anger and blame on to the world, the anger fed it and the delicious, delicious blame allowed it to banquet like a king. When the parasite led me towards self-harm and sexual self-harm, it fed like a winter lion on my pain and then devoured my energy for days afterwards when I marinated in self-hatred and self-disgust and self-loathing.

When I became a bouncer, in a well-reasoned but ultimately perverted attempt to control the parasite in me by attacking all the parasites in the world, the violence I inflicted on others and the violence they inflicted upon me was a literal feast for the enemy within.

Pain feeds pain.

Drama feeds drama.

Violence feeds violence.

I tried everything to remove this "suffering."

I did not see my abuser for twenty years, but he had left his envoy in me, and across time and space he and his parasite were able to vampire my essential energies with simple arousals towards perverted sex, uncontrollable rage, self-pity, guilt, and judgment; all of the vices.

I was an open safe and all of my treasures were looted on a daily basis, not just by him, not just by his *demon* but by every passing energy-form looking to dine out free on the seminal energies of the personality Geoff Thompson.

It also acted unkindly and abusively in the world, as me and through me, accumulating large karmic bills that I had to pick up and repay.

When I finally woke up, I saw what was happening.

When I forgave my abuser, I gave him back his "coals of fire," I took back my spirit, my will, I reconnected to my source and the healing proper began.

I am not saying forgive because it is good for your abuser.

I am not saying forgive because he needs your mercy.

I am not saying let him off.

I am saying *set yourself free* by letting him go.

I am saying *don't cling to the implement of your own torture and then pretend it is powerful.*

I am saying *don't be duped into anger and hate* by thinking it offers you control or proffers you power; it does neither: it steals from you and it creates debt in your name.

When you feed anger and hate you empower anger and hate, in you and in the world. Don't put petrol on a fire and kid yourself that you are trying to douse the flames.

Compassion dissolves evil.

In fact, it is even more powerful than that, it converts it to Love.

Hate becomes the oil that lights the lamp.

Don't take my word for it, try it for yourself. Be your own proof.

The poet Rumi said it more succinctly than I:

Fear knocked on the door, love answered; there was no one there.

I mentioned before about conceptualization.

We place a label on negative emotions, we call them hate, we call them anger and fear and this conceptualization creates a form in its likeness, a hate or dislike for a reviled person or a particular group or a specific situation. When we give a concept form it automatically develops an aspect, this too in its own kind: fear makes us fearful, hate makes us hateful, towards the conceptualized object or person. Anger actively encourages us to use our elected enemy as a punch bag. If we are able to look at all these negative emotions without conceptualization, we will see that they are just neutral energy forms with a label that either we have placed on them or someone else has placed on them for us.

The popular media do this all the time.

They choose a person or a group that they dislike (this is usually for personal or political purposes), then they publish all sorts of heinous or extreme and subjective stories about them on their front pages and encourage us to hate them. Suddenly we find ourselves with an enemy that we don't even know, a foe that has been sold to us by propaganda, by positioned people with an agenda.

Conceptualization is projected onto us enough times already by those with an agenda without us projecting it onto ourselves.

The Buddha articulated this to one of his disciples when he described himself as "freed from denotation by consciousness."

His awareness (or consciousness) of the conceptualization of words or energies, allowed him to become free from their meaning, good or bad, and instead he was able to look at everything as it is: pure unformed energy.

If we too are able to de-label these neutral energy forms, strip them of their conceptualizations, their denotations, all we'll be left with is raw energy. Energy that we can choose to engage or ignore, repurpose, or eschew.

We can turn that molten energy-essence into positive fuel.

If we are expertly practiced, we can break down any conceptualized energy form (evil, hate, fear) into its component parts and smelt it into pure love. When we are able to do this (and it will take time and practice) we can honestly say that we have mastery, we have won free will, and the will to be free.

Surely this must be worth every effort.

To be free from the tyranny of hate and anger and find emancipation from the enemy within, now then, that is worthy of all our study and all our practice.

From my own experience, I can tell you that free will and freedom, personal autonomy, has been an unfolding experience. I have won it piecemeal, it did not happen overnight, it did not come to me fully formed and all at once.

The Israelites (mentioned earlier) were enslaved for hundreds of years by the Pharaoh of Egypt. They did not win their emancipation without the help of plagues and droughts sent by God, and forty years of roaming in the desert. This biblical story tells us that, even when we do eventually become free from the slavish enemy of resentment, it will still take time and practice before that freedom is felt as an abiding force, before it becomes our constant, and even then, it will have to be protected and preserved, we will have to fight to keep it every day of our lives.

I think it helps if we can see our individual self as a collection of territories, each of which has to be reclaimed in order to win back our empire. We should not expect to be freed from bondage just because we read one book, it's wiser to treat it as a process and start with (what is known as) **the small forgiveness**; the small forgiveness is the hurt that people inflict upon us: the words, the unkindness, even the heinous acts. We work our way from the outer edges inwards, removing and healing each emotional stain and slight and wound until we come to the instruments of abuse: people. Once we have given over the acts, we can then begin to forgive (from our minds) those who deliver the acts. This is done with the firm assurance that they are not the root-collar cause of our harm – though it is done through them and on their watch, and for this they must take responsibility – rather, if we follow the bread-trail back, we find that whilst they *are* the bewitched transmitters of evil, they are not the principle of evil itself. This is why we are able find compassion for them, and for this reason we can, in all good conscience, give them over. I remember doing an interview for my friend Brian Rose, on his podcast, *London Real*. When I told him that I felt compassion for the man who abused me, he asked directly, "Why?" Without even thinking I replied, "Because he was a victim too." It was the first time I had ever accessed this level of arcana, it was when I truly understood that the abuser was not my real enemy, he was merely one of myriad, expropriated human petri dishes, through which the microorganisms of evil are cultured and spread.

It is tempting to hate those that do us harm, but if we make that mistake, we will become infected by the virus of hate ourselves, and the disease of evil that races through their veins will take up residence in ours. It is the easiest thing in the world to hate the haters, but the moment we do so, we unconsciously join their legion, because to hate anyone, is to become a vessel for hate, and that does nothing but feed and spread the source of hate itself. This is why we are warned again and again by the higher religious reports never to resist or be overcome by evil because what we resist will persist: rather we are advised to overcome evil with good. The abuser is nearly always presented to us as the *big forgiveness*, but I know this to be a red herring, it is the black magician's sleight of hand, a cunning deceit employed to confuse, with a miasma of convincing distractions. It is the orchestrator of the harm, the wizard behind the curtain that we are called to expose and censor, the power that possesses the weak and uses them as vessels to implement its evil agenda, in man, as man, and through man. What often confounds our ability to heal is the fact that we are trying to forgive at the level of the symptom, rather than its point of origin. No matter how harsh the symptom, or how ugly its effects, we should never make the mistake of believing that we can cure an ill at the site of its manifestation, any more than we can change the content of a horror movie at the level of the cinema screen. Al-Ghazali reminds us in his *Letter to a Disciple* that "medicine of a disease is to first remove the root of the disease." The root is not the pilfering demons that cause havoc in our psyche, using us dually as an open buffet and a human plaything; rather, the rootstock is the Satan himself, who commands these parasitical thought-forms. Even the sharpest scalpel in the surgery will not remove a cancer if its blade is put to the blemished skin and not to the diseased organ.

St. Paul (the "ambassador in chains"), in his letters to the

Ephesians (6:12), offers us a stark and unambiguous reminder that "... our struggle is not against flesh and blood, but against the rulers, against the authorities, against the powers of this dark world and against the spiritual forces of evil in the heavenly realms."

Your protection against these principalities is "the belt of truth buckled around your waist... the breastplate of righteousness in place." More plainly put: we deem our body and mind inhospitable for any form of negativity by making virtue our gold standard. If we live with love, and project joy, and do charities, we will reach a spiritual altitude where demons can find no docking point. As for the war on the temptations themselves, the footslogs of abuse that still approach or rise looking for unholy intercourse, the technique of choiceless awareness is ever "the shield of faith, with which you can extinguish all the flaming arrows of the evil one."

Reality (to repeat and repeat again) exists at the level of engagement, if we refuse vice our attention, we deny evil its life.

Notice when the complaint rises in your mind and refuse to engage it.

We win back our small territories from the instruments, grow our inner-army, and build up to the big forgiveness.

As already outlined, the big forgiveness, you might say *the only forgiveness* is that we forgive (and prevent) from our minds not only the foot-soldiers of the Pharaoh, we forgive the Pharaoh himself: we forgive not only the instrument of our abuse, but also the unseen hand that directs its course: we forgive not just the marionettes who enact bad works against us, we forgive the puppeteer who pulls all the strings.

In other words, we recognize that all manifestations of evil have a source outside of us, and if we can trace them back, we can take the weed out at the root. We can do this by taking on one small evil at a time (which often, and for a time we must) or by taking on the source of evil itself: like the great earth, we can practice self-protection against all negative attacks by hermetically sealing ourselves with the human form of (what is known as) a magnetosphere. To quote current science, this is a "Van Allen radiation belt, a zone of energetic charged particles, most of which originate from the solar wind, that are captured by and held around a planet by the planets magnetosphere. Earth has two such belts, and sometimes others may be temporarily created."

This might sound complicated, but all it is suggesting is that we protect ourselves from evil by filling our inside and surrounding our outside with love. This demands that everything we think, say and do has its genesis in love.

We are already magnetic beings, but what is it that we are attracting?

We attract according to our most dominant state. If that state is negative, we attract, or allow negative elements. All we have to do is reverse the process, by courting only love, and all negatives will be squashed like flies on a high speed windshield.

Reason Ten is entirely dedicated to the magnetosphere of love.

Each small victory will win you courage and strength and wisdom and guile and knowing until your *good* heavily outweighs your bad. Human acts of virtue strengthen and increase human virtue. When human acts of virtue become your abiding state, they attract (what is known in Catholicism as) infused virtues. In other words, the more we help ourselves, the more we are helped by God.

Eventually you will reach a critical mass where the good inside you overwhelms the bad and you become absolute, a united territory with the armed guards of earned knowing on every turret, and at every city gate, and these will constitute your own personal Van Allen belt.

What we contain within, will radiate out; how concentrated our love is on the inside, will determine how well protected we are on the outside.

When we reach this level of understanding, we no longer perceive the adverse force, or the opposition, as an enemy at all, rather they are divine messengers, they act as an early alarm call, a divine shock that alerts us to a fracture in our shield. The moment we heed the warning, and reestablish our shields, these forces will retreat. They must. According to the great Iman Al-Ghazali, when we fall out of alignment, we are "noticed" instantly by these forces. They are attracted to breaks in our guard, just as rainwater naturally gravitates towards a crack in a roof tile. If we stay in the dead center of virtue, we are unseen by the opposition: virtue or *charity* is our cloak of invisibility. Conversely (as already stated) when we remain under the protective cloak, we are noticed by and infused with the higher forces of grace.

In Reason Nine, I have dedicated a whole chapter to the opposition.

My first lesson in changing state was proffered by an accidental teacher called Danny.

In my early days of ascent in the martial arts ranks, when I was writing articles in all the magazines and making a name for myself, Danny (who was a senior martial arts teacher at the time, a stalwart) took a grave dislike to me and decided to make me his sworn enemy. My work was very controversial. I was teaching a method of practical and honest martial arts that went against *you might say offended* the mores; many of the established gurus took a dislike to me. Danny was not alone there, although he had taken his hatred of me to a very personal level. He was a brilliant man, but he was unkind, he was lettered, but he was not self-knowing. He published scathing and critical letters about me in the magazines where I was a resident columnist, and he generally blackened my name wherever he went. I was angry. I was a young buck, I was a practiced martial artist, a nightclub bouncer, *a buccaneer of great renown*, my ego was the size of Birmingham, so of course I was offended. Actually, I was incensed. I wanted to call him out, confront him face to face but... Danny was an old friend and teacher to my own mentor Peter, a man that I loved and respected. Peter asked me not to confront Danny as a personal favor and I of course agreed. But this left me with a dilemma: Danny was still slandering me in the martial arts press, and people were starting to talk, they were starting to ask questions: "Why is Geoff Thompson letting him get away with this?" Even my own senior students were beginning to question why I was letting these blatant insults go. I can remember walking through my local park with Danny's insults rattling around my head like a half-brick in a cement mixer. My mind was taking me to all sorts of imagined scenarios of conflict between me and him. I am embarrassed to say that my arsenal at the time was limited entirely to the physical – Henry Kissinger I was not. I was used to working with hardy men on violent nightclub doors, men who spoke with their fists and didn't complain if the fight went against them and they ended up in the A&E (emergency) department of the local hospital. I had yet to develop a respectable line in badinage. I was not practiced in dialectics and debate. Where I came from an insult was a challenge to fight, and if you threw the verbal gauntlet, you'd better be prepared to back it up with your fists. But I was so loyal to Peter that I absolutely closed the door to a physical response with Danny, I would not break my promise to him.

This enforced restriction "encouraged" me to find another way to defeat my enemy. I knew there had to be one, but if there was, it was not immediately evident. In a moment of spontaneous inspiration, I decided to read up on Danny. This is something I'd been turning to, of late: when a situation perplexed me, I took to the library and tried to solve the problem by getting as much information as possible. If I read up on Danny (he was a published author, and much had been written about him) I'd get to know him better, who he was, where he came from, and what he stood for. I knew there was a good man in there somewhere, because he was Peter's first teacher, and Peter greatly admired him, loved him even. I knew that he had a wife that loved him too, and young children that adored him. They did not see him as an enemy, he was not a monster to them, nor to his many students who were both brilliant and dedicated to their teacher. Anyone that has a loving family, and loyal students, and old friends determined to protect them must have some redeeming features, and I intended to find them.

One of the problems with conceptualizing a person into an enemy (no matter how justified it might seem) is that their form and their aspect will quickly follow suit, and before we know it all we can see before us is a manifestation of evil. But no one can be all bad, and the more we explore their hidden aspects, the more we will be able to break the perceptual distortion, see a complete man, and not just a one-dimensional fiend. Danny's behavior towards me had implanted (or revealed) a dark filter in my psyche, and it was through this damaged Perspex that I viewed him. I knew that if I could lift this veil, he would become changed in my eyes, and I would be able to see him as he really was. This is hard to do because our hardwired survival mechanism wants to home in directly on a potential threat, enlarge it, and prepare to either defeat or escape it. I had to really discipline myself, I had to take charge *as it were*, grab the reins from my knuckle-dragging lower self, and drive my mind to find something more objective about this man, something kind and redeeming. The more I studied Danny (and believe me, this was not my initial intent) the more I came to admire him, like him even, eventually I have to admit that I felt love for him, the love you might feel for a revered warrior or a hero or an elder statesman. He was a pioneer of the external martial arts. He was one of the first occidentals ever to train in the home of karate, Japan. For those of us in the martial arts at the time (the 1980s) Japan was the Mecca, and whilst all of us wanted to sojourn there and learn from the masters, most of us never made it beyond the end of our own street; instead we settled for the closest class to us, usually a small gathering of white suits in a local church hall.

Danny did make it, and he brought back knowledge.

Apparently when he was in the East, he was treated very badly, even attacked and beaten up by Japanese students who did not appreciate Gaijin (outsiders, foreigners) in their country, let alone their dojo. But he stuck with it, he endured, and when he came back home to Britain, he became one of the most revered teachers of his generation.

I loved that.

I so admired everything he did.

In the end I didn't care that he was attacking me in the magazines, it was secondary to my admiration for him. I have to reiterate that this happened very gradually and almost by accident. As I sit here now, thirty years later, I can still feel my admiration for Danny, I can still feel the bubble of excitement that his hero's journey ignited in me, I can still feel the smile rise on my face and the love alight in my heart for this beautiful man.

One day – after yet another unkind letter – one of my senior students asked me, concerned, "What are you going to do about Danny?" I smiled and said, "I am going to forgive him." And it was never spoken about again.

Love overpowered hate.

A few years later Danny died from cancer.

I was sad when I heard the news.

One of my greatest teachers.

I never got to meet him in person, and he never knew what a powerful effect he had on me.

Forgiveness, in its true form, is an irresistible force.

It works.

I have living proof, and it was first given to me by Danny, and later replicated again and again, with other antagonists, who tempted me with hate-baiting, but were converted to friendship by my good-grace.

It is possible, autonomy, but we must acknowledge that we are imprisoned before we can even begin to set ourselves free. We have to realize that we have fallen for the bait-of-hate and placed walls and bars around ourselves.

So, the fourth reason to forgive is simple... we will never experience autonomy while we are connected or bonded to another by anger or hate. It is our resentment – our ignorance – that houses and feeds our jailer.

This leads me nicely to the fifth reason to forgive: the hate trap.

We must not tolerate hate in our body, in our mind or in our life.

Hate is a trap, but it can also be a gift, because the moment it rises in us or approaches, it betrays itself, it allows us to know its nature and reveals its location, and if we trace the energy back to its source, it shows us how we are able to either convert it to a higher energy or cast it back into the abyss.

Every problem comes complete with its own solution.

We just have to know where and how to find it.

Budo Practice

If freedom means understanding the obstacles that stand between you and your goal and removing them, then autonomy is the exercising of this freedom in self-determined living. We become empowered when we go from knowing to doing, and the dynamic of our life radically changes. As a martial artist I won freedom from fear by climbing the grades from white belt right up to black belt and beyond. This gave me the transferable skills to exercise autonomy in other areas of my life. Pre-black belt, when I was scared, I was ignorant of my own biological (adrenal) response to confrontation; I was literally afraid of everything. I was like a slave in my very own kingdom. When I won back my sovereignty, I was able to use my muscular courage to do the things I'd always wanted to do – write, give up work, train full time, study, travel, teach etc. I traversed a world with myriad, stifling laws, and matriculated into a density with very few laws and restrictions. In this budo practice I invite you to switch on your autonomy by writing down and actualizing your freedom. One of the things my eldest daughter Kerry learned through her own process of individuation (bringing the unconscious into conscious knowing) was that she always wanted to be a writer but was prevented from doing so by the many obstacles (the karma) that fearful conditioning threw in her path. Once these were cleaned she was able to see clearly, and with her newly born clarity, she was able to begin the process of becoming a scribe: at the time of completing this book (2021), she has just successfully completed a master's degree in creative writing.

What have you always wanted to do?

What have you put on hold because of your story?

What is the one thing that escaped you, that you perhaps planned to do before your life was so rudely interrupted by crisis.

Write it down.

Begin it.

Remember what I mentioned in the last chapter – if the purpose is true, there will be resistance: resistance is your free fuel supply, it is your gratis workforce, you need it, so use it.

Begin, begin, begin it now.

When you begin something the whole dynamic of your life will change. You are no longer *thinking* about doing a degree/ starting a business/running a marathon, you are actually doing it. You will change with the dynamic. I can't even begin to describe how powerful it feels to go from saying, "I want to be a professional martial arts teacher," to saying, "I am a professional martial arts teacher." Or from saying, "I would love to write a book," to "I have written a book."

Listen, everyone is going to start a business, everyone is going to write a book, everyone says that they are going to run a marathon or get in shape: words are cheap, and if you say them often enough without acting on them, they become absolutely worthless. In the end even you won't believe them. When you act upon them your reality changes, you change, and of course, once you complete something, that becomes a strong refence point for the next goal and the next goal and the next goal after that.

There is no limit to your potential to grow and learn.

What can you begin today, now, this moment?

What can you action?

Reason Five: The Hate Trap

Hate is a trap.

Fear is a trap.

Anger and rage and resentment are baited traps that most of humanity falls into.

It is rare that you watch a TV program or read a book or enter a conversation where, at some point in the procedure, you do not feel yourself being baited by hate. Much of the Hollywood canon, when it comes to action movies, is based on building the audience into a frenzy of hatred (towards the antagonist/s) until, by the last act, the viewer is hyped to revel and cheer and rejoice when the protagonist, the good guy, shoots him dead. The revenge can be visceral, bloody, and heinous and still the watcher, *revved up* and baited by the clever dialogue of the writer and subtle direction and skillful editing and heightened score, cheers when the bad guy gets it in the face. Whether it's the big budget blockbuster, the rolling news or the daily rounds of television soaps, the public are fed and watered on a daily diet of drama, melodrama and conflict. We think we are watching a piece of quality television; we are not, we are feeding on the sounds and the sights of distorted storytelling.

I happened upon an episode of *Celebrity Gogglebox* recently where celebrated and loved faces from music, stage and screen were filmed watching the highlights of a movie called *Thelma and Louise*. In one scene we witness Thelma, the younger, more naïve of the two friends, nearly being raped by a man she'd just met in a bar, only to be saved at the last minute by her older, wiser friend. Louise puts a gun to the neck of the potential assailant and warns him in no uncertain terms to back off. He backs off, but not before the audience are aroused by the injustice into the state of hatred. Just as the girls are about to exit the scene, no lasting harm done, the would-be rapist shouts after them, "I should have just fucked her." When an enraged Louise – insanely angry – shoots him dead, every one of the *Gogglebox* celebrities without exception cheered and shouted in support of the killing, most of them jumped to their feet in jubilation.

They celebrated because they'd been baited by clever storytelling to the point where, as long as they were convinced the antagonist was evil and really deserved it, they condoned and revelled in the killing of another human being.

Hate is bait for the low intellect.

It is a trap, and many fall into it, delighted with themselves that they have an opinion, even if that opinion is not their own.

The current master of hate in modern movies (regularly awarded the greatest prize the film world has to offer for his efforts) layers hate over the arc of his stories so crudely and so obviously it is a wonder that the intelligent cinema goer doesn't stand up from his seat, throw popcorn at the screen *incredulous* and shout, "Really?"

We have become so desensitized to hate and the rhetoric of hate, even from our leaders and politicians, that violent pornography in the guise of televisual drama – organized and scripted hatred – can be beamed into our front rooms every night and we do not even blink an eyelid.

I remember a time some years ago after I'd gone through a hugely challenging reformation process, an experience that physically and mentally brought me to my knees. Around this time, I visited the cinema to watch a film called *Sin City*, an adaptation of a famous graphic novel about four individuals who cross paths when they try to solve their personal problems and fight against violence in the wretched town of Basin City, Washington. It was a forty-million-dollar porn fest where the violence used to defeat violence was more heinous than the original offence.

I was only ten minutes into the film when I had to get up

from my seat and leave.

It was a physical assault on my soul. I felt it as an actual attack. My ego had been so decimated by my recent cleansing that my soul, my authentic spirit, was on the skin. My intuition assured me that, "This is what hatred does to the soul."

Nothing was ever so clear to me than this.

The ego (of which I had none at the time) will eat hate for breakfast, dinner, and tea but the soul finds it indigestible, in fact it is tortured by it.

The false ego feeds on hate. It grows fat and strong on hate, and this is the reason why anger and hate and war are sold to the masses as righteous entertainment. Hate is a nose bag: it feeds the horse-ego obese and keeps the soul emaciated and tortured and in the dark.

Hate is bait, and it leads us into a trap.

On *Gogglebox*, intelligent men, and women, some of them respected public figures and elected politicians, swallowed the wriggling worm, hanging from the broadcaster's hook. They fell for the clumsy bait of an acclaimed film maker and jubilantly celebrated killing from the comfort of their own front rooms.

Hate feeds the parasite in you.

The parasite in you acts as a hub, it contains a hive of insect-like thought-forms that collect human nectar for the queen bee who resides in a non-local frequency of negativity.

Much of our comedy today, too, is based on the crude and the rude and the carnal. The names of known celebrities are regularly corralled by the host and his guests in TV studios and then "roasted" for public viewing, for our entertainment: we eat them for supper.

It is bait that feeds the hungry ghost in all of us, a beast that will not, that cannot, be sated.

You might be thinking (or saying) that I sound like a prude.

Of course, that's the first house ghost right there, that is the first line of defense for a germ that feeds in the darkness and thrives on anonymity.

You stand up, you say what you see, you warn people about the hidden danger of unconscious viewing, and you are called a prude.

I have been called worse things than this.

I am no prude, but I am prudent: there is a difference.

I once housed one of these creatures in me.

To feed it I was violent, I was gross, I was pornographic, I was base, I was judgmental, I was insecure, and I would inflict violence on people at the drop of a hat if I felt that I'd been threatened or disrespected. This biggest thing I learned from this unfortunate period of my life – a great metaphysical secret – was the fact that everything I did to others I did to myself.

I was an ignorant fool.

I felt powerful and strong.

I was neither: I was weak and insecure.

Violence – by man or by nation – is usually sold as strength, but anyone with even a mote of intelligence can see that violence is always a sign of insecurity and weakness.

I learned the hard way that in order to deliver violence, I had to first process its caustic chemistry in every cell of my body. As well as starting a negative chain of causation in the revealed world, I also triggered an inner avalanche, in the hidden world, where the energy I produced to inflict violence on others was pickling my insides like an acid bath. Believing that violence – thought, said or done – would solve the problem of violence was like drinking poison and hoping that my enemy might fall over dead.

More importantly, when we court any kind of vice, we destabilize the natural balance of our inner world and thus we destabilize the natural balance of the universe.

So far, I have been referring to this force as good and evil, dark and light, the beauty and the beast. These are the common terms we use when referring to man's potential for both good and evil. In Judaism, this polarity is explained in the allegory of *the tree of good and evil*, and *the tree of life*. The tree of good and evil represents the left side of our nature, our dark side (what the Jews call the "evil inclination"), our greedy, selfish aspect that wants to receive for the self alone. The tree of life represents the right side, our inclination towards good, the generous, selfless aspect that desires to receive only in order to share with others. In reality, in the ideal scenario, we recognize both polarities and find a balance in the center column, between the two forces, like a filament placed between and connecting the negative and positive terminals of a light bulb. Both sides are necessary, both terminals of energy are ordained, but they need to work together in order to create a glow.

If we lean too much to the right, we may be kindly, but our kindness has no spine and shows no restraint, which leaves it weak and ineffective.

If we fall to the left, we become severe and judgmental: this is the realm of the ego, and all he cares about is himself, which automatically disconnects us from our source.

There can be no light in this human realm without both the negative and the positive forces, but they demand a stable, tempered, and uniting force. In the case of the light bulb, this force is the filament. Both the negative and positive terminals are impotent until they are united in balance by the conducting capability of the filament: it is the filament that enables the bulb to create light, in fact it is the filament that actually glows and becomes a light.

This process is commonly known; what is less known is that the filament is made from a thin strip of Tungsten, a metal with an abnormally high melting point, which allows it to receive (and act as a conductor for) large flows of electricity – both negative and positive terminals simultaneously – and convert them into light without being consumed and burned up in the process. This high melting point is no accident, it has been created this way so that it can safely conduct powerful forces of energy: the tungsten is developed from ore and placed through exacting processes of extreme heat and testing chemical reactions, so that the metal is able to endure high temperatures without being consumed.

There are other factors to consider of course: the bulb itself needs to be hermetically sealed in an airtight vacuum in order to prevent the filament from being exposed to the air and completely burnt out: and inert gasses are inserted into the bulb to add to this protection. The filament is the most important factor in the creation of light, it is the corpus Christi: all the other elements are there to aid and protect and facilitate the tungsten, so that it can produce maximum light without being consumed in the process.

In the human infrastructure it is our conscious will (known as the working arm of the soul) acting as the uniting filament between opposing forces that allows us to create light. And like the tungsten filament, we too have to undergo our "stations" of rigorous testing and painful process before we are able to develop the "abnormally high melting point" necessary to conduct the powerful forces or good and evil and convert them into spiritual light. WWII death-camp survivor Dr. Viktor Frankl said that, "What is to give light must endure burning": this is surely what he must have meant, regarding the human filament, the soul.

As I briefly mentioned somewhere else, this book is an example of the said alchemy, the creation of light through the burning of the soul. I am writing this book now, at my desk, on a note pad. I have negative forces in me and around me that violently oppose the creation of this work. I have positive forces in me and around me too, that actively promote it. Both forces, no matter how seemingly powerful, are impotent without the uniting filament of my developed will. When I sit down to write, tremendous forces try to stop me, magnificent forces try to encourage me, but nothing can come of these energies if I have not developed the will and the wisdom and the intention to make myself sit down, pick up a pen and write.

Both forces are consumed, you might say converted and transfigured, in the volition of making this work.

That which is exposed to light, itself becomes a light.

You are reading the alchemical result of the process in question.

You are looking at and breathing in and feeding on the dark and the light in the transitional form of the written word. There is a fine balance in the universe that keeps the earth spinning and makes the planets align. We are a microcosm of the universe, and our own balance is just as vital. If we lean too much to the right (the good) we lose balance and we become ineffectual beings; mercy without judgment is weak, it is an improper mix of forces. If we lean too much to the left (the negative) we again lose balance, and the dark floods in and we are all judgment with no mercy. In the Holy Qur'an (surah 55.7-9) this balance is spelled out for us: "And the heavens he raised high and he set up a balance, in order that you may not transgress (due) balance. And observe the weight with equity, and do not make the balance deficient."

The surahs (chapters of the Qur'an) are considered to be attributes of God, they are regarded as remedies to our ills.

Our ills are only born when we fall out of balance.

On the one side we have the emaciated preacher, speaking *the word* from a lofty pulpit, but unable to live the word in the cut-and-thrust of everyday life. This is the socks-and-sandals brigade, New Age spiritual aspirants who want to change the world but haven't developed the will to change their socks once a day.

On the other side, we have the dark cynic, the nihilist who sees no purpose and no paradise for those who do good, and no hell regions for those who flaunt the law.

One has too much left, the other has too much right: balance is missing presumed dead. Be in no doubt, if we don't find balance within ourselves, our larger body (the earth, the universe) will eventually redress and bring everything back to balance for us.

In a long-winded way, I am saying this: when you fall into the hate trap *or any kind of vice*, you fall out of balance and you allow the dark, negative terminal of energy to dominate your life, with anger, resentment, depression, hopelessness etc. These forces need to be gathered in, they need to be managed, they need to be balanced proportionately and directed by you and they will not be balanced if you engage or identify with any form of anger or rancor.

The reason this balancing act is imperative is not just because of negative causation; it is vital also because, when we receive selfishly, what we receive is diminished on reception, it is no more. When we receive from a selfless desire, in order to share (for the common good), what we receive is not diminished by sharing, in fact it is increased.

I have shared a great secret here with you (which means it will be increased, and not diminished): what we receive in order to share, is magnified by the sharing. What we receive for the self alone, is exhausted on reception.

In this moving universe of fixed rules, this is perhaps the greatest law of them all, it is the secret to universal, perpetual motion.

Priests, men and women of faith will tell you that evil is very real, it exists in the world and to deny it is to allow it by omission.

They are both right and wrong.

There is evil, but it is better known as a negative terminal of energy.

It is ordained.

God – the universal imperative – created, to quote the Qur'an: "Men and Jinn (devils), you and you."

If God is omnipotent and omniscient and omnipresent, then of course He is all things: He is everything.

The quote does not separate Men and Jinn as *you and him* or *you and it*; it describes them as *you and you*.

Men and jinn are one.

The angel and the demon are one.

The light and the dark are one.

The negative and the positive share the same space, in you, because they are you. When they are in balance, to paraphrase Milton, they can create a heaven out of hell. When they are out of balance, they will create a hell out of any heaven.

Balance is the key.

It is what nature teaches.

It is the lesson implicitly taught to us by the stars and the planets.

It is what we see when we look through a telescope into the dark, night skies.

We *are* the living, breathing, self-levelling universe ever seeking balance.

Resentment in all its disguises destabilizes us.

Even if we demonize the popular hate-figures, the voice of government officialdom, the face of the despot, the behavior of the greedy banker, or the violent fundamentalist. If we hate them, we destabilize our own balance because hate is a trap.

Even when it appears to be justified, hate rebounds on itself.

To hate anyone is to hate yourself.

To hate others is to become hate yourself because your axis of power will tilt to the side you favor and to the degree of your default.

It destabilizes, it disturbs the balance so that evil (Jinn, the negative terminal) can prevail. Once you choose to see one thing through a glass darkly, you cannot help but to see all things through the same filter.

There is no evil in the world, only a lack of balance between light and dark; both are universal forces.

If we fail to heed this instruction, if we refuse to receive the remedy, we will deny our own dark side and when it rises up and acts out in the world we will (like Dr. Frankenstein) abandon and deny the monster of our own making and he will wreak havoc on the townspeople. We will fall into denial, lose our autonomy and (as Jung assures us) put the happenings of our world down to fate.

When we forgive, we are not letting people off, we are simply recognizing that an imbalance of energy, orchestrated by someone who is also unbalanced, has corrupted us. The energy signature manifesting as depression, anger, rage, dissonance etc. has become stuck to us. To forgive is to recognize this anomaly, and resist labelling it as good or bad: we simply remove (or reframe or convert) the offending shadow and manually bring ourselves back to balance.

In psychology this is known as homeostasis, our natural physiological balance.

Our biology, as I mentioned earlier in the book, is compromised when we allow in the vice of hatred or fear (disguised as a righteous indignation) to become our voice of reason.

We are not offering pardon to our abuser, we are simply removing their product, we are redressing our own balance, we are purging the germ and bringing ourselves back to the still center. We are doing this by ourselves, with ourselves and for ourselves.

It is for us the forgiveness, it is not for the recipient of our grace that we give it over, it is for our own equilibrium that we retrieve our sanity and either hand back the hate to the haters, or, if we have enough skills, convert it in the process of positive volition.

How do we do this?

Firstly, by recognizing and understanding and believing the

law and the process of the law.

We do this by refusing to engage hate in all its forms; by refusing to identify hate as part of our vernacular. This is not to deny that hate rises in us, or that it bids for our attention from an inside or outside stimulus, rather it is to recognize its approach and deny it our emotional engagement, our identification.

I am not saying, either, that we cannot cogitate on this energy if it hovers at the doorway of our heart, looking for an entry point. We may well have to engage in an internal dialectic in order to dismiss its claim to asylum in us. Sometimes negative emotions storm the doors (as it were) and before we know it the hate is in us, and it is then more a matter of getting it out again (or converting it), rather than denying it entry or talking it down. This can be a big, complicated job, because once it gets in, once it is habituated, it hijacks elements of our personality, develops its own internal voice and disguises (even identifies) itself as us. At this late juncture it takes a person of elevated self-knowing to distinguish between the false bluster of hate, and the sage, sane voice of the Self.

When I worked as a nightclub bouncer, we had a solid, highly effective policy on club security: **we stopped the trouble at the door**.

When we sensed that a customer might be a future problem if we allowed them entry (if they were drunk, if they were barred, if they were agitated or troublesome, or they had a bad reputation) we simply said no! We stopped the trouble at the door because we knew that if we didn't, if we let them in, at some point during the evening they would create problems for us in the club. By that time, they will have connected with other people of a similar ilk: one man can quickly become one army in the confined space of a busy drinking establishment. What might be a small issue at the doorway of a club with one person can quickly grow into a riot inside the establishment with more enemies than the door staff can safely handle.

At the door we stopped, we monitored, we discerned, we discriminated, and we knocked people back if we thought they might be a threat to club security. If they argued, we would use polite but unemotional dialogue to qualify our censor. We entered into longer dialectics only if it was absolutely necessary, and even then, we maintained a strong emotional distance, and we did not allow them to penetrate our protective shield of professionalism. We were polite but firm. We would not be threatened or bribed or coerced or tricked into *letting the wrong ones* in.

Our decision, once made, was final.

Guarding the mind-door works on the same principle.

We guard our personal will, *our kingdom* like we are guarding a safe full of bullion: we choose the thoughts we engage wisely, knowing that the wrong cognitions will pilfer our treasure, we enter into dialects only if the thoughts bidding for our attention are too strong to ignore: and if they storm the doors, and get in, and pirate our will, we get them out again by fair means or foul, and as quickly as is humanly possible.

Hatred will find any justification to take up a squat in our minds and bodies.

If we find ourselves following a legal path to bring our abusers to justice, we can (and we must) still do so without allowing the poison of hate to enter our hearts. Even if we are in the process of bringing our abuser before a court of law, we can still do so without the engagement of or identification with negative emotions.

To fathom this fully, we will probably have to make this our life's work.

To understand the balance of energies, strip away all the negative conceptualizations and seek our rights, with truth and justice in mind, we will necessarily have to deny feelings of hate and abandon all thoughts of revenge.

As I said (and I reiterate) we do this for our own benefit,

for our own health and well-being, ultimately, we do it for our own sanity. It is not for the recipient of our forgiveness that we forgive, it is for us, it is for us, it is entirely for us.

Ironically, if we work from a place of virtue, what works for us will also benefit all of mankind.

We must never lose sight of the fact that we are all human and we have all erred; to one degree or another, "all are guilty" the Talmud assures us. I have yet to meet a man or woman who does not have at least one dead body buried under the patio (metaphorically speaking), that, at some point, will have to be exhumed and accounted for. When this happens (and it will happen) we too will hope and wish and pray for mercy for the "murders" of our past.

Thought, word or deed, small or large, corporeal murder, or assassination of character, our wrongs are still our wrongs; they are separated only by degree. An accumulation of small "insignificant" sins are just as damaging and corrosive as one large error. Murder with a bullet, death by tabloid, revenge via a Twitter post, spilling blood with a knife or drawing blood with the razor edge of public shaming, we have all abused, therefore we all need mercy, and we can only ever be forgiven to the degree that we forgive others.

Al-Ghazali told his student in his epistle (*Letter to a Disciple*) that he was "afraid not to forgive," because he "feared not to be forgiven."

We set the tolerance.

Us.

We set the tolerance with our own decrees, and with the level of judgment we heap onto others.

To reiterate: we cannot forgive but we can give it over, and we can repent our own wrongs.

We cannot judge but we can ask to be judged.

We do not destroy evil, but we can recognize it as a living energy in need of balance or conversion.

Practice mercy.

Practice gratitude.

Practice compassion.

In the Holy Qur'an there are 99 different names of Allah, all are considered to be divine attributes of God. The first name is Ar-Rahman, which is classed as the adornment of the whole Qur'an: every *good* in this work of God is encompassed in Ar-Rahman, which translates as: grace, mercy, compassion.

Whilst I am aware that the world-bibles might seem peripheral to the concept of forgiveness, they really are not: in fact, these books of elevated and didactic philosophy are integral to the salvation of the erring human. These are not merely arbitrary words plucked randomly from an ancient text, they are highly pragmatic formulas, they are non-local powers, they are attributes of Law that, if understood, if practiced, will rebalance any negative emotions and bring the body back to homeostasis.

They are high-frequency energies, spirit-in-ink that will neutralize all energies below them.

Compassion (as mentioned) is the king of these higher frequencies, and it is the sixth reason why we should forgive.

When we offer (the remedy of) compassion to others, especially those who persecute us, the reward to us is received compassion.

There is a great line in the Billie Eilish *Bond* theme (*No Time to Die*) that says, "just goes to show, that the blood you bleed is just the blood you owe."

In my own words I would say: "Just goes to show, that the seed you plant is just the yield you sow."

What we give, is what we get.

Budo Practice

In my martial arts classes I taught the students how to depersonalize strong emotions like anger and hate, I encouraged them to strip the feelings back to their raw neutral state, and then practice either dissolving the remaining energy-form back into the ether or reconstituting it into something positive. Our concepts and beliefs keep us trapped in small lives. Consciousness (our growing awareness of the true nature and origin of things) frees us from denotation (we no longer label things and allow words to determine states). I would like to invite you in this budo practice to make a list of your personal hates, to locate the ones that are most potent and then practice, through a process of negation, stripping away all the associated labels until you are left with nothing but denoted energy.

This is easy in concept, but difficult in process.

I find it difficult. Everyone finds it difficult, certainly in the beginning, because you have to locate the feelings that are coursing through your body and stand in front of them without trying to move them or change them or send them away. This is difficult because we spend most of our lives actively avoiding or evading or covering up uncomfortable feelings. I am encouraging you to do the opposite. I am asking you to be very curious about these feelings, and delve deeply into their true meanings, their origins. Is fear really fear or is it just a rush of physiological hormones, a warm tingle of energy racing through our body that we have learned to associate with dread? Is anxiety really such an avoidable condition, or have we allowed ourselves to become so afraid of uncertainty and discomfort that we have permitted this feeling to shrink our life into a corner.

My beautiful, ambitious, pioneering brother Ray was going to change the world. He was going to write plays and make films and pen books. He died at the age of 42 years (in 1999) from alcoholism without realizing any of these dreams. I was devastated by his death but determined that he was not going to leave us without imparting his wisdom from a life lived in extremes. When Ray felt anxious, he used alcohol to deaden his nerves. In other words, he hid under alcohol. The more he ran and hid, the stronger his anxiety grew, and the more it grew the more alcohol he needed to drown it out. This once gorgeous man went from being a free spirit ready to trip the light fantastic to a depressed alcoholic, frightened to leave his kitchen stool in a shitty flat in one of the filthiest tower blocks in Coventry. As his fear bloated, his word and his world contracted; his terror expanded until all that was left of Ray was a bundle of frayed nerves, prey to every rogue wind. My brother left me with a powerful teaching: if you run from your feelings, or hide from your feelings, or blanket your feelings, your feelings will grow stronger on your running and hiding and covering. If you welcome your feelings, face your feelings, dive into the belly of your feelings like jumping headfirst into the mouth of a cartoon Lion, your feelings with lose their agency. The labels will fall away, and all you will be left with is a harmless, nameless, neutral energy source that you can either claim, bank and repurpose, or you can ignore. If you bank and reprocess them, you can turn the lead into gold. If you ignore them, the feelings, finding no docking point in you, will fall back into the void.

I haven't written fifty books and fifteen films and five stage plays and a musical and thousands of published articles because I was never afraid; I have written them because I was very afraid: I learnt to use this latent energy, this gift, as a natural fuel for the engine.

As I mentioned in the last chapter, sometimes we cannot immediately change the state of our mood, but we can become curious about the way we are feeling. Dr. Viktor Frankl called this technique "paradoxical intention": we deliberately intend the things we fear most to experience. When depression kicked down my mind-door and ransacked my internal abode, instead of cowering (as I had always done before) I took a stand and said, "Come in, have a sit down, do you want a cup of tea, can I introduce you to my wife." When it threatened to intensify its assault on me, I said, "Bring it on: I want more, this is not enough, bring it, bring it, bring it." When the anxiety and dread threatened to stay forever and never leave I said, "Stay as long as you like, you are welcome."

The feelings have a limited reserve of energy, they can sustain themselves for a short time without our engagement, but they cannot last for long. It is a matter of sitting it out. As soon as the feelings arise, we dive right into them, we examine them, we describe them to ourselves: this feeling is hot in my stomach: this feeling is dull in my chest: this feeling is fast and sudden etc. The feelings will try to engage you, they will try and drag you back to mistakes you made in the past, or project you forwards to imagined tragedies, they will insist that a candle flame is an inferno, that a spill of water is a coming flood, that hope is a nonexistent dream, and that illness and death are as close as your neck vein, they will encourage you to withdraw, to hide, to find a fast relief, to run, run, run.

Watch the feelings rise, observe them objectively, invite them in immediately, be brave, be brave, be prepared for them to stay forever, invite them to stay forever. When you are genuinely happy to live with them forever, they will leave instantly.

In the Kabbalah the advanced version of this technique is to hold these negative, parasitical feelings (or beings) captive, bravely, deliberately in your body for several days, and lord over them without emotional engagement, until they are begging to be freed. This (the Rebbe assures us) sends out a powerful message to all other would-be invaders: I am not afraid of you, do not mess with me, if you do this is what happens.

In Chinese philosophy they call this strategy, "slaughtering a chicken in order to train a monkey."

In the Homerian epic, *The Iliad*, it was known as vaunting: on the battlefield, Diomedes and his fellow warriors insulted, and postured over captured, wounded, dying, and even deceased enemy soldiers, so that their comrades, watching from beyond the field of play, could know the savage nature of the territory and be encouraged to retreat before they even entered the arena.

We are assured in *The Tibetan Book of the Dead*, that *recognition and liberation* are instantaneous: when we recognize our power over these entities, we are instantly liberated from them.

If you create no resistance for these energies, they can find no safehouse in you.

Once you are able to denote the feelings, it is really now just a matter of what you do with them. You can either witness them as they rise and fall. Or you can take the labels off them and drive them into the arc of creativity. I practice both methods: if I have a book to write, or a workout to do or a service to perform, I simply relegate the feelings to a background noise (by not engaging or identifying with them) or I drive them directly into the work. I remember being assailed some years ago by a depression that lay heavy at my mind-door, trying to break its way in. I said to my agent: "Get me as many interviews as you can." I had just written a book that needed to be promoted, so I used this latent energy to propel it. The next day I was on *Morning* television, reconstituting the depression into a talk that was watched by millions of people; I turned the darkness of depression into a living light.

You might not be in a position at the moment to spend your anxiety on a national television interview, but where can you use it? Perhaps you can help a neighbor. Could you drive the energy into your garden? Or your mum's garden? People need help, the world is spilling with folk desperate for a kind, strong working arm: when you help them you will help yourself.

In a later chapter I will help you to build an "eye wall," a budo technique that enables you to sit in the eye of any storm when you are dealing with turbulent energies.

Reason Six: Compassion

If we are looking for a formula or remedy to ease or fix or attend our wounds, there is a one-stop-solution, a panacea, and it is called Ar-Rahman.

I mentioned this at the end of the last chapter.

We have (I hope) already established that we must not practice hate: we must avoid anything that draws our attention into the sticky-sweet mouth of a Venus flytrap and our health and our life and our peace of mind deep into its digestive tracts.

The world is relying upon us to regain our equilibrium, of course.

If we are out of plumb, we contribute to the instability of the whole world.

When we rise from our bed every day we should (at least) try to live our life like a saint. Anything less is unworthy of the free air we breathe.

God favors those who strive, the Holy Qur'an instructs us, it does not favor those who do not strive. In other words, our universe is touch-sensitive to us: it responds to each individual human soul.

When we drop a pebble in the world-pond it reacts. It has always been so. It is always so. It will always be so in the future. You are the only one looking through your eyes and if they *see* even a little, you will know that the entire galaxy is within you. You (we) are the universe. When we walk through the streets and the roads and the cities of our world, we are literally walking through ourselves. Everything in the universe is connected, just as the cells within each human body are linked, from the tip of our toes to the top of our crown. Those around us can be lifted and inspired with as little as the upward curve of our mouth, and they can be deflated with as little as the cynical squint of our eyes. I have seen children crushed by the loaded weight of a parent's glare. I have seen grown men weep when their idol offered them a loving embrace.

Kind e-mails and messages and lines in books and songs have prevented suicides.

Unkind Twitter posts have tormented souls and sent them to an early grave.

Please! We all know this.

To revoke this obvious truth is not so much to be in denial as it is to be in a deep coma. If we do not acknowledge our potential even for clumsy power, we run the risk of crushing souls like bugs under the stomping heel of blind ignorance.

See the power you can wield. Accept the power graciously and responsibly and refuse, refuse, refuse to put any noise out into the world that does not come from the Shofar (trumpet) of love.

What I am saying in layman's terms is: don't be a blind fool.

I was the greatest of all blind simpletons for many years when I trod on the weak and called myself mighty. I learned over a time span, lasting decades, that every curse carries a cost, and every slight has a return address written on the back of the envelope. I suffered as mightily and to the exact degree of the unkindness I heaped onto others. When I went through my *many rounds* of deep repentance (see my confessionary memoir *Notes From a Factory Floor* for the blow-by-blow account) I did not, I would not, and I could not deny the truth of reciprocity. I suffered for many years with every form of personal, public, and private damnation. At some points in my life, my ego was so decimated by personal burnout that I was actually able to not only see my soul (in a series of divine visions) but I could see through the eyes of my soul. I witnessed that the pain heaped out by me, was heaped back on me like the damning fires of biblical lore as a consequence of living for so long in a state of denied imbalance.

I am in possession of certainty when it comes to reciprocity, and the power that it wields for both good and for bad.

After much of the karma was cleared with the body and blood of my repentance, with works, with charities, by changing my ways, compassion was infused in me as a grace, and I put my shoulder to the wheel of its service.

Compassion is a certainty I was gifted after many long years of deep repentance.

I experienced it again and again until it spilled into the knowing that compassion (Ar-Rahman) is the formula or remedy for dissolving the shadow that haunts us, it turns the thorns (to paraphrase Richard Rose) into milk.

The opening formula of the Holy Qur'an is compassion.

I have mentioned this several times I know.

It bears repeating.

This non-local attribute holds metaphysical power.

Hearing it only once or twice will not be enough to make it your constant.

I intend to keep repeating it, to remind you, to remind me.

In the holy book Allah talks about all of his creations, from the sun and the moon to the humans and the Jinn. These pairs of opposites work in tandem: men and jinn (you and you) no less than the sun and the moon. All of the myriad bibles from the many cultures I have studied proffer the same remedy to those seeking escape from the adverse forces. They advise us from a place of expanded knowing, that warring on our enemy only strengthens its arsenal, just as a boa tightens its hold in direct proportion to the struggle of its prey, and quicksand swallows its victim to the exact degree of his struggle for escape.

Ar-Rahman is called the Most Gracious, All Merciful, Lord of Mercy, The Beneficent, the Mercy Giver, The Compassionate.

Maimonides (Moses ben Maimon, a medieval Sephardic Jewish philosopher), in his *thirteen attributes of mercy*, advises, when dealing with persecutors, to "be god-like in your mercy: forgive before offence has been taken: pardon in the aftermath of abuse."

(I remind you that) this is done for you, not for them.

Your instinct might be urging you to attack in your own defense, but your mercy is calling you to forgive for your own salvation. Maimon implores us to find compassion, to act God-like and bring the smother of love to the fire of your rage.

That is hard to do, I hear you say.

I disagree.

It is not hard to be compassionate to those who assail us, what *is* difficult is to see compassion as a practical solution.

Let me tell you a story that was shared with me, to illustrate my certainty.

I met a lovely man called Chris Lubbe. I have mentioned Chris elsewhere. Our meeting was ordained: he had particular stories to share with me and I had a specific message for him.

The fates are master-matchmakers: they love to bring people together, when a particular exchange of knowledge will benefit the greater good of all.

Chris was a close friend of Nelson Mandela, I said this much, he was a fellow dissident in apartheid South Africa. Chris told me that while they were incarcerated on Robben Island, all of the political prisoners were routinely attacked and tortured by white South African guards. The guards hated the "terrorist" prisoners, and the prisoners hated the racist guards, right back. This hatred fueled every beating and every inhumane act, until one day, in the midst of yet another torture session, Nelson Mandela had a revelation. By this time, he'd been in prison for some years and many of the new guards, his erstwhile enemies, were young men, too young (he realized) to have been around when Mandela was politically active in South Africa. Certainly, they were not old enough to know anything about Mandela personally, other than what they had read, heard, been told, or taught at home and at school: probably a rich combination of all the above.

They were too young to have witnessed him for themselves.

Mandela could see that these men hated him because they'd been taught to hate him. All they knew was hate, it was their inheritance and they blindly accepted it without question. The moment he realized this he became filled with compassion for them. His own hatred was swallowed up by the revelation.

Recognition and liberation were instantaneous.

He suddenly understood that the young, white, South African guards were as much victims of apartheid as he and his fellow dissidents. The moment he was gifted true compassion – and this had taken some time – he could no longer hate his torturers and (he told Chris, who told me) when he no longer fueled their hate with his own hate, when he replaced fear with understanding and compassion, they could no longer torture him.

This sudden knowing was a gifted grace, no doubt, but the catalyst to infused virtue, is practiced virtue: Mandela was a studious and diligent thinker, who made deep enquiry into truth his habitus. And as Aquinas reminds us, "acts produced by an infused habit do not cause a habit, but strengthen the already existing habit, just as remedies of medicine given to a man who is naturally healthy, do not cause a kind of health, but give new strength to the health he had before."

Hate needs hate in order to exist.

Without the feed, it died. Or *you could say* it was converted.

Compassion for the torturer turned into compassion for the tortured.

The slayed are wounded in body, Augustine assures us, but the slayer is wounded in his spirit.

When we are able to see that those who abuse us are also victims of shadow, we are able to find compassion.

Mandela suffered, that is beyond doubt. But his suffering was the necessary catalyst to trigger the awakening of compassion. It helped him to remove the hate and return to his own still center. He may never have found this without the opportunity to understand, to find compassion, and ultimately to forgive.

Suffering does not exist in the still center, it does not, *it cannot*; in that place "nothing impermanent appears. No illness, no remedies, no infirmities, no medicine."

When you find your own still center, those in close proximity to you will be sucked into the vacuum of your singularity, and their hatred will be undone by the antigen of Love. For Mandela it was as literal as it was immediate; as soon as he was able to find true compassion for his captors, they could no longer hurt on him. His frequency was so balanced that, like a tuning fork, all frequencies in close proximity were brought into symphony with it.

My beautiful sister died very recently (February 2020) from alcoholism.

She had suffered badly from this disease for over two decades before it finally took her life. She did not like the drink, but the drink certainly liked her: she was compelled to drink. She was overbalanced by this dark spirit until there was nothing left of her, only hanging clothes on a bag of bones and the addictive compulsion to poison (what was left of) her body with alcohol.

Many people who drink, my sister amongst them, are judged for their addiction. All I felt for her was compassion, massive, heartrending, tear-jerking compassion.

I knew she was a victim of the drink.

I knew she was possessed by the drink and neither I, my doting mother, her beautiful children, nor the wonderful doctors and nurses at the University Hospital in Coventry, with all our love and all our knowledge could free her from it.

When people are unkind, abusive, critical, offensive, when they attack me, when they attack society, I feel the same compassion. I feel compassion because they are victims, just as much as the people they target with their abuse.

They do not know themselves.

They are literally, *not* themselves.

To paraphrase Christ on the broken hill, when he was spat on and judged by two thieves on neighboring crosses: "Forgive them, Lord, for they know not what they do."

Anyone who enacts a crime is a victim of evil, an accessory to evil, and whilst their crimes cannot be justified and must be stopped and their actions brought to justice, we should never make the error of treating them any different from the way we would treat anyone who is a victim of disease: with understanding, and with as much compassion as our knowing will allow us.

The compassion comes from knowing (more on knowing, "Yaqeen," in a later chapter) what is occurring.

When a child in a fever lashes out, we protect ourselves *of course*, but we do not lose compassion for the child, because we know that the assault is the result of the malady.

Much of humanity – certainly, those who live in hate – is in a malady of sorts, and this makes everyone a potential threat. I have been attacked and pilloried and demeaned by family members and by my oldest and dearest friends when my growing spirituality clashed with their stagnant, egoic identity. We are warned by the Messiah in the New Testament that those with the Christ energy will be attacked even in their own household. I know firsthand that the very closest of friends can become the keenest of enemies, and absolutely convince themselves that their poor-choice actions are somehow honorable and righteous. You defeat them, friend and foe, with radical, in-your-face, full-fat, concentrated compassion.

One old friend (I'll call him M) rang me some time ago to report that another close friend (let's call him E) was saying unkind things about me. He thought I should know, even though his call was more gossip and agenda-led than it was thoughtful report. E was a beautiful, dynamic friend and former business partner who I loved very much. I told M (the caller) that, "I love E. I'm sure he did say those things about me, but I don't think he meant them. He is clearly not himself at the moment." I spoke with compassion because I felt compassion. The line went quiet. M, defeated by my honesty and kindness, apologized profusely for bothering me, and admitted that he should never have called in the first place. He said he regretted ever telling me what E had said.

I killed both M and E with compassion.

I knew that E had been very bitter about some of my recent successes, he had probably convinced himself that he'd been "left behind" (he had said as much online) and that I had forgotten him. None of this was true, but his imbalance convinced him otherwise, so he made a metaphoric voodoo doll of me and stuck pins into the body with Facebook and Twitter posts.

It did not affect me.

I loved him.

I still love him.

My compassion swept through the bones of his hate like fire.

When I bumped into him some time later, I told him how much I loved him, and if there had been a convenient hole, I think he might have found his hands and knees and had himself a little hibernation.

Compassion is not just a word we pluck from the sky and place at the end of every sentence. Compassion is Ar-Rahman, it is a holy attribute, one of the many arms of Law reaching out of the universe to assist us. When we are in possession of compassion we are cloaked in the armor of angels, we are immunized by the vaccine of Truth.

Compassion is Love, working through us.

It is truth working as us.

It is grace permeating every pore of our body.

Challenging the force of compassion would be like trying to take on the whole universe.

But how do we own this attribute?

How do we endow ourselves with the protection of compassion?

When we are brimming over with fear, when our veins are like a bobsleigh racetrack for the high-speed hormone adrenalin, how do we find compassion? Where is it?

It might help to understand that *compassion is who we are.*

It is our backboard, it is our ground of being, it is the force that platforms and supports all of our myriad programs and perceptions and cognitions and conceptualizations, it allows them to exist.

It is the only thing that is constant; in fact, it is the constant.

It is the only thing that is real.

If we can't immediately see it, it is only because the penny is covering the sun, our hurt is blocking out compassion so that we can't view it, so we can't access it. Whilst we may not immediately be able to see or feel or access compassion, we *can* see the hate, we can feel the judgment, the dissonance, the envy, the greed, the blame, and the fear: it coats our eyes like a haze of scales. We can readily and clearly see all the things in us, and in society, that are not compassion.

In fact, they are anti-compassion.

So why not start by removing these obscurations, one by one, from our beliefs, from our thinking, from our talking, and from our actions. When we stop engaging the phenomenon of emotions and thoughts and just watch (or observe, or witness) we will see these temporal phenomena eventually fall away to reveal the only thing that *is* constant, the only thing that does not change: the indivisible Absolute.

"I am Hashem," the Zohar reports, "I do not change."

This is compassion.

It should be sought with all our might.

All lesser things should be eschewed in order to reveal this prize.

The Absolute is like an orb with infinite arms and hands,

many and countless attributes, reaching its charity into our reality, formulas and remedies and antiviruses for healing the differing ills of the human condition.

The greatest of these arms is compassion.

We can reach out and grasp it the very moment we let go of the pseudo remedy of vengeance.

Whilst vengeance might not be ours for the taking, there is no need to be concerned about justice: all accounts are settled, in full span, and in the full span of time.

Vengeance will be repaid; albeit not always by us.

Once we have grasped the concept of compassion (as a remedy for us, and not a pardon for them), we are only a stone's throw from the source of compassion. We can grasp its hand and follow its trail home to *the world to come* (more on the world to come in a later chapter).

As well as nurturing compassion, we can also practice gratitude.

One of the things we forget when we are locked in the angst of our wounds is how many blessings we have. They are blocked from our eyes like veils covering a lamp. The depression will tell you in its own unique, nihilistic voice that there is no light, or if there is, it will not shine again anytime soon or, if it does, it will not shine for us.

We should never take advice from a shadow: it lies.

Blake assures us that "the eagle never lost so much time as when he stopped to take direction from the crow."

Melancholy can be a very convincing cellmate, but it lies and distracts many a soul from their path when it insists that they can never be free from its sorrowful grasp. The Holy Prophet reminds us again in the surahs that "we should announce our gratitude for the resources, fruits, trees, oxygen, fragrant plants, fresh and salt water, pearls, ships, the delights of the garden of paradise, replete with shading branches, flowering sprigs, fruit, maidens, couches, cushions and fine carpets."

The creator tells us to count these blessings, and asks again and again at the end of every surah, "Which one of your Sustainer's powers can you disavow?"

When we remind ourselves daily – as we must – how blessed we are, despite the problems we may be experiencing, when we deny the dark voice of ingratitude by openly voicing our thanks, this too will clear the obscuration and allow the light of compassion to shine through.

This is not easy I know, but it is pregnant with efficacy.

I have seen it work.

I have made it work in the most challenging of situations.

When I have been up to my squeezy-bottle neck in adversity and everything in me and around me was encouraging me to moan and bleat and complain about my situation, I practiced gratitude not only for the fine things I had in my life, but even more so for the current difficulties: they are *after all* an opportunity to grow.

In my last encounter with the adverse forces, when my life was moment-to-moment anxiety and existential fear, and I was sorely tempted to do everything in my power to run away from it, I said to my wife every day, several times a day, "I want this. I am grateful for this opportunity to remove fear and reveal what lies behind it (love). I have been avoiding this confrontation with my shadow for too many years, it's time to make a stand."

When all other options are taken away from you, and the usual defenses fail to bring you remedy, you are forced to either acquiesce or find (within the restriction) a new form of power, a greater attribute to heal.

The problem comes complete with its own solution.

The remedy is presented before the illness arrives.

Before it will reveal its secret, however, we will have to turn in instead of turning away, we must be prepared to absorb 99% of its threat (to paraphrase Morihei Ueshiba), before it will give up its secret.

This takes the utmost courage.

Suffering is a gift because it offers you the opportunity to access higher levels of consciousness. These are levels of being that you might never have looked for, had the challenge not cornered you with distress. The moment you realize it as a painful-gift, the moment you offer gratitude for your opportunity, hope shines through, the suffering lessens in acknowledgement of your discovery, and the whole universe leans its shoulder to the wheel.

In my private, advanced martial arts classes, where we boasted several world class players, *restriction* was the order of the day. We were searching for Ki in our techniques (Ki is the hidden universal power), and we created specific and difficult restrictions in order to draw it out. In fact, as we got more practiced in this method of training, we made the whole class an area of severe restriction, so that we were forced to abandon our usual way of performing technique: this enabled us to develop the most extraordinary power in a punch, in a kick, in a throw or a groundwork technique. We also started to use the restriction method in our everyday lives, in the pursuit of Ki. We deliberately courted difficult *often life-threatening* experiences, in order to encourage forward this mysterious energy. One example of this was when I took a job as a nightclub bouncer, in order to reveal arcana. The more we were restricted, the more we were able to see into the hidden realms of our art. One of the gifts of this practice was expanded awareness: we were suddenly able to see that life was already offering us organic restrictions, that we could use to mine for power. If our health or our wealth or our relationships were offering us restriction, instead of railing against this seemingly random anomaly we offered gratitude for it, we turned into the difficulty, and we released the treasure it was holding.

Through this method of forced or enforced or sought-after restriction I personally was able to take myself to the world stage in martial arts and in writing. I was able to use the financial restrictions I was experiencing at the time, to reveal the secrets of the fiscal world and earn and employ divine money as a living growing energy. I was able to use my restricted intellect (I left school without qualifications) as an entry point to higher knowledge: and I was able to use the restriction of historical abuse (and all the suffering it contained), to reveal the compassion-cure, and in doing so reveal my authentic self. I was even able to use the fixed law of causation as a powerful restriction: by employing this natural obstruction as a divine whetstone, I was able to sharpen all my working tools, and fashion a prolific life for myself and for others.

Suffering need not be the harbinger of doom, it can become a messenger of hope, a call to arms, it can offer an opportunity to reveal *the treasure in the ruin*, a bounty that you would not have discovered in any other way or under any other circumstance.

So, you are suffering.

Welcome to planet earth.

We are all suffering.

Life is suffering.

That is why we are here, to shape our souls on the anvil of adversity.

The sages choose the hard way in order to win the top prize.

What an opportunity.

The crisis you are facing right now is a decision away from becoming an opportunity to grow.

Only you can make that call.

Tell yourself how grateful you are for your suffering, even if you don't immediately believe it, tell yourself and tell yourself again until you do.

There is a lovely old Japanese saying that I love: "The iron-ore thinks itself needlessly tortured as it goes through the furnace, but the tempered blade looks back and knows better."

Compassion may seem as though it is only an attribute of

the Whole, but if it contains a part of the Absolute, then it must contain all of the Absolute, just as each broken fragment of a hologram contains the whole picture.

We do not possess compassion; we are merely a vessel through which it can travel. If we want compassion, all we need to do is find a place or a person or a situation to share it with, the more freely the better. Compassion will come through us in abundance when we find a greater need for it than ourselves.

There is a beautiful line in the Zohar, the exegesis of the Torah... "The master sets the table for the servants before he eats himself." It is one of the many hidden secrets in the Old Testament, the cloaked key to abundance. It is a message, a combination, a formula, a remedy hidden in allegory. It is saying that in order for us to receive abundance from above, all we need to do is find someone to serve. When we receive in order to share with others, we will never experience lack. When we call down compassion for our enemy – the neediest recipient of all – compassion, a healing attribute, courses through us, and is processed in every cell and every organ of our body before it is passed on to the recipient of our charity. Compassion for them is compassion for us, compassion for he or she is compassion for you and me. The degree of compassion we receive is restricted only by the degree of compassion we share. If we desire an abundance of this holy grace, all we have to do is find someone who is in dire need of love and share it with them.

"Those who have are given more," Matthew reports in the New Testament (the parable of the talents), "those who have not, even what they have is taken from them."

The parable is showing us that when we invest our grace, we are vouchsafed a greater abundance of grace, but if we do not share it, even what we have is taken from us. If we share, the seed lands on fertile soil. If we do not share, it lands on the path, or is eaten by the birds.

What we do not use, we lose.

99 Reasons to Forgive

One of the reasons we are often unable to access compassion, besides the aforementioned obscurations, is because we are not privy to the secret of the Kabbalic Tree of Life: **to receive in order to share.**

If we wish to receive for the self alone (in the Kabbalah this is the definition of evil, because what is received is terminated on reception), the attribute is either not forthcoming or it is corrupted and spoiled and lost, on or shortly after reception, because it has been poisoned by the selfishness of the receiving host.

"Can there be any other reward for bad than bad?"

"Can there be any other reward for good than good?"

This is a process.

This kind of wisdom, understanding and knowing takes time, it takes an expanded consciousness to be able to see clear and to see true.

It took Mandela decades before he was able to let go of hate and embrace understanding and compassion.

The Buddhist murderer turned saint, Milarepa, killed 35 people: it took him years of repentance before he was gifted the truth.

Saul of Tarsus (later, St. Paul), condemner of Christians and persecutor of the Christ, had to suffer crisis and blindness on the road to Damascus before the way to compassion was revealed to him.

And it is said that the Buddhist Arhat (saint) Angulimala killed 99 people and wore their severed fingers on a hideous necklace before the Buddha converted the murderer, with nothing more than his one-pointed compassion.

There is no better time than now to start processing your wisdom and converting it into understanding and knowing.

One of the techniques I developed to reveal compassion is re-humanization. Before we are able to truly despise people, we first have to dehumanize them.

Reason Six: Compassion

And we don't have to try very hard at this, our persecutors do the bulk of the work for us, with their despicable actions.

As a bouncer I found myself unconsciously dehumanizing people all the time when faced with violent aggressors. When they postured and threatened and it triggered my adrenalin, I went into fight-or-flight mode, and dehumanization happened automatically, it was an organic adjunct to the stress of the situation.

These people were actively trying to harm me.

Some of them wanted to kill me.

They were inhuman, what else could they be?

That's why I was being paid four times the day rate of a skilled day worker, so that I could protect the good majority from this bad minority.

Only... they were not inhuman, not one of them, no matter how bad their behavior. They were people like me and you, they were fathers, they were sons, they were brothers and uncles, they were daddies, they were lovers and husbands.

I didn't see that.

To my eternal shame I did not allow myself to see that. If I had, (I felt) I would not be able to do my job and defend myself and defend my club and defend my customers and protect the drinking license of my employer. It was only after battering a "monster" half to death one night in a bar-front match-fight that I was able to see true: that he was not a monster after all, just a drunk factory worker, displacing a bad day at work into a hard night of drinking and fighting in our club. When he lay unconscious on the floor in a pillow of his own sticky-red, his young pretty girlfriend knelt by his side weeping inconsolably, and pathetically tried to stem the flow of his blood with a small white hanky. When she looked at me and screamed *why?* I did not have an answer.

The monster was no longer a monster.

He was a boyfriend to a girlfriend.

139

He was a father to a baby son, at home waiting for him.

He himself was a son to a mother and a father who would be rushed to his hospital bed at four in the morning to be by his side, just in case he didn't make it through the night.

I know this is an extreme example, but it is often only in extremes that we are able to see what is patently evident in the ordinary. This situation (and many more like it) allowed me to see beyond the veil, it allowed me to see the human in all situations, when those that threaten my peace come-to-scratch dressed as monsters. I remind myself that, no matter how bad they might appear, they are loved by someone, they love someone, others rely on them for their daily bread, and they rely on others too for their succor.

It is easy to hate a monster: it is not so easy to hate a daddy.

Dehumanization is a technique that has been used (and is still being used) in warfare since time immemorial.

In the US/Vietnam conflict, the American soldiers were brainwashed into seeing their enemy as little more than rats on a riverbank. They were placed before large screens and exposed to an overdose of Vietcong atrocities against men, women and children. By the time they reached the front line, the US soldiers did not believe they were killing men with families trying to defend their own country, they thought they were doing the world a favor by destroying vermin.

I taught myself to see Danny (mentioned earlier) as a father and a husband and a friend and a teacher. It was easy to hate Danny, the faceless letter writer who compared me to a cockroach you might find in your salad. It was near impossible to hate the Danny that kissed his wife goodnight and took his kids to school in the morning. And if I could find no such clarity, if the anger was raging and clouding my view and I could see nothing but an enemy, I would take myself into a deep meditation and ask my Highest Potential to *please show me things as they are*.

This technique has never failed me.

It has never failed me but... it is a brave and courageous request to make, because the revelation will come, and it might not be what you were hoping for or expecting.

It might reveal things to you that are extremely unsettling.

This is why the Christ asked two of his prospective followers, who requested seats at his right and left hand sides in heaven: "Are you able to drink from the bitter cup of suffering I am about to drink?" (Matthew 20:22) He was not just asking them if they could suffer the physical pain of the passion, on the "stations of the cross," from Pilate to the broken hill; he was asking them, are you able to handle revelation (or truth) when it is revealed to you, after the soul is purified?

His followers said that they were able, but Christ knew they were not, he knew they would be unable to bear the light of truth without first being "prepared by the Father."

When my old friend B betrayed me in the most indefensible manner (some years ago) and in doing so dealt a coup de grâce to our thirty-year friendship, I was unable to find any good in him. Knowing that the dissonance of the situation had possessed me and was raping my reserves of energy, I went to straight to my prayer and I asked: *please, show me things as they are.*

The *showing* came in a visceral vision of my friend and the fall from grace that he would suffer as a consequence of his actions.

I was left in no doubt of the validity and certainty of these outcomes, and I was bereft: all I wanted to do post-revelation was call him on the phone and implore him to mend his ways immediately. I felt frightened for my old friend, because I knew what was coming and all I could do was feel compassion for him. Our relationship had deteriorated to the point where personal communication was no longer an option. When I did bump into him sometime later and tried to forewarn him, my prophesy fell on deaf ears.

I saw three specific happenings in my vision that I am not

privy to share in this writing. Enough to say that the first two have already come to pass and the third *sadly* is an inevitability. Because of the referred, delayed, and truncated nature of his "falls" they did not appear (to B) directly related to his actions against me, so he refused to acknowledge that they were in any way connected. This denial made it even worse for him: if you can't learn from your prior experiences, it means your future is destined to be an exact replica of your past.

This was not all I was shown: in asking to "see things as they are" I was shown things *exactly* as they are. It was revealed to me that whilst B had committed an indefensible betrayal, I was double guilty of the same crime, if not against him, certainly against people much dearer, and specifically someone closer to home. I was shown that his betrayal was a speck of dust compared to my betrayal of my first wife. I shamelessly failed her with affairs, and with savage lies. I once cruelly accused her of going mad when she confronted me about an affair she suspected I was having. I told her that I was completely innocent, and that she should see a doctor about her paranoia. I said all this, whilst quietly knowing that only one hour after the birth of my son, while my wife was still recovering in hospital, I was only a mile away, in a stranger's house, having sex with another woman.

I asked for truth, and I received the cold hard facts.

Don't throw stones if you live in a house made from glass.

It was lashes to see what a despot I had become, lashes. People thought (and I thought) I was a nice person, a Samaritan, one of the good guys, but I was a despicable liar, a hideous cheat: I was not a good man at all, and it killed me, *it killed me* to see myself so naked.

It is not hard to find compassion for people when you are given a glimpse of their future, and the vision you are shown is not good.

And neither is it hard to read the future when you understand causation.

It is (believe me) very hard to find compassion for yourself, when faced with your own crimes against goodness.

Of course (as I have just demonstrated) what is true in the general is also true in the particular: seeing a vision of B's future massively and urgently encouraged me to double-down on my own integrity (which at the time was missing presumed dead), to be extra-careful of my own actions in the world, because my future disasters are as inevitable as his if I too should fall again from grace.

On a separate occasion, another even closer friend P (I can feel a theme building here!) fell into the trap of betraying me, and rationalized it as an act of public service; I *once again* experienced a pick 'n' mix of negative emotions, chief of which was confusion: *why would a smart, intelligent man fall for such a rookie trap?* When I was due to meet him to discuss things I once again called on my inner tutor and said, "When we meet, please let me see Truth through him." We duly met, and the moment I set eyes on him I saw true: this man was steeped and saddened with regret, I could see by his slumped shoulders and his tired gait that he was as confused about his actions towards me as I was. I felt an overwhelming compassion, and I hugged him.

As we embraced, the strangest thing happened: I heard his thoughts.

I literally heard his inner dialogue going at a hundred miles an hour saying (things like), "I can't believe what I've done; I am so sorry for what I have done, I don't know why I did it. I wish I could change what I did." It was the most astonishing experience, and although he has never consciously voiced his regrets to me, I was left in no doubt that the voice I heard was his, and that hearing it was an answer to my request to "see Truth." After this one encounter the aching compassion I felt dissolved any negative feelings I had for him before our meeting. Although I no longer see him, and we are no longer friends (in the sense that we do not meet or chat anymore) all I felt for him post miracle was love.

When I asked to see True, when meeting P, (again) I saw what was true of him, and I also saw what was true of me. For a time, I had allowed myself the luxury of self-pity, when I thought about how this once loyal brother had turned against me, I marinated in the delicious hurt that his actions had caused me. I childishly suckled on the dummy of sickly-sweet emotion that welled up in me when people said, "I can't believe what he did to you." After seeing true, this never happened again: the moment a feeling of righteous indignation rose, my conscience would remind me very quickly that I too had betrayed, and mine were willful and cruel treacheries. His was a venial sin, mine was mortal. He acted wrongfully, but in ignorance. I understood law, so my actions were fully conscious and willful.[6]

I was also instantly reminded that all the betrayals laid at my door, were my due, nothing more and nothing less.

Once you understand the power of forgiveness, you look to it in all aspects of your life, you even practice preemptive *and* post abuse forgiveness: (to paraphrase Maimonides again) you forgive before offence has been taken, and you pardon in the aftermath of abuse.

The great thing about understanding our limitations with regards to forgiveness is that, by acknowledging where our power is not, we automatically reveal where our true power is, and this is the seventh reason to forgive: repentance.

Budo Practice

Resentment and anger etc. restrict the full expression of love, the pupils of consciousness contract and we are only able to see the monster of our fear and not the living breathing human being behind it. We lose connection with compassion because our autonomic nervous system throws us into survival mode. Our fear (to a large degree) dehumanizes our designated enemy.

I have spoken briefly about this already.

In this exercise I'd like to share with you a technique I use in budo training, where we manually dilate consciousness through an exercise that I call "deliberate seeing." It allows us to see things "as they are" and not as they have become, due to the heavy focus on danger that our sympathetic response has triggered. It is perhaps not commonly known, but when we experience a threatening situation, especially one that involves an abuse on our body or mind, the brain marks the measure and the detail of our experience, for future note. It is not personal; it is an ancient safety mechanism that clicks into place in times of danger. It would definitely have protected our distant ancestors against deadly animals in the wild; but we are not our ancestors, and we are no longer in the wilderness, facing the Saber-Toothed Tiger on a regular basis. Rather we are mostly civilized people, who are still living with an antiquated survival instinct that speaks to us through the alarm of adrenalin and the voice of foreboding: "This is a threat to life," it warns us, "avoid at all costs."

I was groomed and abused by a beloved teacher. I trusted him. Actually, that's not true. Trust did not even come into it. I was eleven years old; I idolized him. Perhaps this is why the abuse came as such a shock to my nervous system, when I woke in the dark middle of the night to find heavy, greedy fingers inside my pyjama bottoms, invading my private parts. The result of this attack was that my survival system logged the situation and scratched the details deep into my psyche, a schema for future reference. Before the abuse this man presented as kind and caring and generous and attentive and charismatic: to me he was as close as family. For the next thirty years after the abuse, I found myself unable to trust people... especially if they presented as kind and caring and generous etc. It left me uneasy around everyone, I trusted no one, not even family members, especially family members. If this man couldn't be trusted, then who could? I became deeply insecure and suffered for decades with psychotic jealousy. When I say psychotic, I mean it in the true sense: people with psychoses lose touch with reality. Two of the main symptoms are delusions and hallucinations. I suffered periodic and severe mental disorders that caused abnormal thinking and distorted perceptions. At its worse, I would be kissing a pretty girl (in my early teens) and suddenly her face would morph into the stubbly features of an adult man, and I would recoil in horror. As a married man, if my wife as much as left the room, I believed *I knew* she was cheating on me. Of course, she wasn't, but in my mind she either was or she would, if not sooner definitely later. Why wouldn't she? I was a piece of shit, even a man I idolized cruelly betrayed me, which to my disturbed mind meant that *if he could do it*, then everyone in time would betray me. It was only when I identified my beliefs as delusional by-products of abuse, the distorted projection of an oversensitive survival mechanism, that I was able to start working on them. One of the things that really helped me was this exercise in expanding consciousness. By understanding that my faulty survival instinct had left me in a condition of negative default, I was able to manually expand my awareness and challenge the assertions that it presented to me as both a real and imminent threat. By stepping outside of the arc of fear, which warned me that absolutely everything was a threat to my well-being, I was able to see that the causal situation (the initial abuse) was both rare and unusual. One sick man abused me at a vulnerable age, when my brain was still plastic and impressionable, but that does not mean that everyone is dangerous, it does not mean that everyone will abuse or betray me. Taking a sober and objective perspective on the situation I was able to consciously acknowledge that I was not eleven years old anymore, I was not a child, I was in no way vulnerable to abuse. I had developed the ability to manage most situations if a threat to my person was raised, and – in the rare circumstance that something did happen, and I was hurt – I was more than capable of handling the worst case scenario. My reptilian brain (the part that operates the survival mechanism) was treating me as though I was a babe in the wilderness, whereas, in reality, I was a capable man in the world, a lump, *I could have a fight* (as they say round these parts), and if people did try to affront me, they did so at their own peril.

I was able to look at my abuser too, with a clearer view: he was a damaged man with a sick mind, no doubt, but he was also a son, and an uncle, and a teacher and a friend to many people. Someone loved and cared for this man. And I know from the little history I have of him, that outside of his abuse, he did many good charities. I had also been graced with a profound understanding of the world in which I found myself, I understood law, and I knew two things for certain about cause and effect: 1) my abuser would have been abused himself at some point in his past; in a world of causation, there is no effect without an equal and opposite cause. This means that as much as I was a victim of him, he was also a victim of someone else. 2) His actions in the world would fall into the law of compensation, and at some point, in time, he would have to pay for his crimes. Both of these points when fully processed (and it took me time to understand this) triggered a spontaneous compassion for the man that I carried as a mortal enemy for over three decades. Compassion was the antidote that eventually allowed me to dispel both the abuse and the abuser from my psyche.

Neither does it pardon him from his actions. In a moving world governed by the unmoving cross of fixed law, everyone has to account for their own behavior, and the punishment they dish out, will be met with an equal and opposite return.

This exercise, this knowledge does not condone the wrongs that people do, but it does allow us to forgive them from our mind. The sooner we can do that, the sooner we will be able to retreat and heal, and the sooner they will be forced to untangle from us and atone their sins.

As I mentioned earlier (and this too is an expansion of consciousness) after I forgave my great nemesis, I realized that I was no saint myself, I had lived a profligate and violent life. I needed to be forgiven for my own errors. In the Lord's prayer, it says, "forgive us our trespasses, as we forgive those who trespass against us..." It is divine direction, it is holy edification, it is Consciousness instructing us that we will be forgiven to the degree that we are able to forgive others; it is us that set the level of mercy.

If we are able to step outside of our very powerful emotions for a brief moment, life will offer us a fuller perspective not only on our own situation, but on all situations. Once you understand causation, you will never read a newspaper, or watch a news bulletin, or see a random story of abuse in the same light again.

We are all guilty.

To conclude this budo practice, I would like to invite you to write a confessionary inventory of your own faults.

You already know the faults of others; they are the reason you and I are sharing page space. But what about your faults?

I went through this deeply personal exercise many years ago, it took a lot of courage to look in the honest mirror and see what a deviant I had been at times.

Now I would ask you to locate and write down as many positives as possible about the object of your resentment.

This process of dilation through inventory overrides the contracting effect of adrenalin and manually expands consciousness. It is a virtue practice that rehumanizes both us and our enemy. It allows us (as I just said) to access the antidote of compassion for others and for ourselves.

Ultimately, we are aiming to encourage and invite in compassion, not just for people in general, but also for society's outsiders, the great fallen, those who have committed (even) heinous crimes. I see compassion as (often) a painful Grace, an infused and divine gift that allows us to see the humanity (and the suffering) behind the eyes of even the worst people. I am helped in this matter because I was a violent criminal myself, or should I say that, for a time, I was possessed by criminal elements, which means I find it impossible not to see myself in all people, the good, the bad and the ugly. With compassion being a grace, we can't develop it (as such), any more than we can summon the wind to blow, but we can do the preparatory work (as outlined in these pages) of hoisting up our virtue-sails in anticipation of its arrival.

Once we are in possession of this gift, the best advice I can offer is to prize your compassion, and protect its integrity, and share it liberally: it is an attribute of God within you, it is God working through you, so (as much as you can) try not to impede it, or allow the unkindness of the cynical and the ignorant to impede it for you, just let it flow for everyone. The more you are able to do this, and to the exact degree of your giving, more will be added unto you. One friend wrote to me only today, perturbed, and dissonant: this beautiful man worked in a prison looking after serious criminals, and whilst he felt a great compassion for the people in his care, his fellow workmates did not share the same ethos. Their motto was (to quote): "Give them fuck all, and plenty of it." Luckily (I advised him) this is an easy enough fix: extend your compassion to them, for they too are victims of the dark trickster. And the crueler they are, the more compassionate you should become. Offer your gift to everyone, even those who are called to be healers and betray their Hippocratic oath with the poison of judgment. Be careful too (I continued) because those who judge unkindly will try to tempt you into the same illiterate vice: judgment of them and their behavior. My parting direction to this lovely man was this: "Give them compassion, and plenty of it."

Note: You will have noticed that at the end of each chapter I have asked you to write things down. Please take the instruction, even if you don't initially understand why, even (and especially) if you think that, in your case, this is an unnecessary exercise. The pen (as you will find) opens a third eye, it is not only your spokesperson, but also a powerful, metaphysical tool that your intuition can use to channel arcana from the teacherless teachings.

In budo, the pen is the magic wand: don't be ignorant of this, and do not be afraid to wave it.

Reason Seven: Repentance

We came into this book, you and I, thinking that we were going to learn how to forgive, only to discover early doors that our claim to the throne of great pardon is a spurious one. And whilst it may be obvious that there are people in the world who do need to be brought to justice and should be judicially punished, we cannot discount ourselves from that group.

To be a resident on the great earth is to have made mistakes.

Even if our failings are of a small, hardly noticeable nature, they still add up over time to an accumulated mass of compound debt. The reason we are offered the formula of repentance in all the great bibles and in every world-mythology is because we err as human beings in a million subtle (and not so subtle) ways, and we continue to do so. The bibles, the better philosophical reports, and ancient myth give us hope in the form of repentance, and this hope excludes no one.

The opportunity to repent is a divine gift, it is a grace.

It is also a great revelation. Our gift is infused, but not until we remove the fallacy of omnipotence: we do not administrate over the worldly court of human sin, this is not a mortal endowment, we are not the Caesar at the coliseum, able to offer favor by royal decree or death by the sword.

Milarepa, murderer turned saint, killed 35 people and was able – through repentance – to find refuge and sainthood in the *still center*.

And he did this in one lifetime.

Saul of Tarsus was a diehard Christian persecutor who healed his own imbalance with the remedy of repentance and became St. Paul, one of the most important voices in Christian liturgy.

I know I mentioned these great saints at the end of the last chapter, the repeat is deliberate.

People who think that their sin is beyond repair need to read this again and again.

There is a common and rarely challenged belief that some people are so evil that they cannot be saved. Many men and women perish in societal prisons (or the prisons of social belief) because they accept the lie that they are shameless and helpless and beyond redemption. Many of them die in sin not because there is no hope; rather they die because there *is* a remedy, but no one has taught it to them.

They can be forgiven not seven times but seventy times seven.[7]

Repentance is the gift to humanity, for the sinner and the saint alike.

As for the men and women who have fallen from the way, they have more potential for spiritual ascension than those who have not lived in extremes.

In the New Testament, when the tax collectors and sinners were gathering around to hear Jesus talk, the Pharisees and the teachers of the law muttered, "This man welcomes sinners and eats with them." On hearing this, the Christ gave many parable-like examples of repentant power, and concluded by assuring his critics that, "there will be more rejoicing in heaven over one sinner who repents than over ninety-nine righteous persons who do not need to repent." (Luke 15:7)

Not only was the prodigal son welcomed home and rejoiced by his father, and the fatted calf sacrificed in his honor, but the father commanded his servants to dress his son in "the first robe," which is considered in biblical symbolism to be "the mantel of wisdom" from which all the virtues flow together.

In simple terms this means that when we remove the shroud or the cloak of sin, we prepare ourselves to be adorned in the garb of wisdom, we turn away from the path of error, and return to the way of truth.

In the Jewish tradition, one of the Hebrew words for sin is chet, which means "to go astray." Repentance is called *teshuvah*, a Hebrew word that translates as "returning."

Thus, the idea of repentance in Jewish thought is a return to the path of righteousness.

When I visited men in prisons around the country, giving talks and presentations to the inmates, I was able to personally witness the glaring validity of this truth for myself, it was undeniable, it was inspiring, and it was right in front of me. Most people wander through free-society in quiet denial of the hundred subtle murders they commit every day with their thoughts, with their words and with their deeds.

They never seek repentance because they don't think they've done anything wrong.

To the folk in jail, surrounded by the manifest evidence of their astray – the cast iron doors and steel bars and burly guards with nightsticks – it cannot be denied.

The prisoner awakens every day surrounded by the visible evidence of the consequence of their actions.

He (or she) also awakens to the savage assail of his own conscience. If you had ever met and spoken with these folks, the lost sheep, our great fallen, you would be immediately disturbed by the overwhelming force of depression and remorse, and regret, and deep, deep hopelessness many of them awaken to every day. It is impossible – irrespective of the nature of their crimes – not to feel compassion for them, or grateful for your own priceless liberty, and keenly fearful of the wrath of negative causation.

Many of these people know they need to change.

They see that the nine-inch solid prison walls are built block-by-block by the many harms they have caused.

They cannot ignore or hide from the fact that their imprisonment is the result of their crime.

This puts them leagues ahead of their "law-abiding" counterparts, because they at least know they've done wrong, even if they don't yet know why they did it and how to fix it.

The prodigal sons of society are encouraged and welcomed by the law of compensation, because they have a lot of ignorance to convert, and there is no better oil for the lamp than the burnt offering of past error.

This is what Christ is teaching us through the Eucharist in the Upper Room at the Last Supper, the night before his crucifixion in Rome. He is offering us a symbolic reminder that sin can be cleansed through the body-and-blood sacrifice of our charity. In other words, he is saying, if you sacrifice yourself – your time, your energy, your comfort, your need for personal profit – in the loving service of others, your own sin will be removed in the process, it will vanish as though it never existed.

The cross is the symbol of cleansing sin, through personal sacrifice.

And when I say that we are cleansing sin, I am suggesting that we are removing *the doer* of sin, the trickster, the parasite of evil that is resident in us.

When we take a medicine, we are using it to remove a disease.

The disease is not the person, the disease is merely possessing the person.

When we kill the disease, we recover the person to his true self.

It is good to meditate deeply on this last statement.

The more we have wronged and created darkness in the world, the more fuel or sin we have for the fire, and so the more potential we have to create a light.

We do not just cleanse our sin, our error; we convert the residue of evil into a spirit of light. I am not suggesting that this conversion only creates a temporary flash that glows for a limited time and is then extinguished. Rather I am talking about converting evil into *"a light"*: a permanent spirit, born from sin, delivered from evil, and sent out into the world as a living comforter that will intercede in the lives of anyone genuinely, honestly looking for repair.

When Christ sacrificed himself on the cross to pay for all our sins, he was actually leaving us with a powerful and didactic methodology for redressing our wrongs, by sacrificing ourselves in loving service to others. He was saying: this is the formula, this is the route home, this is the repair, this is the return, this is the three-jeweled refuge and not only are the worst offenders welcome, they are more welcome than anyone else, and their return but will be celebrated, because they are the ones that have the most potential, the most raw material, to convert into a healing light. They are welcomed, not despite their sin, rather, because of it.

One of the reasons I have been able to create so prolifically in my own life (fifty published books, fifteen multi-award-winning films etc.) is because I carried so much negative, often violent baggage. I used the (dark spirit of) the bad deeds from my past to create the bright reality of my present moment.

I literally burned the sin-fuel of my karma in the volition of my work.

If you read any of my books, or watch any of my many films, or attend a stage play that I have written, you will be witnessing an exorcism, my living atonement: it is in every word, in every line, in every paragraph and scene and act.

Repentance is not a sickly-sweet religious aphorism: it is a muscular, metaphysical (painful) transformation, a crucifixion of the negative, and a resurrection into the positive: this is the literal transformation of the material into the spiritual. This is open to everyone, especially to those who have lived depraved lives: after all, they are the ones with all the oil to burn, they have direct access to the living fuel of transfiguration.

There is a reason why all the great works of religion hail and welcome the prodigal son: he is returning, he is repenting, he is repairing, he is finding refuge, he or she is coming home. And the prerequisite to repenting of course is that we have to make the burnt sacrifice in order to complete our journey, we cannot find the stillness and quiet without first eschewing or converting the chaos and tumult.

Not too many years ago a close friend of mine had to go to court for a crime she committed during a depressive period of absolute madness. I went with her to court as a loyal friend, as an advocate and advisor, and to offer a character reference.

She was extremely anxious, to the point of nervous exhaustion.

Her case had been pending for nearly two years, and during those long and punishing months of waiting, of doubt, of regret and deep depression she lost much: her marriage, her integrity and her job to name just three. Many of her fickler friends abandoned their compassion and threw her under the wheels of fast-train-message-board-judgment: she was cut in half by the cowardly betrayal of people she had broken bread with just weeks before.

The potential outcome of her trial was as uncertain as her friends.

There was a chance she might meet with a sympathetic judge, and receive a lenient sentence, but (she was professionally advised) a more realistic outcome was prison. She was told to prepare herself for a custodial sentence.

Just moments before she entered the courtroom to stand trial, when her fear spiked, and the blood drained from her grave-grey face, I saw an opening and I spoke some words of intuitive wisdom. I whispered them directly into her ear with a quiet urgency: *When you talk to your solicitor, when you talk to the prosecution, when you talk to the judge in court, when you talk to anyone, take full responsibility for your crime, do not displace, or blame or project, tell them that the fault was yours and yours alone, assure them that you want and expect to be held to full account. Tell them that you will accept their judgment (whatever it is) without argument or complaint. Apologize from the bottom of your heart for your crime, thank them for their time, and thank them for their patience and for their kindness; leave them in no doubt that this is the first and last time you ever intend to be in a court of law.*

I added that, if her emotion became overwhelming in court, and she felt the urge to weep, she should abandon all pride and let the tears flow. Often our prosecutors and judges need to see our regret, physically manifest, before they know that our remorse is true.

I assured her that whilst I could not predict the exact detail of her sentence, I was certain that, if she was sincere in her repentance, the outcome would be optimum. I was absolutely certain that if she surrendered her future to the higher courts, she would be looked after by the lower.

She took my advice: she apologized, she thanked everyone she dealt with for their time and patience, she took full responsibility for her actions, she blamed no one, only she was culpable, and she surrendered the outcome to the judge.

She also wept inconsolably. Two years of bitter regret flooded the courtroom. Everyone was deeply moved, because everyone could see that her contrition was soul deep, it was genuine.

I have to tell you that we witnessed a miracle that day.

Everyone involved in her case, even the prosecuting council, implored the judge for leniency, and asked that she receive a noncustodial sentence.

And that was how it went down.

The judge – a man with a reputation for severity – gave her "one chance" and sentenced her to eighteen months of community service and fined her in accordance with her crime.

Repentance is a powerful gift.

It works, but it cannot be faked: it is powerful, but it cannot be mimicked: it is potent but only if it is heartfelt and sincere. It is available to everyone (with no exceptions) because everyone makes mistakes; **it is human to err.**

If we deny repentance to anyone, we must be prepared to deny it to everyone, including those we love dearly, including ourselves. As I said, we are all guilty. Our crimes are only separated by degree. Repentance is a universal law, and we all have access to it, no matter how severe our crime. Like the sun in the sky above, it shines on everyone equally, it does not offer more to a king and less to a pauper, it does not favor the priestly and deny the prisoner.

Repentance is absolute, it is an attribute of God, so if it is true in the general, then of course it must be true in the particular. In other words, if it is available to anyone, then it stands to reason that it is available to everyone.

Seeking its redemptive powers is an individual choice we can all make.

It is not governed by a political body, or a particular group, no one church or religion can lay claim to this force, or determine its administration, certainly its power does not lie in the hands of the victim of a crime. Though we might seek it, and as much as we may crave it, we do not need the forgiveness of our victim, in order to absolve an abuse: if we wait for that we wait in vain because it is not within their remit to resolve our wrongs.

It is, however, within our power to repent. Ultimately, that is the only power we can lay claim to, and it is the only force that can bring us home.

This doesn't mean either that we cannot or should not offer apology and redress and justice to those that we have harmed. When I first awoke to the repentance-potential I spent two years genuinely and imploringly apologizing to all the many people I had hurt in my wayward past, but I was not looking for them to forgive me (in the sense of *pardoning* my actions). Even at this fledgling stage of expanding awareness, I knew they could not offer me pardon. My apology was a public confession, it was my way of bringing my errors to the light, accepting sole responsibility for my actions and their consequences, and declaring my undying regret.

I was not looking for them to ease my conscience or suture

my gaping guilt-wound. On the contrary, I was offering them the ultimate shot at redress: to give me back the abuse I laid upon them, by forgiving me from their minds, by untangling themselves from me, and offering me over to God. What I was asking for with my apology – albeit unconsciously – was that they accept my apologies (for their own good), and in doing so free themselves from any grudge that bound them to me, so that they could repair back to their own center, and I could be released from our unholy tie and seek repentance.

If I requested forgiveness at all, I was simply asking them to sever their bond to me and give me over to reciprocity.

This is why, if someone asks for your forgiveness, it is wise and healthy to give it to them: if they ask to be forgiven, they are (consciously or unconsciously) recognizing that they are tethered to you by the wound – they possess you (at least in part) – and they are asking you to sever the link, and "give them over" to karma so that you (and they) can repair.

They are asking to be delivered.

They are offering you escape from possession.

They are encouraging you to disentangle yourself from them and be free.

Accepting someone's heartfelt plea for forgiveness is the intelligent thing to do, because it means (in effect) they are offering to release you from their grip, and you are accepting.

Similarly, if you have wronged someone, asking for forgiveness (if circumstance allows) is also the smart option, not because they "can let you off" or pardon you, rather because they can let you go. When you understand what forgiveness actually means, you ask for it soberly and in the full knowing that you are accepting culpability and requesting universal judgment for your crime: not from them, but from the Great Arbitrator, reciprocity. It is a brave and noble thing to ask someone for forgiveness, and accepting forgiveness is the height of intelligence, because you know that grace is the key to your freedom from the tyranny of abuse.

Many years ago, when I was promoting one of my books, an interviewer, very skeptical of my transition from hard man of repute to a man of love and peace, asked me, "Repentance! Isn't that a soft option? Say you're sorry, make a public apology, move on, no harm done, isn't that the easy way out?" I replied (and I am paraphrasing), "I have pitted myself against professional fighters, criminals, men that can maim, with a single punch *they can kill*. I punished myself with Hemlock, slow suicide served across a club bar in pint jugs. I hid in pornography, I smothered my shame in violence, I hid in bar fights with strangers, and road-rage incidents with innocent members of the public. Do you know what repentance means?" I asked him. "It means to stop causing harm, and start going home, it means to return, and I am more afraid of that than I am of facing down killers on nightclub doors. So, to answer your question (I said), no, it's not a soft option, not for men like me. When you have lived as unkindly as I have, there is no easy option, the way back is all pain."

Asking for forgiveness is offering a gift to the recipient of your crime.

Accepting forgiveness is escaping the prison of abusive entanglement.

The knot that binds the abusive to the abused is molecular. This description is lifted directly from Wikipedia: "Quantum entanglement is a physical phenomenon that occurs when a pair or group of particles is generated, interact, or share spatial proximity in a way such that the quantum state of each particle of the pair or group cannot be described independently of the state of the others, including when the particles are separated by a large distance."

Whilst you hold a resentment for anyone, you can no longer "be described independently of the state of the other(s)" even when you are separated by a great distance.

The man that abused me as a boy was still abusing me thirty years later, even though I had not seen him in as many years, and even though we were separated by time and space and place. His abuse lived in me. I was possessed by it. It acted in me, and through me and as me. I could not be described as independent of it or of him. The abuse, the entanglement was evident even though we were separated by three decades of chronological time and a large geographical distance. And this remained the case until I was able to recognize the perpetual nature of unprocessed abuse and "give him over." When I offered my forgiveness and he accepted (by asking to shake my hand), I severed our link, I gave him over to his own fate.

That is why I forgave him. And that is why he accepted.

The prodigal converts much darkness on his return to center.

This is why he is the favored son, the celebrated home-comer.

Those who unkindly judge the criminal, the perjurer, the violent, those that discriminate and decree that forgiveness has limitations, and that "some" are unworthy of mercy, have forgotten this truth, and they need to read this again and again because they too have fallen into the false belief that *anyone* can be exempt from salvation. It is not true, and the scriptures, the mythologies, the great philosophers of lore (and my own personal experience) attest to this in their liturgy. (I find that) it is often the case with redeemed monsters in theology and mythology, that their extremis is written large into history just to demonstrate the law in general: if they can be redeemed *anyone* can. I believe they are included in the pantheon as proof of leniency; they are the exaggerated examples of divine mercy.

No one is a hope lost.

We should all remind ourselves of the precedent set in all the good books with regards to the conversion of the material into the spiritual.

The bigger the criminal, the greater the welcome.

I am certain of this.

What is a bad man but a good man's student; what is a good man but a bad man's teacher.

And please, you must never worry whether a person's repentance is genuine or not. If it is genuine, it will be registered in the higher courts, and if it is not, it will be spat out by the holy discriminate.

We must concern ourselves only with our own virtue and leave each person's destiny, "thread, spun, measured, and cut" (Clotho, Lachesis, and Atropos) to the fates.

In Islam, another of the 99 names of Allah is At Tawwab.

It is yet one more attribute, one more reaching hand, one more formula or remedy to bring us back to balance. At Tawwab means *repentance* and repentance means to return, to be restored, to be "repeatedly summoned or called."

The attribute of At Tawwab is literally translated as "The acceptor of repentance."

The great Iman Al-Ghazali translates At Tawwab as "he who constantly turns man to repentance." He states that At Tawwab is "the one who keeps facilitating the causes of repentance for his creatures time and time again by showing them some of his warnings and revealing to them some of his deterrents and actions with the intent that they, having been appraised of the dangers of their sins, might be filled with fear by His frightening them and subsequently turned to repentance through (His) accepting (the evidence) of their penitence, the Favor of God most high (once again) reverts to them."

At Tawwab – the remedy – should not be read or translated naively.

It is not a soft option for a hard crime: return is full of life-threatening challenge and danger and suffering.

In Homer's mythological allegory (*The Odyssey*), our hero Odysseus (mentioned earlier) is more challenged on his ten-year perilous return from the Trojan Wars to the refuge of Ithaca (his home) than he is at any other part of his journey.

Even when he finally makes it back to his kingdom, barely alive, his work is still not finished. He is so changed and transformed by the regeneration of his epic quest that no one, not his wife Penelope, not his subjects, not even his servants and most ardent supporters, recognize him. He is a stranger in his own home, which has been besieged in his absence by thieves and criminals and men of war.

No part of the journey is easy, not least the return home.

At Tawwab is not *asking for forgiveness* and *receiving it without any work*.

Asking for forgiveness and seeking repentance are quite different.

The "formula" of At Tawwab requires a necessary step to forgiveness.

An individual must make a sincere attempt to repent for a sin and vow never to return to it. The law, Gaia (mother earth), the *great leveller*, gives us respite, it offers us time to request forgiveness. This amorphous force only accepts repentance when the request is true, and through infinite mercy she can cleanse the stain so thoroughly, that "it will be as though there was no sin at all."

People often criticize me when I say that I have compassion for those who have abused me.

I have compassion because I understand the law, and I categorically know what is coming to the recipients of my grace. I know the pain and the torment and the suffering that they will have to undergo in order to repent. I know because I had to do it myself. I wouldn't wish the torture and suffering I experienced on anyone. Even the great diehard Kabbalists proclaim, after their own regeneration, that whilst they are eternally grateful for the cleansing experience, they would never want to go through it again.

I feel compassion for those who have fallen, no matter how heinous their crime.

I offer gratitude every day for the formula of repentance because, one day, it might be me that falls again, it might be my mother, or my brother, or my daughter, or my son who suffers a falling.

We all fall.

We all need grace.

I have suffered so many falls of biblical proportion that I am left in no doubt of the possibility of repentance and the pain of returning home.

The man who sexually abused me when I was a boy escaped the lawful consequences of his crime for thirty years. He denied his deeds for three long decades. When the truth finally caught up with him (as it must) he hung himself in a lonely hotel room in London.

I was spilling over with compassion when I heard this.

He had hurt me yes, he had damaged me, of course, but he was still someone's son, he was still someone's friend, there were people out there who loved him. And I knew, I absolutely knew that a man who takes his own life, does so because the suffering of living in anticipation of justice is far greater than his fear of death.

I felt compassion, not just because he suffered: his victims suffered more, I personally suffered for thirty years because of his actions. I felt compassion because he'd been given thirty years' worth of chances, he'd been gifted three decades to get his shit together and willingly return to good, but he did not take it.

He lost his life with all of its priceless potential because he could not repent, even though the opportunity was open to him and offered to him many, many times over his thirty-year reign.

I feel compassion for him and all the criminals that I have spoken to in prisons around the country because I know from my own experience what they will have to go through in order to redress.

I know because I am them.

I have committed grave crimes.

On my hands and knees, I have willingly repented, and I too never want to go through that again. When I see the ignorant and the arrogant and the insanely defiant, I feel nothing but compassion, because the further they stray from truth, the harder it is to get back.

To all you kids out there in your prison cells, in the tenements and the projects, or in your gilded cages (in Bond Street, on Downing Street, at the White House), don't let anyone tell you that all hope is lost for you. It is not true. It is never too late; you are never *too* lost. You are never too old or too broken or too far from home to repent, to return, to find refuge, to repair. You think your opportunities are lost, maybe your prison guards are telling you that you're irredeemable, that you have no chance, and there is no reprieve for a man, a woman, *a beast like you*, but they are all ignorant and they are all wrong. Not only is there hope for you – the murderer, the robber, the thief, the pedophile, the greedy banker, the corrupt politician, the violent fundamentalist – there is hope for everyone.

I know too that my inclusion of the pedophile in the list of potential will ruffle feathers like a fox in a hen house. I know that even the hardened criminal has his twisted standards of morality and decrees crimes of a sexual nature (especially against children) as unpardonable.

All crime against all people is equally gratuitous.

When I knock a man to the ground and kick out his teeth (which to my shame I have done many times) his children are not exempt from the pain inflicted on their daddy, his wife is not spared the torment, neither are his parents, nor the rest of this connected universe. If I have an affair and leave my wife for another woman, I would be an ignorant fool if I thought for even a second that my kids would not suffer for my infidelity: when you cheat on your wife, or your husband you cheat on your children too. When we choose selfish and harmful actions in the pursuit of personal gain or pleasure, we take everyone we love to the dogs with us, *everyone* close is abused by proxy of our actions.

When I punch you, I bloody your child.

When I steal from you, I steal from your mother and your sister and your wife.

When I bring my life into disrepute, everyone I love is brought into disrepute with me.

I violently damaged a man in a bar fight one night when I was a bouncer. I'd allowed myself to dehumanize him first – he was my enemy, he was aggressive, he deserved my wrath – then I battered him until he was unconscious. I left him lying in a pool of his own blood while "admirers" bought me beers at the bar and patted my back like a winner and asked me to tell my "war story" one more time so that they could share the cup of glory from the safety of a club bar.

The next day I was strolling through the center of my home city, and I saw him *this monster*, walking wounded, pushing a pram, two young daughters each holding a bar of the frame, his sad wife one step behind surveying what was left of her husband's face.

When I made him an enemy the night before, I had not imagined him with a new baby or two young daughters or a pretty wife. In the bright of morn, my enemy was gone, and all my compassion saw now was a battered factory worker, a defeated husband, a limping daddy.

Be in no doubt that all crime is a crime against the child.

And all repentance must be accepted as the beginning of the cessation of that violence.

This chapter is about repentance, your repentance and mine because "all are guilty": there is not a soul on this spinning planet who is not in dire need of it.

If we exclude *one* from its potential, we must exclude all.

It is not for us *weak intellects* to judge who is worthy of forgiveness and who is not.

It is none of our business.

It is the business of reciprocity to settle its own accounts and if we allow ourselves the arrogance of playing arbitrator, we will have to exclude everyone from the list, including ourselves.

I remember an occasion when an old and dear friend of mine (I'll call him S), a splendid martial arts teacher, fell out of alignment and committed a crime. He was cornered for his remiss and door-stepped by the popular tabloid press, who named-and-shamed him on the front covers of their newspaper.

No complaints from me.

This is reciprocity doing its job through the red tops, and it was only working publicly because my friend had not taken the many opportunities to repent in private. Karma is patient. It will often give us lots of time and many chances to do the right thing, hoping we will *return* of our own free will and by our own volition. The problem with S came afterwards when people who I knew to be equally corrupt disowned him, eschewed him and joined in the savage attacks that followed on the Wild, Wild West that is the World Wide Web.

I felt compassion for S.

I knew he'd been out of balance for some years, and I tried to convince him that he needed to change, but he was not ready yet to listen. I didn't know that he was perjuring himself, this information only came to light afterwards when the news went national, and his life went southwards.

I rang him and said, "S. This is when you find out who your friends are. Call me if I can help." I did not condone what he did. Far from it. But I did not judge him either, how could I, a man like me who has broken too many commandments.

A couple of days later (and this is the gist of my story) a "concerned" person wrote to me, he mentioned that I still had some historical articles on my website written by S and that I should remove them as they "threaten the integrity of you and your site."

What he was actually saying was, "Publicly denounce S the same as everyone else, join in the online beating, or you are condoning what he did and who he is, and that will make you just as bad as him."

What he did was nothing to do with me.

And who is he?

He's my friend, that's who he is.

I was too busy trying to right my own wrongs to concern myself with the misdeeds of S or anyone else for that matter. I wrote back to this concerned citizen. I told him that I intended to leave S's work on my platform[8] because if I removed all the people from my site that'd made a mistake, I would have to remove everyone, including myself. I concluded by saying that "removing S from my site is the only thing that would threaten my integrity."

The man wrote back a few days later and (to his credit) said, "Yes, I think you are right."

If repentance excludes anyone, it excludes everyone, including me, including you.

Therefore, the seventh reason to forgive is repentance because its potential is our savior.

We can only be forgiven to the degree we forgive others.

We can only utilize repentance to the level we admit *everyone* access to the same mercy.

I'd like to repeat something here that I made mention of earlier in the book. I believe it is important. In this chapter, in this book, I have often employed the language of religion, the language of God, whether that be Allah, Christ or Krishna. If the language offends, please, feel free to change any of those names and put in the name that better suits you: science, reciprocity, cause-and-effect etc. And, if you don't want to personalize the law as I have in this book, by all means just think of it as *an energy*, or *a density*, or *a frequency*. It is a law, and within this law, within this realm there are attributes or formulas or combinations or remedies and practices that we can employ *not to forgive others* but to seek forgiveness for ourselves.

I am certain of these laws.

I have been gifted the grace of *knowing*. This fixed cross allows me *some* access to the moving, reeling currents of the universe. This certainty is there for anyone, and there is a specific method I've learned, a process of work that greatly encourages Yaqeen (knowing/certainty) to infuse us with its grace.

And this is next reason to forgive, reason 8: **knowing**.

Budo Practice

When people err against us, and we have developed a deeper understanding of causation, we realize that their venial or mortal sin is not just against us, it is also against universal law. We can't pardon them; all we can do is give it over to a Power that can. What we can do, however, is repent our own crimes. I have repeated this (I am aware) many times throughout the book. It is often only through constant repetition that truth will first penetrate and then settle. In case you think you have not committed a crime: I count amongst these, indiscretions that you have made against both yourself and your neighbor. Whether you think ill of someone, or voice unkind and unqualified opinions, or act in a way unbefitting to your human nature, you have assaulted your neighbor, just as you have wounded your own private self: the soul is injured by any flirtation with vice. And neither does it distinguish between small and large sins: any association with vice is a violence against the soul, because it either wounds the soul (venial sin) or detaches it from the source of Love (mortal sin).

It is common to believe also that thinking a thing does not constitute a crime, even if we allow the foreign thought to run riot in our imagination. We pride ourselves on the fact that we did not voice the slight, neither did we act upon it. Psychology and theology agree that, as far as the unseeing, unconscious brain is concerned, *if we have thought it, we have done it.* In many ways the negative thought is more pernicious because it is closest to the soul, and so has more impact on our inner life.

Please remember too that everything we do in the budo practice is for one reason and one reason alone: we are removing obstacles that stifle or stop our ability to unfold to our fullest potential. Anything other than this is a by-product of our initial intention. When I forgive someone, I am not trying to be a "great bloke" or a good citizen, or a kind Samaritan, I have no interest in these middling side-shows: I am simply and brutally and clinically removing anything and everything from my being and from my life that impedes my ability to blossom and fruit as a full human being.

In the collective religious canon, it is agreed that to repent means to repair, or to return to love. In the budo addendum of this chapter I would like to encourage you to take the list of personal wrongs that you made in the previous chapter and start working on their repair. As I have made mention several times already, whilst we cannot wield any lasting influence over the wrongs of others, we certainly can and must right the wrongs that we ourselves have inflicted. When I realized (for instance) that watching sexual pornography was "the first betrayal" of my wife, and of my own spiritual integrity (when we imbibe porn, we invite vampires across the threshold) and that, in accessing porn, I was playing an active role in abusing those so shamelessly abused on screen: when I understood this, I repented or repaired by exercising my will to no longer watch any form of sexual or violent pornography. Similarly, once I ascertained that jealousy (of which I previously suffered very badly) was a semi-autonomous thought-form, grafted onto my psyche by the man who abused me as a boy, I oversaw its removal by never allowing myself to engage or identify with jealous feelings or thoughts if they rose in my consciousness. By becoming an objective observer of these emotions, I was able to remove them from my mind, via the aforementioned practice of individuation. I watched the feelings rise. I felt the strong inclination to identify with and act upon them. I used my causal will to eschew the passion, and then I watched – over time – as the feelings grew weak, became emaciated and eventually fell away like an old scab.

This demands courage, it takes patience, and it often needs time.

It has its own process: it will not be hurried.

If you can work on repairing your own faults, on a daily, sometimes an hourly basis, you will find that your external resentments will dissipate in direct proportion to your inner work.

Reason Eight: Knowing – "the world to come"

When I suffered with depression as a young man, I wrote down my pyramid of fears and scaled the steps until I reached the top (see my book *Fear: The Friend of Exceptional People*). The confident, practiced, erudite man that stood on the pinnacle was definitely not the same frightened, nervous, anxious, depressive that trembled on the bottom step, all that time before.

I was new.

I was changed.

I was different.

It wasn't just me that was changed, my whole reality was box-fresh new.

Before the pyramid, I worked as menial labor in a factory, I processed acids in a chemical plant, I collected glasses in a club bar, I cleaned windows on my local council estate, or I swept floors around oily lathes in a local engineering factory.

This was the limiting world I found myself in.

It was the only work that undereducated boys like me could procure.

Post-pyramid, I was teaching large classes of martial arts students: I was guarding doors in one of the toughest cities in Europe: I had a strong following of (paying) students: I left the 9-5 reality I was born into and embarked on a new life as a full-time teacher, a burgeoning writer and serious student of the world-classroom.

My tiny life with its limiting prospects transformed into a living, growing, eschatological wonderland of opportunity and excitement.

Knowing was the specific attribute that changed everything for me.

Knowing can be received by anyone who is prepared to do

the work.

When I say "knowing," I am not talking about wisdom.

Wisdom is good for your aphorisms; it is nice to write down in a book or a poem or say aloud in a speech to an audience. It is useful if you want to impress and entertain your friends, but wisdom *on its own* does not change anything.

Understanding too has its benefits, but it is still impotent in a world that demands action above all else.

We can understand the world and the people in the world and its phenomena: *understanding* is the expected standard for a university degree, and a lot of it might even win you a 1st or a post-grad MA with distinction or PhD. Understanding can take you to the level of intellectual professor (and beyond) but of what use is understanding if it is incapable of transporting you to *the world to come*?

In my martial arts lineage, I can direct you to a glut of people who would spin your swede with an intellectual understanding of their system, but they still couldn't make their art work in a scrap outside the chip-shop on a Friday night; many of them can't even use their vast learning to change their thick waistlines (I was one of them), let alone transform the world around them. I also know the most physically able, skillfully dangerous men and women who still haven't gone beyond duality, who still see the *self* and the *other* as separate, who are still prepared to attack a (supposed) enemy rather than trace the genesis of their adversary back to the seed in themselves.

They have yet to find out who they are beyond the vast wardrobe of unconvincing costumes and heinous masks: they are yet to unveil the true Self, their unique and authentic identity.

Some people have wisdom.

They may even have progressed their sage learning into a fundamental understanding, but it has not yet alchemized into the rare gold of *knowing*.

Knowing is not a matter of belief. Knowing is certainty.

Knowing is also a direct communion with your authentic self, the true you.

Knowing is vital *specifically* because there is only one aspect within us that can truly know, that can legitimately experience the attribute of certainty and that is the authentic self.

When you experience certainty, you are introduced to this true, individual, amorphous identify, and once the connection has been made it has been made forever.

Certainty is a gift, it is a grace that never leaves us once it has been found.

This is why, in Islamic mysticism (as I mentioned previously), *certainty* is considered to be one of the 99 names of Allah (Yaqeen).

Whilst it constitutes our own personal connection to the self, it is also in direct intercourse with the source of the source of all being, the root of the root, a direct plug-in to the powerhouse of power, the Ein Sof (The Infinite).

In simple metaphor, this would be like discovering a plug-and-lead and connecting your finite battery-powered radio to the infinite mains electric.

Once you have a plug-and-lead, you can connect any electrical item to the font of power.

Once you are connected, you no longer have to worry about the limitations of human energy, divine energy will power all your endeavors from within.

It means we are no longer working from the small library of our limited human understanding. Once we connect to the self (through knowing or certainty) we are connected to the boundless energy and infinite knowledge of the whole universe. At this level we go beyond concepts and precepts, we transcend rules and regulations, ethics, and morals, we even (eventually) bypass karma and dharma *and the self*: here, we work as a direct Universal instrument. Our lesser will/self is scarified to the

Greater Will, and we work not only for the Divine, but as the Divine.

This is why knowing is rare gift, it is a grace: it is worth every sacrifice, every burnt offering, it is worth seven pounds of your animal flesh to get even a glimpse of it.

Knowing is the discovery of, and bond with, the self, and the self is not only *a* point of reference for every subsequent thing you do in this life, it is your only point of reference, it is the blueprint of the whole universe. You get to it by removing all the ignorance, the detritus, the lies, the half-lies, the distractions, and the conspiracies. It exists as a backboard just beyond the helter-skelter of your busy ambitious life.

When we get rid of the noise, we witness the still quiet center. This is the home of the self.

When we forgive, as in "remove something from our mind," we clear the clutter, and we access a clear view. When we repent, we return step-by-step to the refuge of clarity.

The mystic Richard Rose said that we can't guarantee these revelations of certainty, they are (what he termed) **happy accidents**. We cannot make them happen, but we can use all of our experience, our wisdom and our understanding to make ourselves *accident prone*.

I didn't climb my pyramid of fears with any sense of guaranteed success, all I took with me on that heady-ascent was a powerful intuition, a strong feeling that if I embraced all the things I feared, if I challenged their autonomy and tested their truth by merging with them, by absorbing 99% of their wild bluster, they would give up their tenancy in my body and mind and *something* would happen, something new would be revealed.

And so it was.

That *something new* was what I have come to understand as certainty, knowing or (in Judaic terms) "the world to come."

The world to come is not *just* the nether world that we find post-mortem; we do not have to literally die in order to be reborn. The world to come is the *new world*, the fabled garden, the Eden, the land (the will) that we enter post ignorance.

When I studied Judaism (specifically the Torah, the Kabbalah, the Zohar, and the Tanya) it made mention again and again of the promised rewards in the world to come.

The world to come!

I can remember thinking, *is that it?*

Do I have to wait until I die before I see the rewards for my labor, the returns of my charity and self-sacrifice?

It was not until the very end of (that particular round of) my study of the Zohar, when I processed and reduced my copious notes from seventy pages down to one concentrated line of text that the spiritual knowing truly entered me: the world to come can be experienced in the here and now, in fact I was already experiencing the world to come, I was in it.

The world to come is not post-mortem, it is post knowledge. It is certainty of causation that destroys both death, and the bringer of death (in the biblical sense).

1 Corinthians (15:25-26) tells us that "He must reign until he has put all his enemies under his Feet. The last enemy to be destroyed is death."

"Enemies under his feet" in this aphorism is referring to the hates and resentments (the vices), and the "last enemy" means death of the false ego (or what the Kabbalists call the "evil inclination"), who, in the act of selfish desire, deals death onto whatever he receives. When we subjugate the ego, not only is death destroyed, but the precipitant of death is dissolved also. If there is no false ego, no self, there is no selfish desire, if there is no selfish desire, there is no longer death. At this level we receive only in order to share, which means that everything we receive is increased.

Acquiring certainty of this process transformed me.

Step by step, I grew from a timid aspirant, as frightened by my own potential as I was excited, to a free, conscious man, no longer ambitious to achieve for myself, but hungry to receive in order to share.

Knowing transformed me and everything around me so radically that the old me and the new me, the old life and my current reality were so profoundly different that it would be difficult to connect one with the other if you stood us together in an identity parade.

The world to come is the reality you access, the self-willed existence you enter once you disembark the vehicle of ignorance and alight at knowing.

Knowing *or certainty* is the result of *radical reduction*, getting rid of everything that is not self, it means to jettison the flabby ostentation that parades as us, until all we are left with is a raw, indivisible, fat-free, hench self: this becomes your *geometric point*, the infinitesimal, invisible point that all your future realities are built from.

In Eastern mysticism they talk a lot about developing a "center" (or finding a center) and building your world from that place. The still center is the self, and the self (to repeat) is the only point of reference.

Through my study of the Judaic liturgy, I was gifted a wondrous modality for developing or encouraging the happy accident.

It is called **Chabad** (which is an acronym for Chochma, Binah and Da'at).

Chabad (pronounced *habad*) is a three-point process for creating or encouraging certainty. The triptych are known as chochma (pronounced *hochma*), binah and da'at. When I first discovered Chabad (which I will describe shortly) I realized that I had already been using this methodology to access knowing. It was only in retrospect that I was able to fully comprehend that *knowing*, as developed on my fear pyramid by disproving and converting spurious fears, took me from world to world, from the world that was to the world to come.

I travelled from the world of the prisoner to the free world of wonder.

What Chabad enabled me to do was identify my own organic process, crystallize my empirical learning, systemize it and use as it a standard modality, a methodology that would enable me to become as *accident prone* as possible.

On the Kabbalic Tree of Life, the top three spheres (or levels) are kefer (the crown), chochma (wisdom) and binah (understanding). Wisdom arrives (from the crown and) into chochma as a burst of light, an inspiration, the seed of a great idea, or insight, or remedy, or solution.

Chochma is considered to be creative or *the creative spark*.

Like the seed of a great oak, chochma is potential, it holds the complete schematic of every root and trunk and branch and leaf and fruit, but the seed needs to be planted in fertile soil to nurture and develop.

In Kabbalic terms this nurturing soil is binah (understanding).

If chochma is seen as creative, then binah is developmental.

We take the intuitive, creative spark, we place it into the engine of our cognition, we develop it, we expand it, we deepen it, we follow all the intuitive leads and commands it sends us – to read a particular book, listen to a certain lecture, or talk to a specific teacher – and we fully immerse ourselves in the process of binah until eventually, usually when we least expect it, often when we become absolutely exhausted by the work, it tips into (what is known as) da'at, which is *knowledge*, or certainty.

Let me give you a quick example of how this works practically.

When I was heavily into the revealed martial arts, I once spent eighteen months, training full-time under the greatest occidental Judoka of his generation, Neil Adams. I bought five judo suits and I trained three times a day, with my own students, and with a dozen Olympic level judokas. As you can imagine, my ascent was as steep as it was rapid.

I got two cauliflower ears for my troubles.

Pretty much on day one of my training under Neil, he told me the secret to great judo: grip. He assured me that whoever dominated the grip (our grip on the lapel and sleeve of our opponent's jacket) dominated the fight.

It made no sense to me at all.

It was Greek.

I can remember squinting my eyebrows into a confused question mark and thinking, *grip?!* I did not get it. I wanted to learn new throws, fancy groundwork techniques, the flashy, ostentatious arm-bars and joint-locks and strangles and chokes. I wanted an impressive repertoire; what use was grip to a young fighter like me in a hurry for power?

Neil was twice silver medalist at the Olympics, three time world champion, five time European champion; people literally travelled from around the world to be on the mat with this incredible, pioneering judoka, so I put my ignorance to one side, and I took all the instruction he could offer me on grip (even though I didn't understand it). I even read his classic judo book about mastering grip. None of it seemed to settle. My judo improved, but not exponentially. I won my black belt in an exacting grading in Wales under the legendary 9th Dan Alan Petherbridge, but my understanding of grip, developed from the initial sparks of inspiration that came from Neil, did not spill into knowing. My judo game was good, but it was not great. Something was missing. Then, one session, some sixteen months in, when I had to sit on the side of the mat due to an elbow injury, I watched Neil and his top student Simon practicing randori (sparring). For what seemed like an eternity, these two gladiators fought for grip (in judo this is known as grip-fighting). The moment one of the fighters managed to secure a grip, he immediately dominated the match, threw his opponent and the fight was won.

I was mesmerized by the beauty and the skill and the flow of their play, it was inspirational.

Then I experienced a moment of clarity.

Watching them fight for grip tipped something in me and my wisdom and my understanding became *knowing* instantly. It was the most wonderful feeling, a spiritual high, to suddenly be in possession of certainty.

In a flash of insight, I knew exactly what grip was.

I was transported into *the world to come*.

The next time I went on the mat I fought a member of the Olympic squad and, with my newly found certainty regarding grip, he was unable to throw this 45-year-old "accidental judoka" for a full ten minutes. In the end, he was so exasperated about his inability to get past my grip that he stormed off the mat in frustration.

From that moment onwards, on any mat, with any level of player, I could use that magic and be absolutely in my element. The feeling of grip has never left me. Ever since that day, I have been able to use my gift to control most fighters with ease, because I am in possession of certainty, and they are not.

I am trying to articulate a feeling that words cannot describe, enough to say that this attribute, this grace transformed my game. When I walk through the city or the streets, this working knowledge sits in me like a powerful second body, it has its own eye, and it allows me to see true; I am so certain of its efficacy that just the confidence of knowing it's there enables me to refrain from ever using it.

As I sit here now writing these words, I can feel the attribute of Yaqeen in me from skin to marrow. My fitness may fade in time and my sharpness on the mat might dull, but the feeling of grip, the certainty and control of grip, the *knowing* will never leave me. And not only that: when I take a grip (even when I just imagine taking a grip) I feel an immediate divine connection, a spiritual high, a joy that permeates my whole being.

The thing with certainty, is that you never quite know when

(or even if) it will arrive, but once it does, you will have it forever. It's a process of crystallization, like pouring sugar into a cup of water: we know at some point the water will transform into a crystal, but we are not quite sure when. Ultimately, just one final, single grain of sugar will trigger the transfiguration, but we don't know which one it will be.

I was teaching a large group of martial artists on my annual course. One of my old doormen friends came to watch this particular year. Looking at the 200 students packed into a Coventry sports hall, people who had travelled from across the globe to train with me, he commented disparagingly, "I don't know why you bother with these people; they're not listening, they are never going to get it." He was suggesting that the course was full of weekend warriors, men and women who were not serious about their art, and so were never going to crystallize into seasoned combatants. I said to him, "I hold this same course every year, and every year two or three of these people transform, and it is not usually the ones you expect." I reminded him too that when I was working under his guidance as a bouncer, I too was "a greenhorn," I too looked as though I was never going to get it. But then one night, everything just suddenly fell into place for me, "and now I am talking to tens of thousands of people, all around the world." Some people need to hear the truth fifty times before the sugar crystallizes in the water: I may be the first person to tell them, in which case they have a long way to go, and it can appear to the unknowing eye that they are an impossible case. Alternatively, I may have the honor of being the person who delivers the fiftieth sermon and get to witness their *miraculous* transformation. In the latter case, people will no doubt credit me with their instant transition but of course I know that there were 49 investments of truth that precipitated my timely delivery.

When the true truth finally lands, it feels so potent you do not doubt that the hand of God is in it, and it is both seen and felt and sensed by others too. You can stop a room dead with a display that contains certainty. People will (people have) crossed continents to be in the presence of certainty.

Through the process of Chabad – creative, developmental, conclusive – you can place yourself in the way of certainty, but you cannot rush it, you cannot predict it, you cannot even guarantee that it will arrive but (if and) when it does, you are filled with wonder. Anyone in your proximity will feel the wonder too and it will inspire them to seek the same knowing in themselves.

I have found this certainty in many areas of my life, in the martial arts, in the universal law, in my Self, in the penmanship of my writing, in close relationships, and in talks I deliver where certainty speaks through me. Once you have revealed one divine attribute, once you have found certainty in a particular area, you will know how to find it in any area, in all areas.

This book about forgiveness is a good example of Chabad at work.

I have been thinking and talking about the subject of forgiveness for a long time without fully knowing what it actually is and why the great bibles imbue it with such reverence and power. For the last several years I have been studying the exoteric, the esoteric, the philosophical, the physiological, the psychological, the neurological and all things metaphysical to try and better understand the potency of forgiveness. I wanted to learn the modalities of making forgiveness better understood and better applied in raw situations that call for real resolve. This book is the fruit of a divine spark, a powerful intuition that said to me "know this attribute." I spent thousands of study hours with the rabbis, with the rishis, with the imams and the priests and the shamans and mystics who patiently and religiously schooled me. The tipping point from understanding into knowing occurred two weeks ago. I was in a deep meditation. The clear acoustic of intuition announced from out of Nowhere:

"13 reasons to forgive, write it now!"

I knew that this title was a nod to Maimonides' thirteen precepts of wisdom.

I started writing this book the same day.

This morning when I was taking my three-mile training run around the streets of my city, the same voice made an amendment to the first instruction: "99 reasons to forgive."

This upgrade (from 13 to 99) was a direct connection to the 99 names of Allah in the Holy Qur'an, a bible that I had read and been deeply moved by.

I changed the title the moment I arrived back home, sweat dripping from my brow onto the page as I wrote the words.

Later still, after the third draft was nearly completed, a subtitle dropped into my consciousness like a silver sixpence falling through water: (99 Reasons to Forgive) "and Revenge Ain't One."

This latter addition felt urgent.

There are so many people who are looking to revenge the wrongs done to them, that it felt vital to stipulate that this was not that kind of book, it was not about vengeance, or revenge. *99 Reasons* has something new to say, something fresh and pragmatic to present, and it needed to be announced proudly on the front cover for all to see.

Suggestions, instructions, guidance, introductions, sometimes out-and-out commands continue to appear, almost on a daily basis. My experience tells me that this will be the case right through to publication day and beyond. I will serendipitously be introduced to publishers, matched with editors and designers, I will also be assigned publicists, and any other personal and professional bodies needed to bring this writing to a public platform.

99 Reasons was only made possible because back in 1992 I was gifted certainty when I received a hard copy of my first published book (*Watch My Back*). The certainty of possibility I received from that publication is mine, *it is in me*. The gift cannot be removed, not by fire nor famine, not by disease or disaster. Certainty is a constant. It is indivisible. It cannot be given away. It cannot be broken up or stolen or bought or sold or bartered for. Neither can it be threatened: it is not influenced by opinion.

It is eternal because it is an attribute of God, who is All.

The Ronin Samurai Musashi said (in *The Book of Five Rings*) that to master one thing is to master all things. The *one thing* mastered becomes the template through which all other things can be realized.

I must reiterate though, that although Chabad is processional, that does not mean it offers any guarantees. One has to be aligned enough to first hear the song of instruction. You have to develop acoustic clarity. The sound of wisdom can be missed if you have too many other conflicting noises gonging in your head. Chochma (wisdom, the creative spark) is undeniably a gift, and no one knows if, when, how or even why it will alight. If and when it comes, it must be heard, it must be seen, it must be touched, it must be planted into binah and developed: for a day, for a week, a year, ten years, maybe *possibly* for an entire lifetime. No one knows how long the development process will take before the understanding becomes certainty. You can place no caveats on it. You must be prepared to push and yield, stop and start, slow down or move as fast as your neurons will allow when the instruction to do so arrives. If you push when you should yield, race when you should crawl, talk when you should listen, you will either break the process, break *yourself* in the process, stall the process or lose hope and faith in (or sight of) the process all together.

This is not a university degree program.

There is no specific course with prescribed units and set class times and a bunch of rules that, if followed, will near guarantee you a degree. With Chabad, the creative, the developmental and conclusion, there is no actual set physical structure, no preestablished road map to follow, no peer review, no guarantee of a job at the end of your course if you get a distinction. In fact, there is no guarantee of anything other than this... if you follow the process, something might happen, sooner or later, in a week's time, a month's time or even ten years' time, but when it does happen, even once, you will be in *the world to come* with keys to the kingdom.

Nothing will ever be the same again after you receive certainty, even once.

This is a book about forgiveness: what has certainty got to do with forgiveness?

Certainty is the constant that is hidden from you by negative, unprocessed human cognition, by perceptions of resentment.

Filters block you from certainty, they cloud the clear view.

Clean the filter, and the whole world changes.

Remove the obstacle and you will see for yourself.

The big obstacle is that people *believe* they have someone to forgive.

They do not.

They believe they have a problem.

They do not.

The only problem is *believing they have a problem*.

There are no problems, only limited perspectives.

They believe they hold the power to pardon.

They do not.

I know that there are people out there right now who may have been violated by others, I know that people have lost loved ones to violence, pensions to scammers, health due to medical incompetence and peace of mind because of unkind acts inflicted on them by indefensible human beings. I know that you may be currently experiencing the most challenging time of your entire existence, you may feel certain that some people, some things just cannot be forgiven.

If that were true, I would not be sitting here now, writing

this book, and passing on my certainty to you. If some people, if some things, fall into the *unforgivable* category, I would have been excommunicated and exiled long ago, along with all my heroes, St. Paul, St. Francis, St. Augustine, Milarepa, and Angulimala. Nelson Mandela would not be here either: he was a terrorist lest we forget, he terrorized people before he reformed and reframed and became a teacher of peace.

Both of these spurious beliefs stand in the way of your right to certainty, like a smeared window obscures a clear view.

If this chapter, this book has triggered a spark of light, a creative urge to understand something, congratulations, you have been gifted a creative seed. You are in possession of chochma (wisdom). Put it to work and be the proof of the words in this book: that you cannot forgive (not even yourself), but you can repent, you cannot pardon others, but you can find compassion for them, and certainly you can work towards your own pardon.

You will have to work harder that you have worked in your whole life.

It will take up all of your hours.

It will ask everything of you.

When you call for certainty as your prize, you are calling for the reaching arm of the Absolute, *no less*, so of course, it is not going to be easy. In the process (of Chabad) you will learn much, not least about opposition; of course, there is always opposition where there is opportunity, and if there is great opposition, then the opportunity will be proportionately rewarding. But opposition is no bad thing, in fact it is an essential ingredient in the creative process, it is energy, a turbo in the engine, and when we stop trying to forgive others and start working on redeeming ourselves, this opposition will present itself either to claim you, or be claimed: it will either eat you, or be eaten by you.

That is your choice, and for this reason, opposition is the

ninth reason for forgiveness.

Budo Practice

The budo didactic for this chapter is the technique already briefly outlined in the previous pages: I learned it from my martial arts training, my time as a working bouncer and from a deep study of exegetical Judaism. As mentioned already, "knowing" – often translated as *absolute certainty* – is a transformative, true world power, and although it is universally seen in budo as a "happy accident" or a gift or grace from God, through the practice of Chabad we can prepare the ground and help ourselves to become more accident prone. Just to reiterate briefly: Chabad is a process of taking a spark of wisdom (the spark of a great idea, a powerful intuition, a hunch) and examining/developing/ digesting it (through study and intellectual rigor) in all its detail until the abstract idea becomes embodied and articulate. Through the process of receiving and developing a wisdom spark (and this might manifest simply as an aching desire to find an answer to a problem), we find a bright new world beyond ignorance, and experience the land of certainty. I was personally able to find forgiveness for the most appalling betrayals through this process.

In this budo practice I would like to invite you to experience Chabad for yourself, and be witness to the awesome attribute of certainty, remembering also that certainty in one area equates to certainty (in potential) in all areas through the same process repeated. Choose a dilemma, a pressing problem, an enigma, something that provokes a strong emotion in you – inspirational or angry or confused – and write it down. This will be your portal into certainty.

I'll give you for-instance: I encountered a man at one of my public talks who was very angry at my specific use of the word God, or even the general use of the word religion. He said, "If there is an all loving God in the universe, why do innocent people suffer?"

It is a common question.

We hear it a lot from people who cannot juxtapose a benevolent creator with the innocent rape and murder of children in war-torn countries, or with the unsolicited violence that seems to occur wholesale in our world.

His question was spilling with anger and accusation: he didn't believe in God but nevertheless he was very angry at the (idea of a) God that allowed so much senseless torture, especially of innocent people.

He used the word "innocent" several times.

His anger and confusion and doubt created a perfect portal for the practice of Chabad. An open wound is also an open doorway. His argument *was* common, but naive, it was oft presented as evidence of a godless universe, and it often stumps even seasoned theologians, who are not sure how to answer such a sensitive question, and, for fear of causing offence, they relegate it to the mysteries, one of those enigmas that we will probably never understand while we are human. But his question was surface level, he had clearly gone for so long without satisfactory retort that he found no necessity to delve any deeper. Faced with the same question some years before, I used the process of Chabad to find some answers for myself, in the hope that I might be able to offer some light on it, if asked again.

Remember what I said before: it is a strange quirk of the brain that it cannot process curiosity and fear at the same time. Just by engaging deep curiosity, you are already diminishing the parasite of anger and fear.

Start with a question.

Proffer it to your inner self, your higher self, your God.

I took my initial spark of genuine curiosity (a gift from chochma) and I placed it into the intellectual machinery of binah (process) and let the engine turn over. After much intense study, poring over books, wading through hundreds of hours of talks and lectures, after a deep scrutiny of my own experiences, I went into a meditation, and I asked: "Why does God allow innocents to suffer?" Before I could even finish the question, an inner voice asked me the same question back: why do you allow innocents to suffer? I was ready to defend my position of chastity in this Platonic dialectic, I was just about to defend myself and say, "I don't allow innocents to suffer," when my conscience reminded me sharply that I was allowing innocents to suffer on a daily basis; when I thought, or said, or did unkind things about/to them, I had a funeral procession of past misdemeanors following me, moments when I not only allowed innocent people to suffer, but through my ignorance and my arrogance I had actually deliberately caused them to suffer. Didn't I allow my own innocent children to suffer when I had affairs on their mum, when I chose my own sensual pleasure, knowing that it would cause them direct and lasting harm?

"What about children who are raped and killed in war-torn countries?" I asked, "What did they do to deserve this?"

"Do you believe in law, in causation?" I was asked.

I did believe in causation, I had seen it in action many times, I could not deny it.

"So, you agree that there is no effect without a direct or indirect cause?"

Yes, of course, the two go together, you can't believe in a universal law and then pretend that certain situations or specific people are exempt from it, just because it suits you.

"If you believe in Law, you know that every situation has a cause, even if you can't immediately see it."

I agreed, but still couldn't see how – for instance – someone can be born with a debilitating illness, when they personally had done nothing wrong; how could they have, they were babies, they were innocent.

I was immediately shown that negative karma or cause is

a universal fatberg, it is the collective detritus not only of one generation of men and women, but a purulent debt accumulated over generations of people living on planet earth. And we all contribute, large or small, consistently, or intermittently, consciously or unconsciously, by accident or by design, every time we act in error. The world, it was explained, was a living collective, a web, connected in all its parts, like the cells in a human body. If I kick a chair in anger, the pain in my stubbed toe will be felt in every cell in my entire organism. The karmic return, the reciprocal agony, will not be restricted to the area of damage; rather, the pain will be felt into all parts, simultaneously even if they were innocent, even though they played no part in the act of kicking the chair.

What is true of the microcosm, is also true of the macrocosm.

The effects of our bodily causes are often truncated, or referred, or displaced into areas of our anatomy that seem completely unconnected to the initial action. A severe problem in your calf muscle may be the referred effect of a trapped nerve in the spine, a bloated gut might be referred from a historical neck injury. A great majority of physical woes – from cancer to organ disease – often find their cause in psychological problems that may be several steps removed and truncated from the malady: so much so that they appear to be completely disparate to our illness. Similarly, atrocities that occur in distant places right across the earth, all have a cause, and the reason we cannot always find it is because everything and everyone is the cause: to find a direct link to anything can often be impossible, because unless you are omniscient and can know everything that ever happened to everyone from the beginning of time, you will never find a single, direct root cause. All we can do (I was assured) is know everything in the general (which is to know causation) and start acting today as though the whole world will meet the bill for your every action (at some level), because it will.

If a bird lands in a tree (da Vinci reminded me) the whole world changes; everything affects everything.

The reason why most people do not practice Chabad (or rigor) is because it is easier to project our anger and rage from a stance of ignorance and pain and personal denial, than it is to realize that what we did before, and what we do now, not only affects everyone in the world, but it will also add to the burgeoning debt – the ancestral curse – left behind for our children, and for our children's children ad infinitum. Until we wake up, realize our mistake, learn the intricacies of law and start living in alignment with it, nothing will change.

There is more to this particular dialogue, much more, but it must remain for now unsaid, because it is peripheral to the tight parameters of this book.

I have to say also, that Chabad is a living being, an egregore that knows you, that knows your situation, and will be able to take you as far and as deep and as wide as you want to go. As part of the rigor, it might direct you towards study, or a guru, or a challenging inner dialogue, it might speak to you in parables, or inform you in allegories or similes or dreams, oftentimes (if it thinks you are up for it) it may lay the truth out in front of you like an open buffet. As I mentioned earlier, about the Christ, who asked the question: "Do you think you can drink from this bitter cup?"

To earn certainty, you have to be prepared not only to do the work, but also face the truth that the work will reveal. You also have to take the instruction without complaint and expect nothing in return. If you go in with a healthy expectation of nothing, something will likely alight when you least expect it.

What can you do the rigor on today?

What can you own?

Can you begin now?

Do it. Do the rigor.

Reason Nine: Opposition

When we are attempting to free ourselves from the tyranny of hate, of resentment, of confusion and anger and fear, while we are working to clear the obscuration that blocks our clear view, **we will meet with opposition.**

If this book has done its job, you should have felt that opposition already.

When I suggest replacing forgiveness with repentance and the offended ego cries out its complaint, you have already met with the first level of resistance.

Mine is a radical view, I know, but hopefully I have qualified my findings in these pages, or the words will have granted you enough "spark" to begin your own investigation.

You should begin your own investigation anyway.

It is not wise or healthy to take anyone's word for anything; you won't own it until you prove it for yourself.

Opposition is real.

It will rise, it will approach, and it will present itself: as outrage: as offence: as violent opposition to anything that is not congruent with your current paradigm. (As I mentioned earlier) this opposition has been called many things: evil, Wetiko, shadow, Satan, demon, pain-body etc.; but I prefer to see it as the natural, if uncomfortable, often dangerous, ultimately assisting, opposing energy, necessary to facilitate growth.

When I was younger, suffering with depression, the opposition felt like pure evil, a three-dimensional monster determined to make my existence a living misery. Often it seemed intent on either stalling my life, possessing my life or actually ending my life: if I had allowed these energies to inhabit me wholesale that could quite easily have been the case. These energies – what the mystic Sri Aurobindo called the "adverse forces" – are like semi-autonomous thought-forms that steal our causal will when we unconsciously identify or emotionally engage with them. In mythological lore they would be called "body snatchers" because they literally steal one or all of our bodies, from the physical, right down to the subtle and causal. The moment we identify with the pain-body – the anger, the self-pity, the sense of injustice – we *become* the pain-body, we are taken over and incarnated into it for the duration of engagement. For one minute, for one hour, for one year, or for one lifetime, we become them, and they become us. We think and believe that their thoughts and beliefs are ours and *they* think and believe that they are us. Often, the shift in personality when we engage these rogue thought-forms is so subtle and so smooth and so covert and so habitual that we hardly notice the gear change. Other times the changeover can be rapid and forceful, like a violent coup, and the people around us are shocked by our sudden and radical mood change. Post fall, when we recover our senses, and by way of apology, we might say something like, "I don't know what came over me: I was out of character: I was not myself: I wasn't thinking straight." Worse than this, is when we (try to) rationalize the character change and blame someone else for our actions, anyone else.

Denial keeps the covert takeover a secret.

It is much easier to blame and project than it is to admit fault.

It is much easier to deny responsibility than it is to say, "Something happened to me, and I was not myself for a moment and I apologize."

No one really wants to admit that they were temporarily possessed by a semi-autonomous thought-form because to admit this is to step beyond the bounds of everything we know, everything we are taught in secular, scientific society. If you start talking to your doctor about semi-autonomous thought-forms invading your body, he might well put you on a course of medication and refer you for a check-up from the neck-up. The hardest thing to accept is that there are unseen energy forms that regularly feed off human emotion (specifically drama and pain) because it points towards madness, it hints at schizophrenia or at the very least mental confusion or delusion.

At this moment in time (2022), as this book goes out to print, the presence of amorphous beings is vehemently denied by science, and God forbid that we should ever openly oppose current scientific understanding.

I am not really interested in science per se in this book.

I am not seeking peer review or validation or acceptance by them or anyone else.

I am simply trying to inspire the potential of balance by sharing what I have learned and earned and have been gifted by grace.

These energies, these adverse forces are there, they are known and accepted (and expected) in and by the more senior members of the esoteric community, but they are quietly ignored by everyone else. This is how they like it, these forces.

They work best in the shadows.

When brought out into the open they are diminished and dissolved by the light. Understanding reduces these forces from full-fat, three-dimensional monsters into paper-thin, two-dimensional cartoons.

Knowledge *certainty* dispels them completely.

The truth is discovered by outsiders in society and ignored by everyone else.

They will deny it, they might even attack it, because the same "unknown" forces use ignorance as a tool to defend their anonymity. We mentioned before about the word or attribute Yaqeen: it tells us that the truth is undeniable, and it is right in front of us.

When I worked as a bouncer, I was not there for the money or the infamy or the attention of pretty females (all right... perhaps a little of the latter). I was an aspiring martial arts student searching for truth, for efficacy. I had been sold a robust and effective (read, *deadly*) system of combat by the demigods of martial arts, but I knew they were lying. Or (at the very least) they were not telling the truth (by this, I mean that they believed what they were saying, but what they were saying was not true). I knew that the truth about martial efficacy was out there, but it was not commonly known in martial arts circles, and it was not usually taught on the dojo floor.

I spent nearly a decade in an environment that did not tolerate anything but the truth. If I was going to survive in this savage realm, I would have to find efficacy and very quickly. The environment itself was my teacher. It molded me into the truth.

It didn't teach me the truth; it revealed and infused the truth into me, and in this revelation, I became the truth.

All I had to do was let go of what I *wanted* to know and embrace instead what I *needed* to know. I *wanted* to know something that did not frighten me, that did not shatter my present paradigm of truth. The latter felt too painful. It was threatening to the ego to be told "everything you think you know is wrong."

The ego wants to control everything, that is where its security lies, and it can't control or be secure in what it doesn't understand or know.

I *needed* to reveal a truth that did not give a rat's arse about paradigms and systems and lineage.

I found the truth about martial efficacy, I drank that bitter cup, and it was simultaneously shattering and liberating.

To accept the incontrovertible truth, I had to go against most of the martial arts community (my own teachers amongst them): it was a painful, if necessary, experience. The truth was so obvious and so immediate I was amazed that I had not been taught it before. It seemed incredulous to me that I had not stumbled upon it twenty years earlier, that it was not common knowledge in the martial arts community.

But here's the thing: in the security world this truth *was* common knowledge.

It was common knowledge, but it was not communicated outside the closely guarded circles of door security. This knowing, the certainty of martial efficacy, made the bouncers and the security specialists into magicians. They were able to neutralize even highly trained martial arts masters with their knowing. The top dog in *this* world had no belt, no teaching certificate, and no online following, they were neither gurus nor gods but if you stood in front of them looking for a little contact, you did so at your own peril.

Why?

Because they had the truth about efficacy in a violent environment, they were certain.

They had knowledge.

The point I am making here is that I found the truth and I took it back to my class and my school and my system and as a result I was labelled *by many* as a liar, as a violent thug, a criminal, and a bully. The truth I found (read *Watch My Back* for comprehensive detail on this) is still not widely understood or articulated or accepted even today, in a martial arts community lost in the miasma of illusion.

It is still known only by a rare few.

This is the narrow gate of biblical instruction.[9]

The opposition I was met with when I started to teach my knowing was immense.

I was barred from a city on the west coast, razed in parliament by an MP as a menace to society, vilified in local newspapers, pilloried by "opposition" in magazines, and criticized and reviled by many of the current martial arts elite. I was accused of faking my credentials, lying about my experiences and I was forced to the periphery like an outsider.

No complaints.

I have to add that I also found a dedicated and loyal following, people who did want the truth, folk who (I thought) would have followed me to the ends of the earth.

As an addendum I must also tell you that as my truth grew and expanded, many of my followers also became unconscious instruments for the opposition: even some of my senior teachers had their strings pulled and became actively opposed to me: many of my most ardent and loyal fans became possessed by hatred, set up anti-Geoff Thompson websites and shared their vitriol online.

People are often not themselves, they contradict their own convictions with every second breath, so you learn to never take the trolling personally, and you learn to never ever buy into the good that people say about you either. Good or bad, they are both imposters, they penetrate your invisibility cloak and leave you "seen," which opens you up to further abuse. If you get high on the praise, the criticism will floor you like a Marciano Suzy Q.

Again, absolutely no complaints.

The degree of opposition can be marked by the level of your truth.

And, as I said earlier in the book, if these forces get past your mind-guard, as painful and cruel as they might present, they are not your enemy they are your teachers, they are showing you where your leaks are.

You will meet opposition when you start to talk about forgiveness from a perspective of truth. Even very smart, highly educated people still turn blank and become childish and churlish and reactionary when you suggest that everyone should be forgiven (even and especially the serious criminal) and that there are invisible forces that will actively, even violently oppose this new regime of truth.

This is because they do not have a developed sense of what forgiveness actually is.

Neither do they understand the full gravity, and the clear and present danger of evil.

I always said to people who attacked me, when they thought I'd let them off because I had forgiven their crime, "If I forgive you be very afraid; it means I have given you over the great leveller, it means I have let you go."

There is bad news and good news (and additional information) regarding opposition. The bad news is that opposition is a bear, and it will eat you (literally) if you don't understand it.

The good news is that once you do understand opposition, *you* can eat *it*.

What eats you, you can eat; what uses you, you can use.

In the great mythological works of Vedanta, demons are seen as carriers of light, and when they are defeated in battle, the nature of the demon is liberated, and the effulgence that it contains is infused into the victor and digested like holy manna. The fighter who is able to defeat all the demons is celebrated and crowned as King. In allegory, this is telling us that when we combat and defeat the evil of nescience, the nature of the ignorance is liberated, and the light or knowing that it obscured is infused into us, enabling us to become sovereign in our own body and mind.

The aforementioned additional information is this: opposition is a natural if unpalatable force in this realm.

This opposition, coming in the shape of thought-forms (or *thought* in general), does not come from within you (though it may have docking points (or *partners*) in your body and mind), it comes from outside. It is non-local, it has its own realm, its own atmosphere. St. Francis calls this opposition *the devil of scripture, the roaming lion* and said that it was always looking to devour the unaware.

It will eat you.

That sounds extreme I know, and if you are new to the esoteric, you may not have heard this expression before. In mysticism it is known by the simile "feeding the bear." If you allow the adverse forces in – the wrong thought, the wrong advice, the wrong belief, the wrong person – it will engage you, take over your thinking, take over your speaking, take over your actions and eventually (if you allow it to) it will take over your whole being: like a parasite or a virus, it will consume you from the inside out.

When you hear statements like, "I was consumed by fear: consumed with worry: eaten up by guilt: devoured by lust/anger/rage," you are hearing an uncommon truth spoken in the common vernacular. The parasite works very much like an Internet troll, or the psychology-led advertising moguls who use provocative bait in the form of garish or pornographic imagery or outrageous/intriguing headlines to encourage click-through. In common parlance this is called "click-bait," and the adverse forces employ the same methods, using your mental engagement and imagination rather than (just) an online forum or the front page of a newspaper or magazine (though they will work through these too). An image or a suggestion or an idea or an arousal will penetrate the open mind: it will entice you to engage or identify with it until the bait becomes a negative internal dialogue. This dialogue triggers psychological arousal. The *bait* might be any number of stimuli: curiosity, anger, intrigue, gossip, conspiracy, judgment, outrage, pity, dissonance, violent arousal, sexual stimulation etc. and it is employed to trigger your emotions and use your senses as an entry point to thought. Negative thinking sparks your central nervous system (adrenal-arousal). Once adrenalin is aroused, imagination takes over and arousal is magnified and heightened until your thoughts spill into spoken words and your spoken words tip into physical actions in the world.

Suddenly you are hooked; you have taken the bait and acted on it.

Without meaning to, you strengthen the adverse forces every time you action them.

You create a bond, a neural pathway, a bridge between your

body of conscious will *autonomy* and the adverse forces. Once you have engaged them, they leave an embryonic parasite within you (a semi-autonomous thought-form or a "partner") that feeds and grows strong from your inner resources. Once this parasitical hub has been established in you, it acts as a connection, and it intermittently docks with the adverse forces in the atmosphere around us. It acts like is an invisible intravenous tube that bleeds and rapes our essential creative energies.

If allowed to, it can completely take over our will, our personal autonomy, it then steals our kingdom. When Prince Arjuna Pandava (in the Gita) goes to war to win back his kingdom from his corrupt cousins, this (control of the causal will), allegorically, is what he is fighting for. When Odysseus fights to win back his palace at Ithaca, overrun by criminal elements, this (metaphorically) is what he is fighting for. When Christ goes into the desert for forty days and forty nights, and battles against the devil, this is what he is fighting for.

The adverse forces run such a covert operation that most people are not even aware that they exist.

They reap our energies by triggering and then riding our senses; this of course is best achieved through pain, through misery, through sadness, through sexual arousal, through overexcitement, through anger and fear and drama and depression and misery. In Eckhart Tolle's seminal book, *The Power of Now*, he calls these adverse forces *pain-bodies* and describes them as "semi-autonomous thought forms" that feed off human drama. He is unambiguous in his assertion that "pain-bodies feed off pain," and they feed off other pain-bodies. These forces do not have to look far to find food; they are fed twenty different horror stories on the news every morning before we even leave for work. The news is no longer the news, it is the "bad news" and bad-news feeds bad news, it feeds and bloats the adverse forces.

Like a muscle, this unholy bond becomes stronger every time it is used.

Whether you are aware of it or not, you also create a covenant with these forces when you engage them. When you identify with them, an unconscious agreement is written in the cells of your body by your engagement and a twisted trade-agreement is made between your own personal will and the adverse forces. Before you know it, your borders are being breached on a daily or hourly basis. For many people, their inner world actually becomes completely borderless, and they lose all control over their body of conscious will, and thus all autonomy and positive agency in the world. In simple analogy, engaging vice is like setting up a direct debit (or a direct withdrawal) between the bank of your own energy reserves and the nature of your negativity (or, the adverse forces). It is like an energy transaction in which one-party (an adverse force) withdraws energy-funds from another party's (bank of) energy: this is typically used for recurring payments.

You set up an agreement the moment you engage in negativity.

Once it has been established, a recurring payment is taken by the nature of your vice.

When I was assaulted at the age of eleven years, my abuser left a parasite in me, a partner, that grew strong on my fear and suffering. Over time it took control of (much of) my autonomy. This inner parasite connected to the mother ship (the *adverse forces* or the *realm of thought* or *the world pain-body*) and encouraged massive conflict and drama and pain in my life.

It fed on this pain.

It grew strong and established itself on this pain.

It was only when I became aware of it that I was able to identify the bond, starve this parasite out, break the covenant and win back my own autonomy. The fear, the pain, the dissonance, the resentments I carried, the blames I nursed, the depressions I endured as a consequence, fed the very forces that I wanted to escape from.

Once I understood the process, I was able to identify the adverse forces, and instead of them consuming me, I consumed them. I used the energies as oil for the lamp, ink for my pen, energy for my workouts, and fuel for my study: I was able to take back sovereignty of my own will and use these rogue forces as workhorses.

When I encourage you to forgive, I am doing so because forgiving these forces from your mind allows you to take back control of your life, it allows you to safeguard the vital energies that are otherwise stolen and consumed by the very force you wish to remove.

Anger is a thief.

Grudge is a thief.

Resentment is a thief.

Revenge is a thief.

Fear is a thief.

Dissonance is a thief.

Rage is a thief.

Judgment is a thief.

Blame is a thief.

Now that you know it is a thief, are you still going to allow it to steal from you?

When you forgive, these adverse forces can no longer feed on you, because they find compassion, love, joy, kindness, altruism, charity, completely unpalatable; goodness is like poison to them, it is a weed killer that goes to the very root of the parasitical plant. This is the reason why I never allow myself to engage or identify with anger. I will not have it in my body; I will not allow it in my life.

In the mythology of *Harry Potter* (specifically *The Prisoner of Azkaban*), this protection was known as the Patronus Charm, a defensive spell which produces a silver animal guardian, used to protect a witch or wizard against the evil Dementors.

When the adverse forces take over even a small aspect of your will, they act in the world, as you and through you. They rise up, they act out, they accumulate karmic debt in the world of form, then they recede back again, temporarily sated, to the realms of the unconscious, leaving you chained to the karma they have caused. They dine out lavishly through your body and leave you to foot the bill.

The debt has to be paid, and like the respectable Dr. Jekyll, you will always be running around trying to settle the debts of your own personal Mr. Hyde.

Once we engage negativity and action it in our minds, the proceeding exertion of energy, in thought, in word and in deed, feeds the bear, it gobbles up your essential energies in a frenzy of drama and suddenly you are depleted.

You are a meal for thought-forms that exist in their own realm, in their own frequency and they enter your body and mind, *your world* and delight on the spilling essence of an unguarded human.

The fact that we do not know this is happening is what allows it to happen all the more. Once we know it is happening, once we understand their game plan, their attack ritual, we can learn to defend the mind-door and protect the seminal energy that is our divine inheritance.

The reason the adverse forces do not want us to know about them is because once they are identified they can no longer enter our domain covertly or at will.

Our knowing is an etheric prana-cloak, it is an amorphous armor, it protects us.

Knowing is the chainmail and plate-armor of the Arthurian Knight.

Knowing that we have a shadow, a dark polarity, gives us power. It means we can use the very forces that would use us, we can feed on the energies that feed on us, the bear can feed us, instead of us feeding the bear.

Our kindness, our goodness, our refusal to engage vice, also protects us, as does our acts of charity in the manifest world.

Once we make ourselves a hard target, these forces will likely wander off and find an easier mark: and there are plenty of those around.

Feeding the Bear

(As I mentioned earlier) a common question posed in the metaphysical classroom is: *are you feeding the bear or is the bear feeding you?*

The adverse forces, as evil as we may like to imagine them, can be converted to forces for good if we are able to understand our enemy, know its strategy and use its own power against it. This is where we make milk from thorns; this is where we are able to use that which uses us. If these forces approach and we have developed the skill to interrupt their attack ritual, if we are able to observe the rise, the approach, the *click-bait* of arousal without engagement, without identification, the very forces that would consume us become consumed under the eye of our powerful knowing.

They are not only devoured by our observance; they are also converted by our action.

My last film (*Retaliation*, starring Orland Bloom) is a good example of *the bear feeding me*. When I first sat down to write the film, I felt immediate and massive opposition; this was the metaphoric bear rising in order to claim or be claimed. The adverse forces did not want me to pen this film because the truth exposes them, it brings them out into the open and stops them from feeding so easily and readily on the unknowing masses: vampires – and they very much are bloodsuckers – are afraid of the scorching light of truth.

They are mortally afraid, because the elementals that use us as food, themselves become food the moment we digest them through the organs of virtuous volition.

With *Retaliation* (a muscular biopic about the power of forgiveness), this opposition came in the form of massive doubt. In the Pentateuch (the Old Testament/the Five Books of Moses) from Exodus right through to Deuteronomy we are forewarned against the forces of doubt. In the five books this army are called Amalek. When the prophet Moses led the Israelites to freedom from the slavery of the Egyptian pharaoh, they were pursued and attacked in the desert by a warring tribe called the Amalek.

Etymologically, Amalek means doubt!

The story of Moses can be read in many ways, but its esoteric meaning is clear: in our bid for freedom from the slavery of ego, we will be assailed by doubt.

When we strive for emancipation, doubt, uncertainty, fear, *the forces of Amalek* will always locate, isolate, and attack the stragglers, those at the back of the march, those struggling to make sense of their swedge, those looking for comfort or those people simply wanting to escape from the difficultly of the path.

Know too that doubt is of the path, it is a necessary and ordained force, charged to keep us constantly moving forward, especially when our will is weakened, and our animal soul is tempting us back to the blind comfort of mindless slavery: this needs to be understood in order to be surpassed.

When I felt these forces rise and approach during the writing of *Retaliation*, I immediately recognized them for what they were. I felt their presence in my emotions and in my central nervous system, I observed their movement through the humors of my body, and I heard their doubting rhetoric as a half-convincing inner voice pretending to be me: I sat down and wrote the film anyway. In the volition of writing *Retaliation*, the adverse forces were vaporized, digested, consumed, and converted through the wick of my pen: the material into the spiritual.

The bear rose in order to feed on me, but I fed on it instead.

The bear approached, in order to use me, I used it instead.

Similarly, when you look at the ink on this page, when you observe the sentences and read the letters and the words and even perhaps the spaces between the words, you are looking at the forces of Amalek converted into the light of instruction ("what is exposed to light, itself becomes a light," Ephesians 5:13). This book is not just alive and speaking to you across time and space, despite the presence of the adverse forces, it is manifest on the page because of them.

Opposition is good.

The Jewish rabbis ask a telling question in reference to the instruments of evil: when Jacob wrestles all night with the angel, on the ladder ascending to heaven (Genesis 32:22-32), is the angel serving God or the enemy? They conclude that the angel is serving "both of the above," the dark side has always been in the employ of the Holy One.

So, opposition is not only to be expected, but also to be understood and welcomed.

Opposition is a food-utility; it is there to be consumed.

Opposition, however, is to be respected and handled with great care: we underestimate it at our peril.

When you lift a dumbbell in the gym to build muscle on your body, it is the presence of the weight pushing against the opposing force of gravity that sculpts your physique. The opposition only becomes an enemy if you don't know the science of these forces: what they are for, why you need them, and how to control and direct them. When your knowing is certain, and your intent is set, all forces, negative or positive, good or bad, are employed in the arc of creation.

I mentioned earlier that the negative thought-forms or adverse forces enter easiest when they already have a parasitical partner implanted in your body and mind. In other words, if you are harboring an adverse force in the form of prejudice, anger, confusion, lust, desire, resentment, guilt, grudge, or *any* unfinished business or unprocessed trauma, it will pick up on that matching frequency and immediately connect with it. It roams the atmosphere, this force, looking for, attracted to, and drawn irresistibly towards *like* frequencies. While you carry anger, you will always attract anger: while you carry pain, you will always attract pain, dissonance will attract dissonance, drama will seek out drama, and violence will draw violence; I know this from painful experience. The man who abused me as a boy implanted the parasite of fear in me, and everywhere I went for the next forty years I attracted fear in all its many guises. I said to my wife one day, "Isn't this city violent? Everywhere I go there is violence." She looked at me with a wily knowing and said, "Geoff, there is a common denominator here, it is everywhere *you* go."

It was true. I was a shit magnet. I attracted violence everywhere I went, even at weddings and christenings and funerals. It was not until I understood this, and I removed the offending party from my body and mind that I stopped attracting violence into my life. I stopped engaging the bug-malware implanted in me by an abusive predator, I stopped identifying with it, I stopped feeding it and the violence avoided me, like a base man confronted by a spoken truth.

Don't take my word for any of this.

Please, take it out for a ride, put it into practice, enquire, and be your own proof.

As I said earlier, when you remove the negativity, you reveal the self.

The self then becomes the geometric point, the only point of reference you will ever need.

I have spent my life converting the dark into light, water into wine, ignorance into knowing, the material into the spiritual, lead into gold. Sometimes I still fall, and the bear tricks me into identification and mercilessly feeds on me, and when it does it is always disproportionately painful. But I notice it keenly and I stop it quickly. I redress the balance as soon as I am alerted to my astray. I put my pain to the pen. I write the inky manna to the parchment. I author my truth, and I leave the pages of my life in the marketplace of the great earth for those that may follow.

Some may follow.

Are you feeding the bear or is the bear feeding you?

Are you consuming or are you being consumed?

Are you using this force, or are you being used by it?

The third part of the triptych (I have alluded to it already) is that this force, as much as we all love to hate on it, is a necessary ingredient, it is a natural force, it is the fire and thorns that circumvent the kingdom.

It keeps the unrighteous out, it allows the righteous in.

We are righteous when we are no longer seduced by anger and hate.

Our job is to educate ourselves about this force, not deny that it exists.

We take ourselves outside of its influence by acquiring Yaqeen (certainty).

I mentioned already that certainty is a happy accident that can be encouraged by the practice of Chabad (creative, developmental, conclusive rigor) and this is a process that will be present for as long as we wear this coat of skin.

The potential to learn is infinite.

This means that study and enquiry and practice need to be forever too.

This work needs lots of fuel, and there can be no better supply than the energy store we carry round with us everywhere we go in the conceptualized form of resentment.

If we can recognize this, we can transform our rich vein of woes and worries into the workhorse of perpetual learning.

Why do you think my life and my output has been so exciting and eventful and prolific?

Because I recognized the innate treasure store that was locked into the rage and confusion I felt in every cell of my body, and I cashed it in. I sat down and I put my rage to the page. I went out and I turned my confusion into fusion, and it fueled the journey.

Like electricity, this energy has the power to zap and kill the clumsy workman dead, but to those who respect its laws and become skilled in managing its force, it can transform realities for the better with its life-enhancing potential.

As a bouncer – probably the most metaphysical experience of my entire life – I was gifted a vision. I did not fully realize it until many years later; I was able to witness the whole process of what is usually an amorphous energy, visibly and in exaggeration. What usually occurs in the hidden realms of our own minds was manifest right before my eyes.

It happened in real time, with real people.

I observed the pinball mayhem of colliding energies. I noted the effect my own energy had upon the people (the energies) around me. I learned how to alter my state manually and consciously in order to guide other energies (in the form of human beings) in the direction I wanted them to go; sometimes I did this to protect them from me (if I felt they were physically out of their depth), sometimes to protect them from themselves, and other times I deliberately commandeered their energy to protect myself from them.

Eying the agitating crowds in the nightclub was like looking through a microscope at the protons and neutrons and electrons swirling around inside an atom. I knew that these people (these energy cells) were being affected, often entangled by me (the observer) and by my energy; I also understood that I could (with practice) control and direct and determine their energy. I knew that I could alter their state, their direction, and their lives, accidentally or deliberately, with my own expectations and with my own actions.

I saw myself primarily as a powerful, amorphous energy form, a particle ("a small, localized object to which can be ascribed several physical or chemical properties such as volume, density or mass"), encased inside a physical body that could act with or against other particles, and the outcome of our encounter – positive, negative, neutral – would be entirely determined by the intent behind my intercession.

I could see in real time what was occurring inside their bodies, and if I chose, I could alter that state with any number of stimuli: with my voice, with my eyes, with my gait, with mudras, with my explicit or implicit intention, or with physical touch. The customers, the positive, the negative *and* the neutral, presented at the door of our club like thought-forms queuing at the doorway of my (body of) conscious will, vying for attention, and looking for entrance to the wonders within.

I realized that the way I managed the door of that club was the way I needed to manage the doorway to my priceless attention.

As a bouncer I did not let anyone in our club who was not fit to be there.

The aggressive, the violent, the drug dealers and the street fighters, the criminals, the gangsters, we knocked them back, wholesale. If necessary, we fought them back, but we did not allow them thoroughfare into our space.

Like the vampires of lore, they needed an invite before they were able to cross our threshold.

If they were negative, we did not extend them a welcome.

They did not get in.

Because we ran a strong door, we won a reputation for having a clean club; this attracted balanced people to our venue who only wanted to have a good time.

To guard a door against the violent and the criminal, the team needed to be awake, they needed to be sober, fighting fit, intelligent, courageous and above all, *knowing*. We needed to be certain about what was going on all around us.

Our stewardship was challenged many times and we had hundreds of pitched and violent battles on the concrete outside our venue, but we never lost the door, and we never lost the club. Lesser teams, in a city that was a Poppy field of drinking establishments, lacked the courage to stop the trouble at the door. They were afraid of the criminal element; they were frightened to refuse entry for fear of reprisal. Subsequently, they courted the violent, they pampered to the gangsters, they tried to curry favor, and in doing so they lost integrity, they lost face, and ultimately, they lost the door.

The battle against opposition in the metaphysical sense was, and is, and always will be no different.

People fail to guard their mind-door because, firstly, they don't consciously know what a mind-door is, they don't acknowledge that we all have one, and thus they fail to realize that there is anything to defend.

We understand it with our kids. We employ this kind of common sense knowing organically and automatically with our children. We do not doubt for a single second that these young developing minds need protecting from forces that they don't understand, or have not yet developed the ability to discriminate against.

No one needs to teach us that vulnerable minds in society are constantly at risk of abuse. We understand the need to be on guard in the protection of our children (and the elderly). Against an undeniable, clear and present danger, we know we need to remain perpetually aware.

We do not, however, understand that we too are under attack, at all times. But not necessarily from the rogue elements visibly present in society; rather ours is the enemy within, the semi-autonomous thought-forms that move in and out of our mind-space – convincingly presenting as us – and pervading our consciousness and harvesting our seminal energies, every waking hour.

The mind-door is the point of attention where we decide what we are going to allow into our minds, and what we are going to refuse entry.

The thoughts that rise in us, the thoughts that approach and bid for our attention, are not ours. Some of them may have set up residence in us, and many of them may swim around inside our head relentlessly, but ultimately thoughts come from the outside, and can enjoy no life within us unless we decide to engage them and allow them into the wonderland of our consciousness.

We just presume that the rogue thoughts and the unkind words and the out-of-character actions are disparate, unruly parts of our nature, quirks in our character, and elements of our own personality, the angels and demons of the human condition.

They are not.

Whenever I was given a busy bar to protect, I knew that fronting the door made me an automatic target for any malcontent, any criminal, any rogue element who might benefit from the bounty of an unpoliced club. I knew this before I started, we all knew it, the knowing was standard. Policing a club door paid top money, and bouncers were revered, respected, feared, and hated in equal measure. The job was taken very seriously, even by the constabulary, but ultimately, all we were guarding was the license of a shitty club.

How much more valuable then, the license of the human will, the agency of a soul in a shell, a living being ensconced within a human skin bag?

The adverse forces have got it made.

While they can access a food supply (our energy) at will, and any time they please, why wouldn't they. Like any virus or parasitic insect, they are always on the lookout for a hearty meal or a tasty snack or a delicious, unguarded pantry. Human energy is already a banquet for the many roaming parasites, and as a society we strive to make vaccines to protect ourselves against these infinitesimal killers. At this present moment in time (2021) the world is uniting to create a vaccine-protection against a new marauder (COVID-19), and as quickly as is humanly possible: it has already killed close to a million people around the world.

But what of the thought virus?

Of course, as yet, this is not a commonly acknowledged killer. Because the sleeping human does not know that he is a free buffet for every hungry ghost roaming the atmosphere, looking for a feed, few feel the need to do anything about it.

We know we must guard our cars, so we put the latest high-tech security systems in place. We know that our houses are vulnerable and valuable to burglars and thieves so we have top spec alarm systems fitted, we keep our doors and windows locked and we might even home a barking dog to alert us against marauding intruders. We know that certain countries, certain districts, certain streets and certain bars are no-go areas, so we escape becoming a victim statistic by avoiding the obvious crime hotspots. We know all this, but the average person has yet to fathom that there is also a hidden threat: an invisible enemy that works by stealth and lurks invisibly.

I won't overburden you with too much detail here, this is merely a relevant chapter in a book specializing in forgiveness. I am giving it chapter space here, to reveal this crime-in-plain-sight so that you can prevent yourself from becoming its next victim in the near or distant future.

My book, *The Divine CEO*, gives a detailed account of the adverse forces and Eckhart Tolle reveals it with even greater clarity in his book *The Power of Now*. If there is an appetite for further enquiry, you would do well to invest in *Dispelling Wetiko*, by Paul Levy, a compelling and comprehensive exposure of the same forces.

I introduce it here, only because it is the 9th reason to forgive.

Resentment and all of its cohorts (fear, dissonance etc.) are engaged emotions that feed rogue forces.

This opposition feeds on negativity, the stronger the better.

Your reward for practicing forgiveness and courting compassion is that it stops these energies dead in their tracks. Compassion, love and joy are as caustic to the pain-body as Dettol (Lysol) is to a germ.

The 9th reason to forgive is freedom from the tyranny of and the slavehood to the forces of negativity. Enough to say that if your thoughts tip towards the negative pole, you have already become a victim of this ghost in the works.

In order to stop it, you first have to see it. Once observed, we are able to cut it off, and keep it back with the weapon of a keen and alert and practiced intellect. For want of constant use, our protective cloak of intelligence is impaired and negative intruders will penetrate and occupy our mind space. They will do this as quickly as rats consume and befoul a barn full of freshly harvested wheat, left unguarded.

Seers are spiritually awake.

When you awaken from a sleep of ego, you see this drama playing out, and you recognize that few are privy to this knowing. You feel ever so slightly insane when you become aware that, deep down, everyone knows that they are quietly under siege, being fattened for the kill like pigs in a pen, but no one wants to be the first to find his voice and whistleblow. Most people are so smothered and confused and controlled by their own designated shadow that they no longer know where they end, and the pain-body begins. The mental fog obscures their view, it prevents them from seeing clearly and thinking concisely and hearing acoustically, so they do not actively rebuff and repudiate unkind, rogue thoughts, they are not even aware that the thoughts are not their own.

As I mentioned elsewhere in the book, the self is your only true point of reference. In the lost gospel of Thomas, Jesus advises his followers that: "When you know yourselves, then you will be known, and you will know that you are the sons of the living Father. But if you do not know yourselves, then you are in poverty, and you are poverty." Before we can even begin to reclaim our autonomy, the self must be known, it must be revealed and fought for and reclaimed *thought by thought, territory by territory, nation by nation,* until the guard on your mind door is as robust as four burly bouncers.

The 9th reason to forgive is that you get to reveal and uncloak the opposition: when you stop feeding the bear, the bear starts feeding you.

This is a process.

It takes time.

It takes wisdom, understanding and ultimately it demands knowledge, certainty.

You must prepare the ground for the grace of Yaqeen if you are to win the war of the inner worlds.

There is one last important ingredient that will help you in your fight for sovereignty...

Love.

The last chapter is the best chapter because it is all about love.

Budo Practice

As a developing martial artist, I innately knew that if I was the top fighter in my class, I was no longer able to grow.

Like a plant or a flower or a tree, we have to matriculate into bigger and bigger pots (eventually from pot to the garden proper) if we want to sponsor maximum growth and avoid becoming root-bound.

In order to grow we need opposition.

Those that grow exponentially, do so because they pit themselves against forces that are always a little greater than their ability to withstand.

When I took my bamboo plants from their small pots and placed them into the soil in my back garden, I worried that the wind and the rain would rip them from the earth. My wife reminded me that they needed the challenge of inclemency: "The wind will force the roots to burrow deeper into the ground," she assured me.

We are human beings, planted in the living soil on the great earth; in order to thrive, we too need the occasional gust in order to quicken our development.

I call this "encouraged growth."

Mine is a similar method to that used by gardeners who enhance the growth of plants and vegetables by restricting their access to light. In gardening terms this is known as "forcing." It's a simple way of tricking nature into early growth.

By placing myself into dark areas of life, where I have access to little or no light (little or no knowledge or skill) I encourage or force new or accelerated growth.

I once gave up work for eighteen months just to practice judo full time; I was the worse player in a dojo that was full of international judoka. I was so bad that the teacher (World Judo Champion Neil Adams) actually stopped the class one session and announced, "Please, everyone, take it easy on Geoff." Because I placed myself in the path of massive opposition, my skills and abilities grew exponentially: within two years I could hold my own in a class of Olympic players. If I'd not understood the concept of "encouraged growth," I could quite easily have judged this class as a torture chamber, and my fellow students, bullies of the first order, tyrants determined to throw me on my head as often as they could. And I have to admit, there were times when I felt as though I was the iron ore going through the furnace, feeling needlessly tortured. Because of my knowing, I was able to constantly remind myself of why I was there: I was there to grow. I "constantly labored, and deliberately suffered" (ref. Gurdjieff) in order to develop at an advanced rate.

I have always made a point of placing myself at the bottom of someone else's class: it acts as a catalyst to elevated learning.

In this budo addendum I would like to encourage you to not

only see opposition as a force for good (even if the opposition is thrust upon you and not chosen), but also encourage you to welcome, even search out opposition as a natural catalyst. This opposition might come in the form of an uncontrollable anger you feel or a fear that has been haunting you, it may be that you are fighting against habits and addictions: this is all manna for the martial artist. We learned to approach it with reverence *and* caution, of course, but also with excitement and gratitude. You may not particularly like where your life has placed you at this moment in time; like the root-bound bamboo tree, forced from its safe pot in the greenhouse, you too might feel mercilessly assailed by the prevailing forces of nature, but I promise you, if you stay with it, your roots will grow thicker, they will burrow deeper, and your power to withstand will become proportionately strong.

When life proffered me depression for instance, I initially railed against my position and blamed the world for my sorry lot, but it did not help, in fact it made things worse: the more I resisted my state, the more my state resisted me.

You have a choice: you can marinate in your misery, waiting to be saved (I have news for you, no one is coming, no one is going to save you) or you can take control and lean into the sharp edges of whatever hurt is pressing on you at this present time. You can't feel any worse than you already feel, so you might as well take some profit from your sorrow: there is always profit in sorrow if we work with it and not against it.

In order to survive my profligate encounters with opposition (fear, depression, the doors, life), I developed – what I call – an "eye wall," that has enabled me to sit protected in the middle of the wildest storms. Actually, it would be more accurate to say that I grew an eye wall as an organic by-product of placing myself deliberately and directly in the path of personal storms, recognized the phenomenon and then adopted it as a deliberate strategy.

What is an eye wall?

Gandhi overcame his debilitating addiction to sex by lying in bed with naked women and training his attention to resist temptation (note: I don't think my wife would buy this as a legitimate training methodology!). I overcame crippling fears, by deliberately placing myself into challenging situations for the same reason: the exercise taught me how to experience the rush of fearful arousal without being captured by its force. At the very center of a hurricane there is an eye (the eye of the storm) and within this eye – impervious to the evident chaos all around it – there is stillness, there is perfect calm and blue skies. What I learned to do, particularly when I was working as a bouncer, was to consciously create an eye wall (almost like an interior castle that I could withdraw my attention in to) so that, even though I may be surrounded on all sides by violence and threat, I could find mental refuge. This technique is effective, whether you are facing external threat as a security specialist, or the internal charge of a depression and anxiety that threatens to destroy you.

In the Old Testament, the eye wall was called an ark:[10] Noah was told by God that a flood[11] was coming and that anyone spiritually unclean would be washed away by the waters and killed. Hashem instructed him to build an ark, withdraw his family to the very center and stay there until the waters had receded. The story of Noah's Ark is a didactic allegory, it is a powerful spiritual strategy explained in a simile. The storm can be whatever is happening in your life right now: the fear, the anxiety, the anger, the rage, the illness or the depression. And the ark (or the eye) is an inner cell that you build at the very center of your being and mentally retreat to, as a protection from the emotional deluge. Most people never build their own personal ark because they lack instruction, they don't even know that the eye wall is an option, let alone a possibility. The powerful thing about working as a bouncer was that the life-threatening situations you faced on a nightly basis were so severe that you either developed an eye wall, or you got dragged into the cyclone, and torn to pieces. Every bouncer that ever worked the doors will have developed an eye wall, and even though most of them were experts in this strategy, I never spoke to one who was consciously aware of what they were doing, all they knew was that they had a safehouse inside them, where they could hold their mind when things came on top. But here's the thing: because they were not consciously aware of their ark, they were unable to employ it as a transferable skill in other areas of their life.

One legend I worked with could hold his center when fighting four violent thugs outside a city bar, but he fell apart like a cheap suit when he lost his day job, because he didn't understand that *threat is threat*, no matter where it comes from, and the process of creating an eye wall was the same. Another stalwart held his shit when faced with a gangster, wielding a sawn-off, but had a mental breakdown when his wife left him, and a subsequent depression stole his center like a rattle from a child: it was the same threat, it was the same rush of terror-hormones, it was just wearing a different hat. The key is being able to construct your eye wall and use it not just in other areas of your life, but in every area of your life.

In order to build the eye wall, and subsequently be protected in the blue-sky-center of any crisis, you have to first become aware of your own *"observer self."*

The following exercise will help you to identify him.

Close your eyes. In your mind, take your attention to your right foot. Hold it there. Your mind will feel the urge to roam. Most people don't use this muscle very often, so it is underdeveloped and weak. Resist this temptation to drift. Hold the attention firmly on your foot. Now move the attention to your left foot, feel the tingle of blood in your skin and muscle and veins, then move it to the left big toe. Hold the attention.

Try and make your big toe throb, as though a rush of blood is being pumped to the very end of your nail.

Did you manage to do it?

You have just located your observer.

The observer is the inner part of you, the self, that directed your attention to your foot/big toe. All you need to do now is put the observer to work and build it like an internal power lifter, so that you can hold your attention in any part of your body or on any object for as long as you choose. Once you have developed a sinewy observer, you can build an eye wall, and retreat to the center of any storm at any time. If you are suffering with fear or anxiety (which attracts your attention like metal filings to a magnet) you can use the observer, like a shepherd, to gather your scattered energy and march it into the center of your being. As confirmed etymologically (see endnote 10) the ark, the center of our being is anatomically located in the trunk, or chest (the heart) area of the human body.

C.S. Lewis condemned a society of "men without chests." He insisted that "without the aid of trained emotions, the intellect is powerless against the animal organism." He also assures us that "in battle it is not syllogisms and logical argument that will keep the reluctant nerves and muscles to their post in the third hour of bombardment. The head rules the belly through the chest. The chest is the seat of magnanimity. This chest magnanimity and sentiment are indispensable liaison officers between cerebral man and visceral man."

And what is magnanimity? It comes from the Latin magnanimitās, from magna "big," and animus "soul, spirit"; it is the virtue of being great of mind and heart. It encompasses, "usually, a refusal to be petty, a willingness to face danger, and actions for noble purposes."

First you engage the observer self, and then the observer situates itself firmly in the chest (or the ark, or as we have called it here, the eye wall), this creates a powerful centripetal force that gathers all the scattered and wayward attention towards itself and holds it there.

The observer is the gatekeeper to your attention, the heart is the holding pen for the same energy.

What is attention?

It is the essence of the human soul, no less.

This seminal energy contains the building blocks to your entire reality. It is invaluable! Why do you think that so many bodies – adverse forces, politicians, bankers, dogmatic religions, TV, Radio, tabloids, the Internet, people, people selling people, people selling commodities – are always vying for your attention? And they are quite happy to trick it or steal it from you if you won't sell it.

And man, do we sell it cheaply.

As little as a salacious newspaper headline can have us lusting our vital attention over the juicy details. The Great Earth is a parasitical-paradise, the demons are only ever one click-bait away from a delicious meal: it would be no exaggeration to say that these adverse forces are trying to steal our attention at all times.

Ask yourself, throughout the day: "Where is my attention, where is my attention, **where** is my attention?"

If it is entangled in resentment, if it is still being syphoned off by an enemy who slighted you ten years ago, twenty years ago, if it is being hijacked by hate or fear or dissonance, then your attention is not your own.

When the attention is stolen by the strong emotions, draw it back to the eye.

If your attention is being seduced by the sirens of passion, draw it back to the neutral center.

If you find your attention wandering inappropriately, rein it back into the ark.

You can practice this technique at any time: eventually you will so value and so prize your attention that you will practice it all the time.

In Christian theology this is called "being in constant prayer."

In other words, our attention is constantly on God (the observer is an attribute of God, so if we are centered on the observer, we are centered on God).

The Quakers call this technique "centering down."

When the cyclone of crisis cuts a path through our life, we draw all our attention inwards and we "center down," we create an ark, we enter the eye, and we stay there until the storm has passed.

In the perfect center of the eye there will be no discomfort at all, nothing. In fact, if we are in the middle of the eye there can be no storm, there can only be peace. But holding dead center consistently takes Olympic level practice and a Titan will.

This means that the ark or eye wall does not always completely shield us from the effects of strong passions, just as elements of a cyclone will seep through the wall now and then and make themselves known. You will always be aware that there is a storm on your periphery, and you may feel the dull, background ache of chaos trying to break through, but it is greatly diminished, it is manageable.

If the art of ark building is perfected, it creates a human black hole at the very center of our being (known in Chinese philosophy as the dantien), or what the Taoists call "the magic bowl": anything that goes into it, is literally disappeared.

On the doors it was not unusual to have to stay in the eye for weeks and months at a stretch, when violence in the club spilled into threats of reprisal at our homes.

If we hold the eye for long enough eventually the external storm will be sucked into and through the eye (as mentioned), into nothingness. I have personally experienced and witnessed this phenomenon many times, it is a miracle to observe. With no engagement, with no identification, with nothing to feed from, all storms eventually dissipate.

In esoteric lore this is accepted as the highest level of practice: it is called "doing nothing."

To sit in the ark, is to do nothing – no engagement, no identification – until the storm has passed.

It is also known as "choiceless awareness." We are aware, we witness, but we make no choices.

Doing nothing, is all of the dharma (to quote Dogen).

If we perfect this one technique, we will become masters, not just of our emotions, but captains of the world.

But of course, doing nothing takes practice, practice, practice.

It took Noah 100 years to build his ark: basically, the parable is warning us that it is a singularly difficult task, and it will take time to achieve.

Oh, and don't expect assistance or understanding from others.

When Noah asked his fellow citizens for help building the ark, they not only refused him, but they also ridiculed him, they thought he was mentally unstable. They didn't believe there would be a flood, so they saw no profit in building an ark.

The story of Noah is giving us a heads-up: don't expect help, or support or even understanding from other people when you say to them, "There's going to be a flood and I have been called to build an ark. Inside myself."

Like lifting weights in the gym. I find that building the resistance and developing your inner strength one small disc at a time is preferable to sliding four x twenty kilo discs onto an Olympic bar and trying to press it off your chest on the first session.

Meditation is a good place to start – it is an excellent way of developing an eye wall, because it demands that we lock our attention on a single word or phrase or object (like a lighted candle or a mantra) and use it to hold our attention there. It also allows us to locate the observer and build a little cerebral muscle on him.

It is said that Sri Aurobindo developed such a powerful eye wall that when a hurricane swept through his Ashram in Pondicherry, India, every building was rocked except the room where he was sat writing, which remained completely calm, and absolutely unaffected.

In conclusion I would say that there is nothing like a real life crisis if you want to force-grow an eye wall: in many respects, you can't have an ark, unless you experience a flood, just as there can be no eye wall without a hurricane.

Reason Ten (to ninety-nine): Love

Until we see the Buddha behind the rabid dog, until we see the Christ behind the diseased leper, we will never be free from illusion.

This is the nicest chapter in the book, but it is also the toughest chapter, to write, to articulate and to implement into our lives because it is all about love.

Love is the 10th reason to forgive.

When we remove the scab of resentment, we reveal the healing wound of love.

There was a famous Buddhist saint called Asanga who made it his life's purpose to sit in meditation day and night so that he could cleanse his mind in order that he might see Maitreya (the Buddha). After twelve years of dedicated effort and with no joy Asanga fell into despair and lost his faith. He suffered the dark night of the soul where purpose was replaced by doubt and deep depression, and there seemed to be no point in anything. Deciding that he'd had enough of seeking, Asanga left the cave that had been his home for over a decade and headed home. On his journey back, bereft and defeated, lost in the wilderness of his own sorrow and perceived failure, he happened upon a rabid dog lying in the street. The dog only had its two front legs, its back legs had been eaten away by disease. Trying to drag itself along the street, the decrepit dog barked at all in close proximity and tried to bite anyone who approached. Asanga witnessed the suffering of the dog and fell immediately into a spontaneous and overwhelming compassion. Whilst everyone else in the busy street walked past and ignored the rabid dog, Asanga got onto his hands and knees and tried to help it and assuage its pain. He was so moved by its hunger and its plight that he even cut a lump of flesh from his own thigh to feed it.

On close inspection he could see that the dog's wounds were

riddled with maggots. As Asanga tried to remove them with his fingers he fell into compassion again, this time for the maggots. He didn't want to hurt the dog but equally he did not want to squash the maggots when he removed them with his clumsy fingers. So, he closed his eyes, and leaned in towards the dog's weeping-wound with the intention of removing the maggots harmlessly with his tongue.

Suddenly the dog disappeared.

In its place stood the Maitreya.

Overwhelmed with love for the Buddha, Asanga bowed and prostrated himself in reverence. Then, in a moment of confusion he said to Maitreya, "I've been meditating in a cave for twelve years, but you never came to me. Why didn't you come to me? Where were you?"

The Buddha replied, "I was always with you, I was never not with you, I have been with you all the time. It was only when you demonstrated compassion for the rabid dog that you were able to see me."

The Buddha was behind the rabid dog.

Charity, works, love, they are more edifying than a library of books.

Those who had not done the work, the internal cleansing, would not have even seen the dog, let alone the deity behind it, much like people walk past rough sleepers every day in towns and cities around the world without seeing them. Those who have done a little cleansing *will* see the rabid dog or the rough sleeper or a distasteful person, but nothing more.

Those who develop compassion for all living creatures will see the Buddha behind the rabid dog: behind all of his distressing disguises they will witness the Tathagata (Buddha).

Similarly, when St. Francis was still an aspirant, he too was given the challenge of finding compassion for the things that repelled him. After confessing his debilitating fear of lepers, God instructed him to find a leper and kiss him on the cracked and bleeding lips. Francis thought this instruction insane and immediately denied the voice and eschewed the instruction, thinking it the work of a devil. When the instruction was repeated again and again, Francis eventually relented, found a leper and embraced it. He described in his writings the smell of the leper, so odorous with his rotting skin that he could taste it, and the sight of the wounds and sores and decaying fingers made him feel immediately repulsed. However, as instructed by the voice of God, he embraced the leper, and when he did, when he kissed his lips and wrapped him in a cloak and lifted him in his arms to carry him to a refuge, the leper disappeared: Francis realized that he was nothing more than a manifestation of his own sins. Before his conversion, Francis had been wealthy, he courted many women, and he went to war twice seeking vainglory. His history was littered with sin and the moment he realized this, he had a vision of the Christ behind the leper.

Compassion for the leper enabled Francis to see the Christ behind the disease. His greatest revelation, however, was still to come: it was only on witnessing (a vision of) Christ that Francis realized the true truth: he was not afraid of the leper, not really, he was not afraid of standing before his own sins, it was not that at all; rather he was greatly but unconsciously afraid of the bitter cup of truth that would be revealed to him on removing both. He was afraid to look at undiluted, unadulterated, pure Love in concentrate.

As it turned out, he need not have worried: the Christ energy that he was exposed to, on kissing the leper, greeted him like an unconditional father embracing his prodigal son.

Compassion is love.

But, as the poet Rumi warns us: "Love is not a subtle argument, the door there is devastation."

When you talk about love, people think you have gone soft, they think you've gone all socks-and-sandals, that you are presenting a soft modality for a hard world problem; not so.

There is no harder problem than love because in order to access love – which is there all the time, it is the Constant – you have to first eschew everything that is not love. And (to reiterate) once love is revealed, the residue of anti-love that might still be resident in you, will be devastated: on contact with love, it is wiped clean, like unprocessed camera film, exposed prematurely to light.

Saying the word love, adding the word to the end of your text or e-mail or birthday message *is not love*. Love is only love when you feel it for all sentient beings, even and especially the ones that repel you.

Love is always there.

It is the backboard to our reality.

It is the dark invisible matter that holds our universe together.

It is the space between words, the silence behind thoughts, the still nothingness that supports and connects and holds together all of our noisy, busy *somethings*, our life.

Love is the most available constant.

It is the only constant.

It is the Yaqeen, the *certainty*, it is At Tawwab the *repentance*, it is Ar-Rahman the *compassion*, As-Shakur the *gratitude*, Al Ghaffar the *all forgiving*. It is *this* and it is all the other 95 names for Allah (the God). They are ever available but often missed in the busy rush to get in, to get out, to get on, to get off, to get rich, to get laid, to get famous or to simply get by. People miss love in all of its 99 attributes because they are so possessed of opinion, of fear, of judgment, of criticism, of envy, of greed, of anger and rage and dissonance.

Much of the world currently lives off these negative energies, and the same energies live off them. The masses feast on the fast-food of fame and fortune and fighting and fornication because they have forgotten that the fine-dining of divine love is not just on the menu, **it is the menu**. They have forgotten about love in the greedy rush for hollow crowns and specious titles and fool's gold.

All vice is "devastated" when it stands before love.

This is not just a matter of adding a few inspiring lines at the end of your company mission statement, nor is it about wearing your charity-coat twice a year or clapping your hands in appreciation for the NHS on a Thursday night at 8pm with all your neighbors. It is none of these things, even though it might include all of the above. It is about shutting your mouth, opening your ears and your eyes and your mind and seeing and hearing and feeling the plight of people's pain and struggle and allowing yourself to be overwhelmed with compassion for their suffering.

Everyone has suffered.

Everyone is suffering.

Everyone will suffer again in the future.

When we open our hearts to compassion *now* for other people – the saint or the sinner, the good citizen, or the barking dog of criminality – we do not just access love for our fellow beings, we access compassion for ourselves. Our whole being is infused with the healing power of love, the elixir of life, when we call it forward for others. I may have said it elsewhere (it stands repeating) but the secret, the blueprint of the universe is delivered in a single line from the Zohar: "The master sets the table for the servants before he eats himself."

If you want love, first find someone who needs love.

If you really want to understand something, anything (it is all available), first set the table by finding a person or persons or a party that needs to understand it more and bring it down for their benefit.

When you call it down for them, you automatically call it down for you.

Do not think that your righteous campaigns to right wrongs in the world will make any difference if you are not working from the source of love.

If there is agenda, it is not love.

If fiscal profit is your secret aim, it is not love.

If personal recognition is important to you, it is not love.

If you are looking for followers, it is not love.

If you desire recognition or accolades for your charity, it is not love.

If you are upset when you or your work are overlooked, it is not love.

If you feel the need to tell people about your charity, it is not love.

If you think yourself special, because of your contribution, it is not love.

If you criticize others, because they are not as kind as you, or as spiritually advanced as you, or as busy doing good as you, it is not love.

If you feel the need to advertise your *giving* in your company brochure, it is not love.

If you find yourself on a judgmental campaign to expose the fraudulent in society when you are still full of sin yourself, do it if you must, but please, don't fool yourself: it is not love.

Your illusory ends do not justify your foolish means.

Stop busying yourself with the tilting lance of judgment; you are not aiming it at monsters, only windmills. You have no right pointing out the mote in a fellow's eye when you still have a plank sticking out of your own eye.

If you really want to help, stop hunting down fallen angels in the world and start dealing with the devil in your own bathroom mirror.

Hate and anger and grudge only muddy the water.

Call on love for the sinner as keenly as you call on love for yourself.

The most splendid acts of charity, even those that raise millions of pounds, are merely "clanging symbols and noisy gongs" if they do not have love.

Find a way to serve with love and compassion if you want your charity to mean something. And lest we forget, it is not the benefactor of our aligned compassion who gets the most from the gift, it is the bestower who receives the greatest reward when the giving comes from love.

The Rabbis of lore were always on the lookout for "charity carriers," needy beings through whom they could earn divine merit by offering holy service.

It is we that benefit when we give from love, and the person who receives our giving allows us to profit from the charity by accepting our gift.

The Rabbis would often spot a needy person in the street begging and say to each other, "Let us put a coin in his bowl and some food in his belly and be the first to win merit through him."

To access love is easy in principle, but extremely hard in practice.

If you want to begin today (I highly recommend you do), start **not** by increasing your list of worthy charities, rather, by reducing your list of unworthy habits.

The best way to help others is first to remove all the personal traits that might harm you and them. As these are reduced, your ability to receive love will expand and the opportunities to capitalize on your charity will become immediately evident.

They say that *reality is, but it is somewhere else.*

That *somewhere else* is love.

And what is love?

It is not an emotion; I know that much.

It is not a sentiment or a feeling, although it may include all of these.

Love is non-local.

Love is its own place.

It is the frequency behind all frequencies, it is the I Am, before science and academia, it is the density at the back of every density; it is not in space or time, but it is space-time; it is not in the known, but you can experience it in the abstract. It is the fabled *kingdom* of the New Testament, it is the Promised Land of Israel, it is the *still center* of Buddhism, it is Zoroaster's Edenic garden, it is the *utopia* of philosophy, the *omega point* of cosmology, the *geometric point* of construction, it is *home* to the travelling pilgrim, it is the *crown* on the tree of life, it is the *fixed cross* behind the clanging chaos of this moving world, it is the Jewish *shamayin*, the *seven lakes of heaven* in the Vedas, the *Jannah* (the final abode of the righteous in Islam) and for the Sikhs it is *the paradise* that can be experienced in the here and now, if you are balanced, if you are in tune with God.

The 10th reason to forgive is Love, because, when we forgive our resentments from our mind, Love is revealed.

Budo Practice

I said to my wife once, "We have too many weeds in the garden." She replied sagely, "We don't have too many weeds, we just don't have enough flowers."

The flowers are our attention. The weeds only occur when we lose our attention, and it drifts, or it is snaffled from us by unnecessary distractions.

We do not need less weeds, we need our attention to be so strong, so firm, so under the control of our conscious will that there's no room for weeds.

Weeds only grow where there is room for weeds to grow.

Love is the only constant, it is the backboard to all of our programs, those learned or inherited concepts and precepts, the entrancing lift-music of our social conditioning. Often when I advise people to practice gratitude every day, or to love their enemies as themselves, the advice falls on deaf ears because they think, "How can I love someone who has hurt me?"

The flower of love can't blossom because the garden of our mind is overrun with weeds.

As my wife suggested, if we hold our attention on the positives, on the flowers, there will be no room and no space for the weeds to grow. St. Thomas Aquinas assures us that virtue is destroyed or lessened through the cessation from act. In other words, if we do not busy our lives with acts of virtue, the void will be filled by the fancies of any negative energy form that happens to pass by.

The budo of this chapter, is this: if Love is the panacea, then ultimately our only job, the one and only thing we need to solve all of our problems is reveal the love that is already there. In the teaching addendum of this final chapter, I would like to encourage you to forensically examine your lives, root out all the inputs that are not coming from a place of love, and clinically remove them, one by one. For instance: the news (morning, noon, and night) is a 24 hour "fear fest." "What bleeds leads" on the television bulletins and in the popular press. It is hard to access love when we are being spoon-fed twenty horror stories every day before breakfast. Using all the tools we have developed in the previous chapters, we have to practice self-observance, and constantly ask ourselves, "Where is my attention?"

Ask yourself too, "Will this food lead me home?"

If we actively studied at university for the number of hours that we passively imbibe negativity through the television screen we would all be Doctors of Philosophy in no time at all.

Remove everything from your existence that you know does not have love at its root and replace it with everything that does.

We do this by mastering our attention.

We choose to invest our attention only in the things that are beneficial, to us and to our world. We can stop watching nihilistic and conspiratorial dramas and start reading inspirational manna. We can stop gossiping about friends and colleagues and people we don't even know and start quietly looking for and talking about and encouraging their qualities. Certainly, we can stop judging them.

If we plant more metaphoric flowers, and stop feeding the weeds, love will become our constant. It will be so concentrated that it will radiate out from our center and form a protective shield all around us.

Do you currently entertain a lot of passions that lead your attention astray?

What is the chief passion amongst them, your weak spot, the Achilles' heel, the trait that quietly and overtly distracts your inner and outer gaze?

If your attention is inside your body, you can work, you are in charge, your autonomy is safeguarded.

If your attention is outside of the body, you can't work, you are impotent, just another automaton, walking blindly with the masses.

(As I mentioned somewhere else) if you strike the shepherd, the sheep will scatter.

I call this the 1-in-10-rule. I learned it from a legendary fighter who ran a bar in one of the roughest districts in England.

I will call him Mr. J.

Mr. J was a notorious character, the breweries in the area hired him like a latter-day Sheriff when one of their saloons experienced problems with the local cowboys. Whenever he took over a new bar, especially in the wild west of Coventry, he knew that his authority would definitely be challenged, often violently and usually within a few days of putting his name above the door. He had a simple process, Mr. J: he observed the bar for the first few days of his new tenancy in order to establish which of the locals constituted the greatest threat: who was the leader? In the last bar he ran (he is retired now) he quickly recognized who the resident gunslinger was, he identified the 1 in 10.

I will call this man Mr. K.

As soon as he identified Mr. K as the dominant threat to his authority, he invited him, very genially, to meet for a "private chat." Immediately after entering the secluded cellar under the bar, Mr. J took off his jacket, and said (I'm paraphrasing), "I can see that you're the loudest noise in my bar, and I can see that a lot of your followers are looking to kick off at the first opportunity. I just want you to know that if any of them make a fuss on my premises, I am going to hold you personally responsible, and I am going to come for you. If you don't like that, take your jacket off and we can settle it here and now, man to man." Usually when offered a one-on-one fight, most bullies become iron mongers and "make a bolt for the door." This was certainly the case with Mr. K, who lost his bottle quick-smart and backed down.

In order that Mr. K did not lose face in front of his followers, Mr. J put his arm around his shoulder as they reentered the bar (so that everyone could see and hear) and told the barmaid to "get my friend here a drink please. On the house."

Mr. K never lost face in front of his friends and Mr. J established his authority in the bar.

By controlling the 1, he automatically controlled the 10.

What is your 1 in 10?

What is the one thing you can control, that will automatically wipe out all lesser opposition?

Write it down.

Make plans to confront it on your own terms.

Make this your daily practice from now on.

If you can control the 1, the 1 will take care of the other 9.

Final Words

This book is not asking you to abandon your responsibilities on the great earth just because reciprocity settles its own accounts.

I am not saying that it is OK for people to treat you badly, or cruelly, or criminally. Reciprocity does call in all receipts, of that I am certain, but that does not deny you the right to justice, or recompense, or apology in the here and now if you have been wronged in the manifest world.

We might very well need to have our say, demand an explanation, have our day in court, or suffer the six stages of grieving and loss, and there is nothing wrong with that, often it is a very necessary point of closure, of healing, of social justice.

Society has its laws, which are sometimes successful in bringing criminals to justice. At other times it is lapse in its duty; often it does not recognize its duty at all, and fails to admit and arrest injustice, even when it happens in plain sight.

Divine law often works through the human judiciary and through the human being, but it does not rely on or need the conscious assistance of either. In the full span of time, wrongs are always righted, credits are always paid, debts are called in and the books are always balanced.

This is a self-levelling universe.

Our own personal ledgers are written with every thought we think, with every word we speak, and with every deed we do. Sooner or later, each soul, responsible for each life, will be called on by law to present their accounts, and the good of their life will be weighed and measured against the bad.

It is down to you to make sure that your balance sheet falls to the good, and not concern yourself too much about the misdeeds of someone else, anyone else. Bad people often redress their negative accounts privately and far away from the eyes of mortal men, out of sight of your witness, but it is always under the eyes of God. Their repentance may happen at the final curtain; they may *return* on the last leg, they could become saints like Milarepa, like Angulimala, like St. Paul, like Mandela, not just despite their violent and murderous history, but because of it.

Equally, the saint may fall at the final hurdle; he may be netted by the trapper in a moment of wild folly or human weakness and ruin a lifetime of good deeds in a moment of wonton excess.

Unless you are omniscient and able to track every action of every soul from cradle to grave, you are never going to know.

This should not concern you.

It is not your job to keep count, or take stock, or hold the world to account.

I have encountered several men like this in my time, playing judge and jury over others when their own life was fat with sin. I am embarrassed to say that I have been one of them, projecting onto others what I am most guilty of myself.

This is an exciting time, this is exciting news, it is unburdening you, it is telling you to let go of the world (you fool), you don't know anything about it, you haven't got a clue.

How do I know that?

Basic psychology will tell you that the men or women who are busy judging the wrongs of others are doing so because they are frightened to get double-busy judging the wrongs of themselves.

A man of arrogant pretention once asked the Dalai Lama, "How are we going to fix this broken world?" The Dalai Lama looked at him for a second with a scrutinizing glare and said pointedly, "Perhaps you should start by fixing *your* broken world."

In Zoroastrian theology, they stipulate the importance of following the Three-Fold Path of Asha (right behavior), which revolves around good thoughts, good words and good deeds with a heavy emphasis on spreading happiness, mostly through charity (Love). It is made clear in the Gathas (hymns said to have been written by the prophet Zoroaster himself and that form the core of the Zoroastrian liturgy) that each human is capable of making choices and is thus responsible for their own actions. The world, it insists, is relying on each individual to live their own good life and balance their own accounts; they are not here to make sure that others balance theirs.

The world might not like you when you get busy mending your own ways, and stop joining their orgy of drama and judgment, but your job, my job, *our work* is not to look to our fellow man for a moral compass, rather it is to take example from the higher authority of our own conscience.

If you are awake, she will speak to you keenly when you fall wide of the narrow path, when you slip into the broad-way of the sleeping masses.

I will leave you if I may with a quote from *Jane Eyre*:

If the whole world despised you, but your own conscience absolved you of guilt, you would not be without friends.

Be well.
Geoff Thompson 2021

P.S. I promised you in the title of this book, *99 Reasons to Forgive*; I only delivered ten. But, of course, you probably already guessed that the other 89, the other 189, 1089 ad infinitum are all included in the 10th reason to forgive: Love.

Every reason to forgive, every reason to live, is in Love.

Appendix: Quantum Entanglement

Before I begin: a little about quantum entanglement, bearing in mind that I am no scientist, and these are merely amateur observations, similes that I hope might help you to disentangle from the abusive experiences of your past.

Wikipedia tells us that

> **Quantum entanglement** is a physical phenomenon that occurs when a pair or group of particles is generated, interact, or share spatial proximity in a way such that the quantum state of each particle of the pair or group cannot be described independently of the state of the others, including when the particles are separated by a large distance.

When I read this, I am reading about my own life.

As I mentioned earlier in the book, I was abused by a beloved teacher when I was a child. You could say that by grooming and abusing me, he forced the two of us into an unholy quantum entanglement: he was in me, literally, in my thoughts, in my mind, in my physical body, in my psyche, and in my memories: actually, he was embedded and entangled into my very cells. Worse than this, he had taken over (much of) my body of conscious will. His abuse stole my autonomy. In Judaic liturgy, personal will is considered to be the literal kingdom of God, the promised land, the land of milk and honey, so in hijacking my will, he took the helm of my fleshy spaceship, he took all of me. And I was equally entangled in him, in his mind and in his conscience, he carried his sin against me and all the other kids he so heinously wounded in every cell of his body too and he would never be free from us (and what he did to us) until we found the courage to break the unholy bond. This became evident when I met him serendipitously decades after the crime and I forgave him from my mind: in doing so I effectively delivered him from my being. Quantumly, I disentangled myself from the particle-demon of abuse.

Before I broke the connecting thread, the two of us could "not be described independently of the state of the other," even when we were separated by a long span of time and by large distances. We still (albeit unconsciously and unknowingly) interacted and shared spatial proximity, even though geographically we lived miles apart and didn't see each other for decades.

How could we not be connected: he was in me; he was a part of me.

In the quantum, entangled particles are so intricately connected that there is no longer even a need for communication between them, the particles can be thought of as one object.

Many of my actions and decisions and directions in life *post abuse* were caused and directed by his negative presence in me. I physically and mentally and sexually abused myself for decades after our encounter because I was entangled with him, albeit unknowingly and against my own will. He had implanted a parasitical elemental in me, a "particle" that regularly took over my will, stole my autonomy, and acted for me, through me, against me, from me and as me for most of my adult life. The worse thing about this entanglement was the fact that – because of the covert nature of abuse – I was not consciously aware of the connection, I no longer knew where I ended, and he began. I was not aware at the time that I had been possessed by (or entangled with) my abuser, I just thought myself a deviant, and my negative actions the result of a disturbed and depraved mind.

How can you remove a cognitional parasite when you don't even know that it is there?

I was loosely aware that, during my periods of self-abuse, I was not myself, and that I didn't want to do the things I was doing, but I could not articulate this enough to locate it as a parasite that needed to be removed. It was only after I was shaken violently awake by the harbinger of depression in my early twenties, that I decided to challenge my unhappy existence and replace fear and depression with a curiosity and enquiry that later became my raison d'être.

You may well ask, why I am introducing quantum entanglement into a book about forgiveness? Because as far as I can see, the squatter of abuse (if not removed) is entanglement at the deepest quantum level of our being. And... the science of unravelling particles that have become entangled might offer some clues as to how we can unpick the abuse that has burrowed itself into and wrapped itself around the organs and sinews and neurons of our being.

There is a beautiful verse in the Kabbalah (I have touched on this elsewhere) that says, "If you would forgive your enemy, first injure him." It sounds oxymoronic I know; if I am going to forgive my enemy, why injure him first? Read as allegory (which the Kabbalists insist we must do with all biblical liturgy) the verse is suggesting that the parasite of abuse by its very nature entangles itself so comprehensively in us that – like a quantumly entangled particle – the abused and the abuser, the parasite and its host can be thought of as one: they are in us, just as a virus or an illness or a disease is in us, and, until it is removed or healed, it effectively is us.

The world pain-body

These entangled particles (or people) are not acting alone: when two particles become entangled (you and your abuser) by an abusive event, they are both the victims of a greater force, they become connected to and entangled with a larger body (a sort of mother ship), a huge and independent matrix of entangled particles (what the mystic Eckhart Tolle calls "the world pain-body" and Sri Aurobindo called "the adverse forces") making up an interwoven community of invisible invaders and influencers.

In this greater, negative "many-bodied entanglement" the whole is greater than the sum of its parts. The particles act together like a single entity whose identity lies not with the individual but on a non-local plane; it becomes (a part of) a negative collective, something larger than itself, and individual autonomy is lost to it.

Entanglement with this singularity would be fine and, in esoteric practice, even encouraged if the surrender was done willingly and to a creative, divine force, whose intentions were benevolent, but of course, the demonic body of adverse forces feeds only on suffering and pain and destruction and so should be repelled at all costs.

This force of evil is an independent amorphous body that invades, possesses, and corrupts the human psyche of (initially) one person, who then *like the walking dead* proceeds to pass the parasite of abuse onto others through their own subsequent acts of cruelty and unkindness. This can be, and it often is fast-spreading like a virus: Nazism, fascism and communism are three potent examples of how brutally and violently and rapidly this "fire" can race through the bones of society when the conditions are right: it acts *as* people and *from* people, but it is not a human force, rather it is a disparate energy source that works through people: it roams the atmospheric plains like the Lion of scripture, hunting for vulnerable prey.

Because it acts as one with us, and it feeds from us, of course it will resist its own removal violently, as though its very life depends upon it, because of course it does: "The Lion perishes (to extend the metaphor) for want of prey." (Job 4:11)

Because it is so deeply entangled in us, we will have to weaken it (or injure it) to make removal – forgiveness – easier.

Postdoc Fellow Georg Endress assures us that, "entanglement is like a thread that goes through every single one of our individual cells, telling them how to connect to one another."

When we have been abused, but have failed to remove the

resident parasite, it connects to us through all of our cells, and feeds off our suffering. When we break the thread with Truth or Love, this injures or weakens the parasite, which makes removal easier.

How can we injure our enemy before we forgive them?

Quantum science has a few proven ideas that might help.

We can injure it greatly by denying it food (our attention), we do this by **observing** the emotions that rise in us (anger, fear, depression, dissonance, rage etc.) without emotionally engaging them or identifying with them. Quantum entanglement only has to be observed by a dispassionate and objective eye (called the "observer" or "witness") for it to disentangle. We watch the emotions rise with curiosity, and with amazement we watch them fall: if they are not engaged, they will eventually perish. As with forgiveness in the conventional sense, we may have to practice this exercise of dispassionate observation or choiceless awareness many times before the emotions completely lose their power, loosen their hold and collapse (see *The Power of Now* by Eckhart Tolle for a comprehensive instruction on this process).

We injure them by changing our **environment**, inner and outer. Entangled states can easily disappear or collapse when the environment changes even slightly. Abuse tends to take place away from public view, in secret locations, in dark places, that is how it is able to thrive. The act of observing an entangled state destroys it, just as abuse that is seen/observed can prevent it from happening in the first place. It is particular environments that encourage and allow entanglement to occur and germinate – changing the environment "encourages" them to untangle.

Abuse of a child stops when the crime is observed and as a consequence the child is removed from harm's way. Similarly, domestic abuse stops when the abused party is removed from the volatile environment. The 16th century Ronin Samurai Miyomato Musashi used a similar process of softening or injury in his many life and death battles with other Samurai. In order to weaken his opponents before the kill, he would "attack the four corners": he would injure their legs and arms, leaving them unable to effectively attack, or properly defend themselves, thus making the finishing blow, the coup de grâce, a mere formality. Similarly, when I worked in security, I often injured potential attackers with psychological attacks (see my book *Watch My Back* for greater detail on this process) before either evicting them from the club or defeating them in a fight (this was only if the opportunity for over-the-table negotiations did not present itself or had already passed). I mentioned earlier about the Homerian strategy of vaunting: mentally defeating the enemy with verbal posturing.

With regard to the man who sexually abused me: to *injure* him before I forgave him proper and in order to break his hold prior to "forgiving him from my mind," I changed my inner environment by courting curiosity and enquiry, by studying, by talking about and practicing the esoteric strategies of metaphysical power. I then changed my outer environment, by removing myself from all places and all people and all situations that contributed to abuse. When I became entangled in the world of violence and crime (as another for-instance) I changed my inner aesthetic by massively educating myself out of an ignorant and insecure mindset. According to the ancient Judaic wisdom of the Zohar "all forces of evil are dominant at night; they rule at night." Allegorically, this means that evil can only exist in ignorance. "Night" is esoteric code for lack of awareness or knowing, just as "light" is code for knowledge or consciousness. "That which is exposed to light must itself become light and everything that is illuminated becomes a light." (Ephesians 5:13)

There are many ways to interpret this multifaceted verse, but the most obvious is this: knowledge dispels ignorance, truth shines a light on falsehood, until falsehood is converted and itself becomes truth.

After I changed my inner aspect, I removed myself from the outer environment that supported it: I stopped studying and training in violent martial arts, I gave up my job as a nightclub bouncer, and I immersed myself wholesale into the word and world of budo.

Changing the environment has a massive effect on entanglement: as I mentioned before, if we take a Lion out of its usual habitat and put it in an environment with no natural prey, it will assuredly die for want of food (unless it goes vegan and develops a penchant for grass and vegetation).

According to the latest in quantum science, the grand solution to entanglement *is* entanglement. We replace a negative entanglement with a positive entanglement. In a neurological quirk of the human species, our brains are incapable of experiencing fear and curiosity at the same time (I mentioned this earlier). I weakened the thread of abusive entanglement with powerful curiosity.

Curiosity *is* an inner environment; it is a state, a positive entanglement. Enquiry too is an inner environment and a distinct state. If fear and curiosity are incapable of existing in the same space at the same time, then by simply changing our perception (from fear to enquiry/from depression to curiosity) we dull or completely remove our fear. Fear feeds from fear, and pain feeds from pain, this dense body of negativity that pervades the atmosphere feeds off all human suffering, but it cannot abide, and it certainly cannot digest the joy present in curiosity or enquiry.

I wanted to know why I was depressed, I wanted to know why I was in pain, why I was so afraid, and why someone who abused me at the age of eleven was still abusing me *remotely, in my mind and in his absence* thirty years later, and many miles apart. Although I was suffering and in pain, this powerful anomaly fascinated me, and I wanted to understand it, I was hungry to know it. Rather than being entangled in thoughts of abuse and injustice, and fantasies of revenge, I instead changed my perception and made my life a full-time study on how one might escape the grip of abuse, and better still find a grander, kinder force to entangle with.

Truth and faith injures entanglement too, and mortally so. On first reading, the attributes of truth and faith might not seem like potent weapons in the war of attrition, but they are mighty tools indeed, certainly if we understand their true properties. In St. Paul's epistles, the letters of advice and instruction he wrote to his followers in Rome (who were facing daily and deadly persecution for their Christian beliefs), he told them: "If your enemy is hungry, feed him; if he is thirsty, give him something to drink. In doing this, you will heap burning coals on his head." (Romans 12:20)

Paul's advice is quantum: it is didactic instruction on how to disentangle from the parasite of fear. In esoteric parlance food and drink are code for *truth* and *faith*. If our enemy is hungry, it means he lacks the "food" of truth. If he is thirsty, it means he lacks the nourishment of faith. When we feed our enemy, when we give him drink, we inject him with both our truth and our faith (the latter being *certainty* in our truth) which act like a poison to them. Remember, ignorance and fear can "only rule at night," they enforce their power only in the dark: In other words, they can only exist in ignorance, so when we shine light on that ignorance with truth, with faith, they are injured, they are weakened, and they are eventually dissolved. When I confronted my abuser, I weakened him first by telling him the truth: "You abused me when I was a boy and you **cked my life." His power over me lay in the fact that he had groomed and gaslighted me to believe that the abuse was my fault, that I sanctioned it, that somehow, I wanted it. He didn't think he was abusing me, he rationalized his behavior by convincing himself that he was developing a relationship with me, and the other kids he abused. This heinous distortion, this blatant lie perpetuated the abuse, and fed the parasite in me and in him, it kept it alive. When I confronted him and told him the truth, that he (and not I) was culpable, that the abuse was all his doing, the lie, the ignorance, his weak rationalization was destroyed. My absolute certainty filled the room, it had a power that could not be rejected or denied. I watched him wither under the "food and drink" of my words. Once he was weakened, once I had injured him, only then did I offer him my forgiveness; I disentangled myself and gave him back to the force of reciprocity. The truth and faith removed the burning coals of his abuse from my being and "heaped" them on his head. In other words, I gave him back his parasite, and in so doing took back the autonomy, the will, the kingdom that he had stolen from me.

In the Hindu canon, Arjuna Pandava is the prince of the world, but his kingdom has been stolen from him by his corrupt cousins (his will/autonomy has been stolen by fear and ignorance). When he goes to war to win his kingdom back, his missile of choice is the fired arrow of truth. His weapon is the Bow of Gandiva, which consists of 108 celestial strings endued with great energy: it contained the strength of one lakh bow (100,000 times the power of a normal bow). The indestructible Gandiva bow is worshiped even by the celestials for its power. Arjuna is also given two infinite quills of arrows.

Allegorically the arrows represent missiles of truth, and the bow, the eye of certainty, or faith. The infinite arrows of truth are fired from the indestructible bow of certainty in order to kill the nefarious enemy, ignorance.

At the very onset of war, in the midst of the battlefield Arjuna falls into (becomes entangled by) the very fear and ignorance that has stolen his will. He is so afraid that he wants to renounce his kingdom and run away. In order to unburden the prince from fear, his friend and charioteer (Lord Krishna/his own higher consciousness) delivers a discourse of powerful truth (called the Bhagavad-Gita), which untangles Arjuna, allows him to enter the battlefield and win back his kingdom.

Lord Krishna offers Arjuna the optimum solution to the problem of quantum entanglement.

Entanglement.

Instead of being entangled in egoic fear and the concepts and precepts and dharma of established warfare, Arjuna is encouraged to entangle (or surrender) himself instead into the higher frequency of consciousness (which in this allegory is represented by Krishna, the Godhead).

Of course, in the Gita proper, the battle and the battleground at Kurukshetra, and the warriors are depicted as historical people and places, and recorded fact. But when you read into the original verses that the Gita is taken from (the Mahabharata and the Srimad Bhagavatam), Kurukshetra (even though it certainly does exist as a city in Northern India) is not described only as a geographical location but as a mental state. Lord Krishna describes the battleground as "the sea of nescience."

Nescience literally means "lack of knowledge or awareness."

Lord Krishna assures (and convinces) Prince Arjuna that "if you surrender to me" crossing the sea of nescience will be as easy as "stepping over the hoof print of a calf in the mud." When the Lord encourages Arjuna to surrender to him, he is (allegorically) telling him to swap negative entanglement for positive entanglement: he invites Arjuna to surrender himself to the *greater knowledge* or *wider awareness*, he encourages him to step outside the prison of his limiting beliefs ("surrender all dharmas"), his fear or ignorance and surrender to (entangle with) consciousness.

The dictionary denotation for consciousness is "a person's awareness or perception of something."

The Buddha said the same, when he told one of his followers that he was "freed from denotation by consciousness."

Denotation is our entanglement with concepts; consciousness is a state in which all concepts are transcended.

We disentangle from every lower state, by becoming deliberately entangled in the highest state.

This may sound simple I know, but as anyone who has become learned knows, while the principle might be fundamental, the process can be painful. As Aeschylus (an ancient Greek Tragedian) tells us, "He who learns must suffer" ("And even in our sleep pain that cannot forget falls drop by drop upon the heart, and in our own despair, against our will, comes wisdom to us by the awful grace of God").

He is talking here about the bitter cup of Christ.

It is the third law of Zeus: "No wisdom without pain."

To birth a new truth, we must first destroy the old paradigm, and many of the people we love and cherish will probably fall (and be lost to us) when we make such a paradigm shift, because if there is one thing the common man is prepared to fight and die for it is his right to defend his own limitations, even if they are steeped in ignorance.

Protection against future entanglement

The best way to protect against (future) entanglement, with suggestion, with conditioning, with abuse or an abuser, with fear or doubt or resentment or threat, is to find a center of certainty within ourselves (what the Buddhist calls the "still center") and entangle so deeply with this singularity, that our quantum computer (us) becomes robust enough so that the "noise" of the world does not perturb or confuse us, or create doubt, which breaks our connection with it.

We do this through the processes (laid out in this book) of disentangling from all aspects that prevent it, not least making sure that the entirety of our life comes from the center of our being. In Buddhism they call this "the three jewels," or the three refuges: these jewels are the teacher, the teaching and the community of likeminded souls. We become powerfully protected when we commit (entangle) our life to all three, to the exclusion of everything else.

When I trained in physical martial arts (for instance) I reached an elite standard of competence and protection because my whole life was dedicated to the learning of practical martial arts: the teachers, the teachings and the community around me were wall-to-wall combat training, this was my life, I lived and breathed it. To reach an elevated level of writing, the same process was observed: I dedicated my whole being to the written word.

When we skirt around the edges of a state – our faith, a commitment, a relationship, an ambition, or goal etc. – it is easily collapsed by negative, external stimulus: it is easy to be pulled out of a positive state if we are not deeply embedded in it, just as it is easy to pull a plant from the soil, if its roots are not deep. The deeper we commit, the more protected we become. Our truth is no longer based on a halfhearted commitment, or a surface wisdom, or intellectual understanding or a classroom education: rather, it is born from earned, experiential, Graced knowing. Our truth then is protected from instability, or what science calls *superposition* (when a wave interferes with or is diffracted by another wave. In other words, when our state is challenged by and made unstable by opposition: criticism, doubt or attack etc.). It is protected from instability because it is so deeply and so widely entangled that it becomes impossible for anyone or anything to disturb or expose it.

As an example: I remember once trying to pull a weed out of the tarmac on the driveway outside my old house. It was a tiny bit of weed, infinitesimally small and weak in comparison to me, and yet no matter how hard I tried to remove the weed it resisted. I later realized (after finally digging into the tarmac) that this tiny weed had burrowed its stem and its roots through the tarmac and the concrete and into the earth below. I was not just trying to pull a weed from my driveway, I was actually trying to lift the tons of tarmac and concrete and earth that it had entangled itself with. There was no longer any real separation between the weed and the tarmac: the weed and the tarmac were essentially one. Later, I used this enlightening piece of information when I decided to put a basketball hoop in the front garden for my son. Rather than simply concreting the metal post into the mud by the side of the house, I dug a hole right next to the driveway so that when I poured the concrete into the hole, I joined (I entangled) it with the concrete driveway underpinning it, which itself was connected to the road, which in turn was tied into the foundation of the whole estate. This hoop could never be pulled out of the ground because it was entangled with thousands of tons of connecting concrete.

Martial arts master and pioneer Morihei Ueshiba (the founder of Aikido) was once asked if he feared being challenged by other fighters (this was after he had become famous, and personal challenges to fight were a real possibility): he smiled and said he was not concerned at all, because if anyone approached him with bad intentions, they would immediately realize that they were taking on the whole universe. Ueshiba was so deeply entangled in the budo of his art, that he had connected to everything, he had become everything, and this was patently apparent to anyone that ventured into his proximity.

This happy conclusion suggests that entanglement to the dark *or* the light of the great earth is an inevitability, something we cannot avoid, just by proxy of our being on spaceship earth: ours is the human condition. But expanded awareness, knowledge and a developed will allow us to at least choose the character of our intercourse, anabolic rather than catabolic, good as opposed to evil, and thread our being into the very fabric of this divine absolute and become something larger than ourselves, something creative and beatific.

Ultimately then, the choice is not whether or not we wish to be entangled, rather it is what do we wish to be entangled with. And of course, as every adept knows, when we choose to entangle ourselves with the light, we find ourselves (as Rumi suggested) in a field of energy beyond good and bad, and ultimately that is the only place to meet.

I know what I have chosen, and my life is a miracle of inspirational possibilities because of it.

Endnotes

1. Budo is the esoteric sector of martial arts; it literally means "without arms."
2. Thomas Aquinas defines free will as the ability to choose, according to wisdom and love, what is truly good. Personal freedom is the result of continually making such choices.
3. In Buddhism this process is known as Dependent Arising and is considered to be all of the Dharma or teaching: "If there is this, there is that. If there is not this, there is not that." Arising phenomena depends entirely on our engagement for its reality.
4. The great psychic Edgar Cayce assures us that the planets do indeed affect our physical being, but (he insists) even the force of all the planets combined are not as powerful as the God-gifted human will... if we chose to exercise it.
5. I have added a specific chapter in the Appendix, all about quantum entanglement.
6. In Catholicism, venial sin is said to wound our relationship with God, whereas mortal sin separates us from Him completely, because it is enacted with full knowing. We are warned, however, that an accumulation of venial sins can also sever our bond to God.
7. The 70x7 expression (Matthew 18:21-22) is symbolic for infinity: it is said that Christians are called to forgive an infinite number of times because that is the number of times they are forgiven by God, and when a Christian fails to forgive, it becomes inconsistent with the infinite forgiveness of God.
8. I first made sure that the articles in question were not perjurious, that they did not contain any mistruths, or misrepresentations or full-fat lies.
9. "Enter in by the narrow gate; for wide is the gate and broad

is the way that leads to destruction, and many are those who enter in by it." (Matthew 7:13)

10. Ark in Hebrew is Tebah, which means "container" or chest, which is in "the trunk of the human body" ("arca" in the Latin bible), a container that protects something sacred. Ark is also related to "arcana, arcanum"; something hidden, a secret known only to those specially informed.

11. The flood is also known esoterically as the "Wet Holocaust" from the Greek meaning "burnt offering."

O-BOOKS

SPIRITUALITY

O is a symbol of the world, of oneness and unity; this eye represents knowledge and insight. We publish titles on general spirituality and living a spiritual life. We aim to inform and help you on your own journey in this life.
If you have enjoyed this book, why not tell other readers by posting a review on your preferred book site?

Recent bestsellers from O-Books are:

Heart of Tantric Sex
Diana Richardson
Revealing Eastern secrets of deep love and intimacy to Western couples.
Paperback: 978-1-90381-637-0 ebook: 978-1-84694-637-0

Crystal Prescriptions
The A-Z guide to over 1,200 symptoms and their healing crystals
Judy Hall
The first in the popular series of eight books, this handy little guide is packed as tight as a pill-bottle with crystal remedies for ailments.
Paperback: 978-1-90504-740-6 ebook: 978-1-84694-629-5

Your Simple Path
Find Happiness in every step
Ian Tucker
A guide to helping us reconnect with what is really important in
our lives.
Paperback: 978-1-78279-349-6 ebook: 978-1-78279-348-9

365 Days of Wisdom
Daily Messages To Inspire You Through The Year
Dadi Janki
Daily messages which cool the mind, warm the heart and guide
you along your journey.
Paperback: 978-1-84694-863-3 ebook: 978-1-84694-864-0

Body of Wisdom
Women's Spiritual Power and How it Serves
Hilary Hart
Bringing together the dreams and experiences of women across
the world with today's most visionary spiritual teachers.
Paperback: 978-1-78099-696-7 ebook: 978-1-78099-695-0

Dying to Be Free
From Enforced Secrecy to Near Death to True Transformation
Hannah Robinson
After an unexpected accident and near-death experience, Hannah
Robinson found herself radically transforming her life, while a
remarkable new insight altered her relationship with her father, a
practising Catholic priest.
Paperback: 978-1-78535-254-6 ebook: 978-1-78535-255-3

The Ecology of the Soul
A Manual of Peace, Power and Personal Growth for Real People
in the Real World
Aidan Walker
Balance your own inner Ecology of the Soul to regain your
natural state of peace, power and wellbeing.
Paperback: 978-1-78279-850-7 ebook: 978-1-78279-849-1

Not I, Not other than I
The Life and Teachings of Russel Williams
Steve Taylor, Russel Williams
The miraculous life and inspiring teachings of one of the World's
greatest living Sages.
Paperback: 978-1-78279-729-6 ebook: 978-1-78279-728-9

On the Other Side of Love
A woman's unconventional journey towards wisdom
Muriel Maufroy
When life has lost all meaning, what do you do?
Paperback: 978-1-78535-281-2 ebook: 978-1-78535-282-9

Practicing A Course In Miracles
A translation of the Workbook in plain language, with
mentor's notes
Elizabeth A. Cronkhite
The practical second and third volumes of The Plain-Language
A Course In Miracles.
Paperback: 978-1-84694-403-1 ebook: 978-1-78099-072-9

Quantum Bliss
The Quantum Mechanics of Happiness, Abundance, and Health
George S. Mentz
Quantum Bliss is the breakthrough summary of success and spirituality secrets that customers have been waiting for.
Paperback: 978-1-78535-203-4 ebook: 978-1-78535-204-1

The Upside Down Mountain
Mags MacKean
A must-read for anyone weary of chasing success and happiness – one woman's inspirational journey swapping the uphill slog for the downhill slope.
Paperback: 978-1-78535-171-6 ebook: 978-1-78535-172-3

Your Personal Tuning Fork
The Endocrine System
Deborah Bates
Discover your body's health secret, the endocrine system, and 'twang' your way to sustainable health!
Paperback: 978-1-84694-503-8 ebook: 978-1-78099-697-4

Readers of ebooks can buy or view any of these bestsellers by clicking on the live link in the title. Most titles are published in paperback and as an ebook. Paperbacks are available in traditional bookshops. Both print and ebook formats are available online.
Find more titles and sign up to our readers' newsletter at http://www.johnhuntpublishing.com/mind-body-spirit
Follow us on Facebook at https://www.facebook.com/OBooks/ and Twitter at https://twitter.com/obooks